ELITISM AND MERITOCRACY IN DEVELOPING COUNTRIES

THE JOHNS HOPKINS STUDIES IN DEVELOPMENT
Vernon W. Ruttan and T. Paul Schultz, Consulting Editors

ELITISM AND MERITOCRACY IN DEVELOPING COUNTRIES

Selection Policies for Higher Education

Robert Klitgaard

The Johns Hopkins University Press

Baltimore and London

The Johns Hopkins University Press
701 West 40th Street
Baltimore, Maryland 21211
The Johns Hopkins Press Ltd., London

∞

The paper used in this publication meets the minimum requirements of American National Standard for Information Sciences—Permanence of Paper for Printed Library Materials, ANSI Z39.48-1984.

Library of Congress Cataloging-in-Publication Data

Klitgaard, Robert E.
　Elitism and meritocracy in developing countries.

　(The Johns Hopkins studies in development)
　Bibliography: p.
　Includes index.
　1. Universities and colleges—Developing countries—Admission.　2. Elite (Social sciences)—Developing countries.　I. Title.　II. Series.
LC2610.K55　1986　　378′.1056′091734　　86-2729
ISBN 0-8018-3269-1 (alk. paper)

O! that estates, degrees, and offices
Were not deriv'd corruptly, and that clear honour
Were purchased by the merit of the wearer.
How many then should cover that stand bare;
How many be commanded that command;
How much low peasantry would then be glean'd
From the true seed of honour; and how much honour
Pick'd from the chaff and ruin of the times
To be new varnish'd!

— William Shakespeare
The Merchant of Venice, act 2, scene 9

Contents

Acknowledgments

Many people and institutions helped me in the course of preparing this book. Ana Teresa Gutiérrez de San Martín was co-author of a teaching case that formed the basis of Chapter 1. Jayjia Hsia, Russell Simpson, Gregory Treverton, and John Weiss provided helpful comments on the Chinese case.

The research on Pakistan reported in chapter 3 was supported by a grant from the Ford Foundation to the Applied Economics Research Centre of the University of Karachi, where I was a Visiting Research Professor from 1975 to 1977. John Cole Cool, Sadequa Dadabhoy, Ahmed Saeed Siddiqui, and Ehsan Rashid assisted with this work in various ways.

Many officials of the University of the Philippines facilitated the research reported in chapter 4. Some of them wish to remain anonymous, but I am able to thank Raul de Guzman, Edgardo S. Pacheco, and Paz G. Ramos.

Chapter 6 is based on work I did in 1982 for the Directorate General of Higher Education in Indonesia. Indro Suwandi, Boesjra Zahir, Toemin Masoem, Muchkiar Suradinata, Ceri Bryant, Nananda Col, and O. Simbolon generously supplied ideas and assistance.

On various drafts of the book, Robert Coulam, Lee J. Cronbach, Peggy Hoover, Richard J. Light, John D. Montgomery, Dwight Perkins, Anders Richter, and Geralyn White made helpful suggestions leading to major improvements, but perhaps not as many as they hoped. In her usual patient and efficient fashion, Constance Tuton provided most of the secretarial services. Thomas C. Schelling and Richard Zeckhauser gave support when it counted. To these friends and colleagues I owe a special vote of thanks.

The writing took place over many points in space and time, and I have enjoyed the hospitality of Graham Allison and my colleagues at Harvard's Kennedy School of Government, Bruce Bushey and the staff of the Ford Foundation in Rio de Janeiro, and Marc Lindenberg and the Instituto Centroamericano de Administración de Empresas in Alajuela, Costa Rica.

A grant from the Russell Sage Foundation enabled me to complete the book. I am especially grateful to Marshall Robinson. The Japanese Corporate Associates Program of the Kennedy School of Government also provided support during the final stages of writing.

The ideas presented here do not necessarily have the endorsement of these colleagues, the various sponsors, or the countries and universities I have studied.

ELITISM AND MERITOCRACY IN DEVELOPING COUNTRIES

INTRODUCTION

"Are you sure you want that title?" a colleague asked me about this book. "Both 'elitism' and 'meritocracy' are dirty words."

It is true that elites, and especially elitism, have few friends among those who study developing countries. An abundant literature describes elites in various settings—who they are, where they come from, what their "class interest" is. Usually these studies criticize elite groups for their reactionary selfishness. The elementary proposition that drives much research is that elite groups try to perpetuate themselves at society's expense. The existence of elites, even in the seemingly benign and unavoidable sense of "the choice or best of anything considered collectively, especially of a group or class of persons," is therefore said to lead to elitism in the sense of a self-conscious, exploitative ruling minority.

In theory, a number of social institutions and policies are supposed to check elitism. One is democracy, another is economic competition, a third is the public redistribution of private wealth and income. Unfortunately, says the literature on elites in developing countries, these policies are often subverted by elite groups. A classic example is what happens to meritocracies.[1]

A merit system is ostensibly anti-elitist. Its purpose is to allocate scarce opportunities to the worthiest aspirants, not to those with the best connections. Examples of merit systems include policies for university admissions and for the selection of recruits for the civil service. Both are devices for selecting a nation's future elite but doing so objectively and openly, with no notion of perpetuating the power of any group. Broadly speaking, meritocracies also might include bidding systems for public contracts, procedures for awarding research grants, and even methods for allocating scarce foreign exchange or import licenses. In each case there are more candidates than positions, and the winners are chosen via a process that, in theory, picks those with the most merit for the task at hand. University admissions, for example, are often based on "academic merit," as measured by examinations and not by willingness to pay or political loyalty or family background.

But do meritocracies work out that way? No, declare many critics. Merit systems get co-opted by elites. Max Weber identified the underlying dilemma:

> Democracy takes an ambivalent stand in the face of specialized examinations, as it does in the face of all the phenomena of bureaucracy—although democracy itself promotes these developments. Special examinations, on the one hand, mean or appear to mean a "selection" of those who qualify from all social strata

1

rather than a rule by notables. On the other hand, democracy fears that a merit system and educational certificates will result in a privileged caste.[2]

The caste metaphor suggests the stratification, inbreeding, and self-perpetuation that occurs when elites control what appears to be selection by merit. Some authors contend that examinations and related devices are particularly insidious means of elite dominance because examinations create the illusion of objectivity and do permit a few people of nonelite background to rise.[3] Indeed, in some circles it has become tautologous that merit svstems are simply another tool of the elite. As one author put it, "Educational systems are a key instrument in ensuring the reproduction of the prevailing social structure and must necessarily adopt a social definition of talent or achievement that favors the maintenance of power and prestige of the privileged group."[4] And so "meritocracy," like "elitism," becomes a dirty word.

What can be done about this sad scenario of pernicious elitism and the breakdown of meritocracies? On such practical matters the usual literature on elites in developing countries is silent or vague. It may be suggested that it would be nice if elites were not needed or if everyone could have elite status or if human relations were transformed so that one person's greater authority or expertise or wealth did not negatively affect other people. Lamentably, we have few examples of these nice things happening. Simply calling for "structural changes" rings hollow. So far, neither the ejection of colonialists nor the erection of revolutionary orders appears to have obviated the need for elites or eradicated elitism.

But even if we have no magic wand, can we not take meritocracy and elitism seriously from a policy perspective? Are there ways to design selection systems to enhance their efficiency, to make them more representative of a society's diverse groups, and to use them to create beneficial incentives? Through selection systems in education and the civil service, public policy affects who will be a country's future elite. How should such decisions be made?

This book provides a framework for addressing these issues. In broadest gauge its subject is how to allocate scarce positions according to some definition of the merit of the candidates. The specific focus is on admissions systems for universities in developing countries. The objective is to provide analytical tools and practical examples that will help to improve selection policies, both in higher education and elsewhere.

Few topics would seem more important for the long-term health of a society. The choice of selection policies affects the quality of a nation's future scientific, economic, and political leadership. The choice influences how much access members of disadvantaged classes, races, regions, sexes, and other social groups will have to elite status. Selection policies create powerful incentives that ripple back through a nation's educational and economic systems.

These issues are encountered in every nation and in various kinds of institutions, but the stakes are especially high in the developing world, and selection for higher education is a conspicuous and crucial example. In the developing countries the needs for capable future leaders are pressing. At the same time, the threat is great that disadvantaged groups will be excluded from the future elite by the operation of a straightforward merit system. When pondering selection criteria, policy-makers may face a choice between narrow, mechanical measures of merit and broader, more relevant criteria that may, however, succumb to subjectivity, influence, and corruption. Selection policies play a symbolic role too. They can be a cause of political as well as academic turmoil.

HOW THE BOOK IS ORGANIZED

The case of the People's Republic of China, which is presented in chapter 1, beautifully illustrates these points. China has had the richest experience of any civilization with systematic procedures for selecting educational and administrative elites. Already at the time of Charlemagne, China had a nationwide examination system. Over the centuries, this system was buffeted by the same forces and tensions now facing other countries: a desire to select "the best," a debate over what "best" should mean, a worry about the representation of various social groups among those selected, and the important fact that policies for choosing elites create incentives back through the educational system.

In 1966, at the outset of the Cultural Revolution, the long-enduring system of selection by academic merit was abolished in China. Installed in its place was a politicized selection process, controlled by the Party instead of the educators, which gave primacy to revolutionary ardor, desire to serve the nation, and class background. I emphasize that the arguments used to justify this radical policy shift were factual as well as normative—it was not just that "values changed." These arguments can be usefully classified under the headings of efficiency, representation, and incentives:

- *Efficiency.* The students selected with the new admissions policy would be better students, better engineers, better leaders for the Revolution.
- *Representation.* The old examination system was biased against workers, peasants, and soldiers. The new system would give these groups much greater representation among those selected.
- *Incentives.* The old system led to abstract learning, irrelevant intellectuals, an unhealthy dominance of teachers over students, and the wrong emphases in high-school curricula.

These arguments have relevance beyond the borders of China.

Eleven years later in 1977, admissions policies shifted again. Entrance examinations were restored. As before, empirical questions, and not solely a change of objectives, were decisive in justifying this move. Simply put, the reformers now said that the arguments used in 1966 had been shown to be false.

DOES ALL THIS IMPLY "ELITISM"?

If we study how to select a few of many candidates for scarce positions, does this not endorse "elitism"? Not in the popular sense of that term. We will not presuppose a definition of what constitutes "quality" among those selected; we will not define an institution's objectives; we will not say how many should be chosen. Our task is, *given* those decisions by a society or institution, helping them do better in achieving their aims, whatever those aims may be.

Philosopher Sidney Hook put the matter in useful perspective:

We must distinguish between standards of achievement that individuals must meet before certain professions are open to them—and from which, both in their own personal interests and in those of society, they can be legitimately barred—and the standard of growth and progress that is applicable to each individual. It is the latter which concerns the teacher. . . . And this means not the elimination or the dilution of subject matter, not the substitution of play for study, not a cafeteria of snap courses—but holding up ever higher goals to be reached by every student until he has attained *his* best. . . .

Education is not a race or a combat or a competition, although, properly implemented, these may be pedagogic devices to add zest to learning. If we must use language of this sort, it is better to have the individual run a race against his own potentialities. . . .

Allied to the conception of education as the process by which prizes and power are won is the view of society as a graded and hierarchically organized system, in which intelligence—not birth, social status, or wealth—is the principle of differentiation. No matter what the principle of differentiation is, if it involves hierarchy, official or unofficial, it involves the likelihood of exploitation. . . .

. . . It should be recognized that as an educational ideal, the pursuit of excellence is perfectly compatible with stress on educational opportunity. . . . Second, we must not identify some types of educational excellence, for which there is a pressing, and perhaps only transitory, social need, with excellence as such. As we have already maintained, emphasis upon them may be justifiable but it should not blind us to the existence of multiple forms of excellence. Third, we should be wary against converting our appreciation of excellence into a *cult,* as if only the excellent is important and nothing else counts. If the term means anything, we cannot all be excellent. But in education we can all do better than we have done.

In the intellectual history of the West, the cult of excellence has sometimes been associated with an ideology which disdains equal social, political, and sometimes human rights of those who are less than excellent. There is an entire family of doctrines which assume that a cultural and educational elite should function as a political and ruling elite. This confuses different issues. . . . The upper ranges of any normal distribution of talent in any field may be referred to as an elite. In this sense, to say that there is a natural aristocracy of talent, on the basis of current biological theory, is a commonplace. Every adequate educational system—which to a democrat means one in which equality of opportunity prevails—ought to enable us to discover this natural aristocracy of talent. But to couple a natural aristocracy of talent with a natural aristocracy of virtue . . . is questionable.

Source: Quotation from Sidney Hook, *Education for Modern Man: A New Perspective* (New York: Knopf, 1963), pp. 39, 40, 41, 43–44. Emphasis in the original.

Their assertions can again be organized according to the dimensions of efficiency, representation, and incentives; and again, the issues raised are of general and not just Chinese interest.

The lesson of the Chinese case is not that selection by examination is good or bad, for China or any other country. Rather, I hope the case fascinates you, the reader, and persuades you that the topic of this book is a critical one, economically and politically, for the developing nations. The chapter also introduces by example the three dimensions of the policy problem, which later chapters study systematically.

Chapter 2 moves from the example of China to a broader, Third World context. The chapter describes the importance of selection systems for higher education in developing countries. Facts are assembled—alas, the data are few and imperfect—about the efficiency of selection, the underrepresentation of groups of various kinds, and incentive effects. The varieties of selection policies used around the world are described.

Chapters 3, 4, and 5 develop tools of analysis and illustrate these tools with real cases. Chapter 3 deals with efficiency. It includes a general discussion of the difficult problems of defining objectives and finding usable measures for them. Then, using a case from Pakistan, general techniques are developed and applied to help policy-makers assess the gains in efficiency from the improved prediction of later performance.

There will be surprises here for many readers. A selection criterion may have what looks like a "weak" correlation with later performance. But in the context of selection, one can easily be misled: using that "weak" predictor may lead to large gains in the performance of those chosen. Chapter 3 presents some techniques for unpacking this anomaly—techniques that are further refined in chapters 4 and 6.

The problem of group representation is analyzed in chapter 4. An important distinction is drawn between *bias* in selection and the *underrepresentation* of groups. The former may imply the latter but, contrary to much popular opinion, the latter does not imply the former. I present techniques for assessing bias. I also tackle another issue. Suppose we want to increase the representation of a certain group through preferential treatment. How should we decide how far to go? What is the optimal degree of "affirmative action"?

In the process of addressing such questions, chapter 4 examines the "democratization" of admissions at the University of the Philippines—one of the few examples in the world of an *experiment* to admit a greater number of underqualified, poor students. The experiment has recently been discontinued, but if its evaluators had used the tools of this chapter it might well have been continued. The Philippines case provides a rich study of policy analysis gone awry, along with some practical examples of how to do better.

It is the difficult task of chapter 5 to scan the virtually uncharted waters of incentive effects in selection. There are some helpful economic models, but they remain in a highly conceptual stage; applying them to real problems will at present lead to qualitative insights rather than empirical estimates. Of particular importance are the incentives created back through the educational system. Also, the threat of corruption must always be kept in mind. Examples from China, the Philippines, and the United States when it was a "developing country" illustrate how important incentive effects can be—and how often they are overlooked or underestimated.

By the end of chapter 5, the major dimensions of making merit work have been analyzed and exemplified. Now it comes time to integrate these dimensions in a policy analysis. This is what chapter 6 attempts, looking at the case of Indonesia. Because of data shortages, the estimates of some key relationships are tenuous; especially with regard to incentive effects, one must rely on informed speculation. But for the major alternatives considered by the government of Indonesia, we are able to give preliminary estimates of their pros and cons in terms of efficiency, representation, and incentives. The Indonesian case helps us to understand the uses and limitations of policy analysis in an environment characterized by poor information—a characteristic of most developing countries.

Of particular interest is an analysis of the academic costs of a possible program of preferential admission for students from the underrepresented islands outside Java. Chapter 6 also presents for the first time a description and analysis of Indonesia's quota system, which limits the enrollment of Indonesians of Chinese descent.

Chapter 7, the final chapter, restates the book's major lessons and extends some of the findings to other examples of policies for allocating scarce positions. The chapter includes some checklists for policy-makers which summarize the major empirical and normative questions that should be asked about each dimension of making merit work. I hope these checklists serve as a convenient starting point for policy-makers and researchers alike.

THE APPROACH OF THIS BOOK

The chapters that follow are unusual in that they draw on tools from several disciplines: psychometrics, economics, and public policy analysis. The tools are presented and combined not for their own sake but in an effort to improve practical decision-making. This means that the presentation is not aimed at specialists, and more than in most applications of social science I will emphasize the limitations as well as the virtues of analysis. At the same time, I hope that specialists in various fields will find certain aspects of the book of particular interest.

Psychometricians will encounter here an application of the classic models associated with names like Cronbach and Gleser, Lord and Novick, and Hunter and Schmidt.[5] Several new twists are added. The possible uses of exploratory data analysis in validity studies are described and briefly illustrated in the appendix to chapter 6. To evaluate the trade-off between efficient selection and preferential treatment, a new approach based on marginal cost analysis is developed and applied in chapters 4 and 6. Most psychometricians will find novel the treatment of the incentive effects of selection, specifically in chapter 5. Those interested in the often parochial debate in the United States over ability testing may find the case of China in chapter 1 mind-expanding. Finally, few studies of selection have examined the *policy* problem in all its real-world complexity, as this book tries to. Psychometricians may therefore be interested to see how far their tools can take us in making real policy choices.

Economists will find examples of what the theoretical literature in economics is coming to call "allocation by contest," as contrasted with the usual economic presumption of allocation by the market. In a variety of settings, the market metaphor is not the best paradigm for allocation problems as they actually exist. Queues and rationing characterize many economic decisions, from hiring to contracting, and candidates' performance relative to each other, rather than their absolute performance, often determines their rewards. The selection problem is a good example, and I believe that for the developing countries understanding the economics of this problem is almost as important as understanding the economics of the competitive market. This book suggests how some of the advances in the economics of signaling and of contests might bear practical fruit. Once again the limitations of theoretical work for real decision-making are illuminated.

A considerable body of research in political science and sociology focuses on elites in developing countries. In contrast to the descriptive nature of most such studies, the focus in this book is prescriptive. True, the descriptions provided here of selection systems in China, the Philippines, and Indonesia have something to say about who elites are in those countries. But the purpose of the research is to help policy-makers do a better job designing selection and admissions systems. I hope this perspective is refreshing for political scientists and sociologists, perhaps encouraging them to direct some of their own research toward policy measures that affect the formation of elites.

Finally, those in the field of international development may find several aspects of this book particularly interesting. One is its topic. Selection policies of all kinds are important, but largely overlooked in the literature on development. Much more work, both analytical and theoretical, needs doing, and I hope the work reported here can kindle additional interest in this category of development problems.

A second aspect of the book is its method. It includes several substantial Asian case studies. Short examples also appear from Brazil, Ecuador, Zambia, Swaziland, the United States, and the Republic of South Africa. It is hoped that by working through real examples, with their inevitably incomplete and disorganized data—for such is policy analysis in the developing countries—we may gain a greater appreciation of what policy analysis can and cannot accomplish. This may be a neglected appreciation in the field of international development. Academic work on development is often too general and too abstract. It seems to be divorced from decisions facing policy-makers in specific contexts, and one may come away from the research without really seeing how it could be applied, or believing that the application would be automatic. This is not to disparage general treatments; indeed, this book provides some tools of broad applicability. But the focus on real cases is there to remind us that the bottom line is practical. How can the dilemmas of elitism and meritocracy be mitigated? If a society wishes to allocate positions according to concepts of "merit" of its choosing, how much can policy analysis help balance the objectives of efficiency, representation, and incentives?

1

THE POLICY PROBLEMS
The Case of the People's Republic
of China

On June 6, 1966, the graduating members of the Peking No. 1 Girls' Middle School wrote a remarkable letter:

> Dear Central Committee of the Party and dear Chairman Mao,
>
> We are students who will soon graduate from senior middle school. In this great cultural revolution, the responsibility falls first of all on our shoulders to smash the old college entrance examination system. We wish to express our views on the existing system of admissions to higher schools.
>
> We hold that the existing system of admittance to higher schools is a continuation of the old feudal examination system dating back thousands of years. It is a most backward and reactionary educational system. It runs counter to the educational policy laid down by Chairman Mao. Chairman Mao says that education must serve the politics of the proletariat and be integrated with productive labour. "Our educational policy must enable everyone who gets an education, to develop morally, intellectually and physically and become a cultured, socialist-minded worker." . . .
>
> Many young people are led not to study for the revolution but to immerse themselves in books for the university entrance examination and to pay no heed to politics. Quite a number of students have been indoctrinated with such gravely reactionary ideas of the exploiting classes as the "book learning stands above all." . . .
>
> We suggest in concrete terms that:
>
> 1. Beginning this year, we abolish the old system of enrolling students to the higher schools.
>
> 2. Graduates from senior middle schools should go straight into the midst of the workers, peasants and soldiers and integrate themselves with the masses. They should first of all get "ideological diplomas" from the working class and the poor and lower-middle peasants. The Party will select the best from among the fine sons and daughters of the proletariat, young people who truly serve the broad masses of workers, peasants, and soldiers, and send them on to higher schools.[1]

This letter, published in the *People's Daily*, was to mark the beginning of a massive change in higher education in China. In particular, entrance examinations were abolished. Admissions decisions were henceforth made through the Communist Party. The idea was to give more weight to personal qualities, such as how well a student would serve the country and the revolution, and no weight to the arbitrary, possibly biased results of a standardized test.

Abandoning entrance examinations was one part of a thorough and radical reform of the Chinese educational system during the Cultural Revolution. Many institutes and all universities were shut down for several years. Teachers were retooled or replaced. Curricula were shortened, simplified, and politicized. Even though the Chinese decision about examinations must be viewed in its distinctive context, the critique of examinations and "academic merit" is instructive beyond Chinese borders. The issues raised are relevant to all selection systems: the efficiency of selection, representation and bias, and incentives. What were the arguments for and against various uses of entrance examinations and "personal qualities"? How might one have assessed these arguments in China in 1966?

THE HISTORY OF EXAMINATIONS IN CHINA

The magnitude of the changes in the selection process for higher education during the Cultural Revolution cannot be understood without some familiarity with China's unique tradition of examinations. For more than a thousand years, selection for the civil service and higher education had primarily been by tests. Indeed, examinations were mentioned before the time of Christ,[2] and by the end of the seventh century an empirewide testing system was in place. The tests were crucial: "For twelve centuries social rank in China has been determined more by qualification for office than by wealth. This qualification, in turn, has been determined by education, and especially by examinations. . . . The question usually put to a stranger of unknown rank was how many examinations he had passed."[3]

There were many tiers of examinations. Success at one level enabled a student to qualify for a particular level of the bureaucracy or to go on to the next level of study. Periodically, examiners from the capital would go out into the provinces to identify and certify those who had distinguished themselves academically. Such students were awarded the *hsui-ts'ai* degree, the rough equivalent of a bachelor's degree, and they were eligible to continue their studies at the provincial colleges.

At the next level were the full provincial examinations, held about every three years. These tests involved three straight days of writing. Only about 1 percent of the candidates passed, and they obtained a *chu-jen*, roughly a master's degree. They could join the provincial government or continue their studies at an imperial college, to prepare themselves for the imperial examinations.

The imperial examinations were as much a test of endurance as of intellect. For seven days, each candidate would reside in an isolated cubicle containing only a brick bed and a desk at which to stand and write. Successful candidates, numbering about two hundred a year and having an average age of about thirty-six, received the *chin-shih*, or doctorate. By about A.D. 1050, the doctoral degree examinations supplied half the replacements necessary to maintain the civil service at then-current levels. Officials with doctorates tended to hold the highest offices in China.[4]

Examinations could be taken in a variety of subjects, including law, history, letters, rituals, or classical study. In each subject, the classics were emphasized as a guide to conduct and a molder of character. The examinations stressed memorization, although the imperial examination in letters also involved essays through which candidates could demonstrate originality and skill in reasoning and expression.[5]

Over the centuries, many debates took place about the relevance of the tests. How well did they assess "intellectual merit"? Examinations were often criticized as being too narrow a measure of academic performance. For example, in the year 1044 the "memorization and written elucidation questions" were dropped. In their stead were questions requiring imaginative solutions and original discussions of the broader meaning of classical texts. But such questions brought their own problems. Questions calling for originality invited subjectivity, and perhaps bias and corruption, in the grading. Examination officials "preferred the safer ground of the traditional compositions, which could be graded objectively, if mechanically, on the basis of set rules."[6]

Another debate over the years concerned how well the examinations served to identify future public leaders. There were a number of criticisms. Some people believed that family background should be taken into account. The prominent statesman Li Ti-yu argued in the ninth century:

> The outstanding officials of the government ought to be the sons of the highest officials. Why? Because from childhood on they are accustomed to this kind of position; their eyes are familiar with court affairs; even if they have not been trained in the ceremonies of the palace, they automatically achieve perfection. Scholars of poor families, even if they have an extraordinary talent, are certainly unable to accustom themselves to [its routine].[7]

The sons of high officials did enjoy many advantages in the selection process. Some were allowed to enter civil office through the *jin* privilege—that is, qualification simply by virtue of the father's position. For example, the sons of officials in the first three ranks could apply for government positions in the seventh rank or below without having to submit to the examinations. The son of a *chin-shih* titleholder could begin in the ninth rank.

At various times, sponsorship by a high official was also needed for medium- and high-level official appointments. The idea was a bit like a strong letter of recommendation, with the added feature that if a person who was recommended or sponsored did poorly later, the recommender himself could be demoted or even corporally punished. The reason to supplement examination results with such sponsorship was to assess character and the other qualities thought desirable for public office.[8]

Nonetheless, for hundreds of years the great majority of civil servants were selected through the examination system. Particularly at the highest levels of government, scholarly certification was very important. "Even those who entered the civil service through *jin-pu,* although relatives or protégés of important officials, still found the examinations important to their careers, and it was not uncommon for such men later to take their *chin-shih* degree."[9] A careful study of the Ming dynasty showed that the examination system did not favor the offspring of the imperial clan.[10] As Karl A. Wittfogel concluded,

> While . . . no definite statement is possible at this point, it may be hazarded that appointment to the empire's leading offices was determined in the main by considerations of personal qualification. Officials hardened in competition and of tested ability seemed to have had a better chance of achieving the highest positions than the privileged sons who more often obtained posts in the middle or upper middle brackets.[11]

The use of meritocratic examinations did not, however, imply equal opportunity for all citizens. Women were excluded, as were merchants, brothel-keepers, and entertainers. The sons of the literati, the nobles, and the mandarins were advantaged in the competition for marks. Of the six imperial colleges operating during most of China's ancient history, only one admitted sons of the common people. Nor could everyone afford the long period of study needed to prepare for examinations, even at lower levels. The wealthy also had access to the best tutors and to their clan's private libraries. Occasionally in Chinese history, university admission and public offices were auctioned off to the highest bidder, and a few offices were made hereditary.

The examination system was sometimes criticized because students from certain regions did worse than others. Some observers blamed this on biased examiners. Others disagreed. While admitting that the distributions of scores differed across provinces and regions, they did not blame the examinations but instead cited geographical inequalities in the educational system.[12] The stakes here were not trivial, as Max Weber observed:

> After 1370, only examined men had claims to offices. At once a fight set in between the various regions, especially between the North and the South. The South even then supplied candidates for examinations who were more cultured, having experienced a more comprehensive environment. But the North was the military foundation stone of the empire. Hence, the emperor intervened and *punished*(!) the examiners who had given the "first place" to a Southerner.[13]

Eventually, separate lists were drawn up for the North, South, and Center regions—in effect, regional quotas.[14]

Despite numerous problems and criticisms, the examination system persisted with only a few changes into the twentieth century. In 1906, a radical shift took place in the content of the exams. It was believed that the traditional tests overemphasized an outmoded form of learning and had led to the neglect of the sciences. China wanted to become modern; the examinations had stressed the classics.[15] The selection system was decentralized, and new subjects received attention. The new tests of "intellectual merit" continued as the method for selecting university students until well after the Communist Revolution.

In 1924, Sun Yat-sen summarized the meritocratic ideology of the Chinese examination system as follows:

> So in Chinese history we find not only those who could fight becoming king; anyone with marked ability, who had made new discoveries or who had achieved great things for mankind, could become king and organize the government. Cooks, physicians, tailors, carpenters, and all others who had special ability had become king. The general psychology of the Chinese is that a man possessing marked ability should become king.[16]

At least, many men had that theoretical opportunity.

THE COMMUNISTS TAKE OVER

When the Communists finally gained control of the country in 1949, they inherited a system of higher education that was inadequate in quantity and emphasis. In all of China in 1950, only 100,000 students were enrolled in higher education. The Communists' modernization plans called for a large pool of trained technical manpower; enrollments at the tertiary level had to be increased. Because qualified secondary school graduates were few, the selection ratios during the first six years of Communist rule were high (table 1). Different fields of study were now emphasized. Scientific and technical institutes multiplied. Liberal arts courses were sharply curtailed.

Examination scores remained the primary criterion for admission. Fields of study and universities varied in their cutoff scores, depending in part on supply and demand. The Ministry of Education ran the examination system, devised provincial quotas, and allocated successful candidates across fields and universities. But with limited pools of qualified applicants, admissions standards could not be overly stringent. In 1955, the journal *People's Education* reported that of those senior middle school graduates who had taken the entrance examinations

TABLE 1. College Acceptances from Those Registering (China, 1952–57)

Year	Number Registering for Exam	Number Accepted for Enrollment	Selection Ratio
1952	73,000	65,900	0.90
1953	81,000	71,400	0.88
1954	134,000	94,000	0.70
1955	177,000	96,200	0.54
1956	350,000	165,600	0.47
1957	250,000	107,000	0.43

Source: Based on data in Robert Taylor, *China's Intellectual Dilemma: Politics and University Enrolment* (Vancouver: University of British Columbia, 1981).

in the previous year and had been admitted to a university, 73 percent had failed the mathematics section and 72 percent had failed the physics portion of the exam.[17]

Selecting primarily on test scores, it was believed, enabled qualified technical cadres to be developed as quickly as possible. But the system led to the underrepresentation of certain important groups: students of lower-class backgrounds did not do as well on the examinations. As a consequence, higher educational resources went disproportionately to the offspring of the old elite. In 1956 Mao Tse-tung observed apologetically: "Although many of our university students are not children from the homes of workers, yet, with a few exceptions they are patriotic and uphold socialism."[18]

It is unclear why working-class students scored lower on the tests. But the Chinese Communist Party (CCP) wanted to broaden the class composition of the universities. It undertook special educational efforts to qualify the children of workers, peasants, cadres, and soldiers:

- In 1950, "rapid middle schools" were started for workers and peasants lacking formal schooling. The accelerated curriculum was designed to prepare these students for college study in only three years. The first 1,680 graduates received their degrees in 1953, and 1,622 went on to college. By 1954, some 51,000 students of worker or peasant background were enrolled in 87 such schools.[19]

- Special refresher courses were available to working revolutionary cadres and vocational school graduates. "Spare-time middle schools" were new paths that might eventually lead to college.

- Preferential admissions policies were adopted. At the margin, those of worker and peasant backgrounds were given an advantage, and some of them who failed the examinations were admitted provisionally. If their academic performance turned out to be adequate, they could remain in college; if not, they were sent back to their production units.[20]

- When many students in the "rapid middle schools" and the refresher courses had trouble mastering the material, the Ministry of Education published an examination outline to help them direct and concentrate their studies. But problems developed. In the race to pass the exams, teaching and learning were directed to the outline. Rote learning became even more prevalent.[21]

The representation of students of lower-class backgrounds increased, even as admissions grew more selective. The percentage of students who were from worker or peasant families increased from 19.1 percent in 1951 to 36.3 percent in 1957. But this gain should be interpreted in light of three facts. First, workers and peasants made up about four-fifths of the country's population, so even after the improvements their underrepresentation in higher education remained severe. Second, worker or peasant students were heavily concentrated in teacher training, agriculture, and forestry; most were studying in the less prestigious local institutions. And third, there is evidence that the majority of the repeaters and dropouts in both secondary and tertiary education were of worker or peasant background.[22]

SWINGS IN PRIORITIES

In 1958, policies shifted again. The Great Leap Forward aimed at increasing production and achieving self-sufficiency, but China must "walk on two legs." It was argued that intellectual formation should not be separated from the world of work. "Overreliance" on theoretical, specialized, and technical education was criticized; henceforth, training was to be more general, more adaptable, and above all more practical. Cadres of all ranks were required to do manual labor for a number of years (or several months a year). Students were now told to acquire more experience with productive labor. By requiring that schooling and work be more interrelated, students' learning would improve; theoretical knowledge would gain from experience with practical applications, and vice versa.

Between 1958 and 1960, there arose hundreds of "Red and Expert" universities where students split their time between study and work. The universities were closely connected to production units, and the proceeds from the students' part-time labor went back to those schools. Thus, the production units helped finance their members' education.[23]

It was hoped that other benefits would also ensue from the Red and Expert universities. Distinctions between manual and mental work would erode. Engaging everyone in the struggle for production would enhance political commitment as it raised output. The gap between the old social classes would narrow.

Admissions standards at the regular universities and colleges were also changed. Examination scores lost importance, while political criteria and political education gained. Workers and peasants received more advantages in the selection process. A special clause in the registration rules of 1959 allowed "workers, peasants, cadres of worker and peasant status to avoid the nationwide joint examinations."[24]

These changes had academic costs. The academic standards of the Red and Expert universities were roughly equivalent to those of regular secondary-level institutions.[25] Increasingly, critics attacked declining standards and levels of preparation in the regular colleges and universities. A Chinese educational journal in 1959 contained a warning:

> If their examination success does not fulfill the lowest acceptance level, we cannot lower the standard to accept them for this would give us no way of guaranteeing the quality of new students and would in turn adversely affect the standard of trained cadres. . . . Such a policy would not be in [their] interest for they would not be able to keep up with their coursework, they might have to drop out or generally damage their own health.[26]

Most of the curricular and admissions reforms adopted during the Great Leap Forward were short-lived. By 1961, many officials were arguing that the academic costs outweighed the benefits. One Western scholar summarized the reaction:

> Quality was the watchword in education in 1961. Less time was to be devoted to political activities and physical labour and more time to teaching. Strong opposition that had developed among the Party leadership and in educational circles to what was felt to be excesses in education during the Leap years came to the fore. It was claimed that productive labour had been allowed to expand at the expense of classroom teaching. A typical manifestation of this opinion was an article entitled "The Work of Schools Must Centre on Teaching," which was first published in the *Guangming Daily* (GMRB) in April and then reprinted in the *People's Daily*. The article claimed that classroom work was the principle form of teaching and learning, and criticized the Leap period by stating:
>
> > "In the midst of leaps forward . . . we must not forget that our schools are schools, in which the normal order of teaching and learning must not be disturbed at random. Those students who should be sent to take part in labour outside must be sent without failure. Those who should not be so sent must remain. . . . Where possible, the sending of students to take part in labour outside must be delayed."
>
> On July 20, the Ministry of Education issued a document entitled "Opinions on Certain Problems Concerning Full-Day Schools," which pointed out that quality in education had deteriorated since 1958 due to excessive productive labour and political activities. It was also pointed out that the time devoted to "social activities" had to be reduced.[27]

By 1962, people of worker or peasant background were no longer given priority in most regular institutions of higher learning. A new directive that year specified that admissions would be carried on solely by selection "from higher grades to lower grades" on the entrance examinations—which once again *everyone* had to take. The emphasis returned to academic quality. Chou En-lai announced the establishment of the key school system of schooling, where students were tracked and streamed on the basis of academic performance from primary school on:

> In developing education in our country we must adopt the method of combining popularization with a raising of quality. . . . Now it is time to improve, consolidate and raise up their level. . . . We must devote relatively more energy to perfecting a number of "key" schools . . . so as to train specialized personnel of higher quality for the state and bring about a rapid rise in our country's scientific and cultural level.[28]

CHANGES WITH THE CULTURAL REVOLUTION

The Cultural Revolution arrived in 1966. It transformed many educational policies. The changes reflected a shift in objectives, but they were defended not just as matters of value or as ideological mandates, but with factual assertions about the results of alternative methods for selection and training. Policy-relevant research played a prominent role, at least in defending the new policies.

Henceforth candidates for higher education were to be chosen on the basis of political correctness, integration into one's unit, and correct class origin—not examination scores. Politics were "put in command" of the selection system. A June 18, 1966, editorial in the *People's Daily* summarized the basic idea: "Beginning this year, a new method of enrollment, a combination of recommendation and selection in which proletarian politics are put first and the mass line is followed, will be put into effect; the best students will be admitted, selected from those . . . recommended by their outstanding moral, intellectual and physical qualities."[29] In January 1967, the Central Committee of the CCP decreed that "all examinations . . . should be abolished. . . . Academic results should be democratically discussed and decided by study sections which is the 'living way' of doing things."[30]

To be eligible to apply to the university, a candidate needed several years of work experience in a commune or a factory. Then he or she would submit an application to the brigade or production unit. Members of these units would then vote whether or not to recommend the candidate. The next step was to gain approval from the political leadership: revolutionary committees consisting of party cadres, workers, and students. In theory, the university or college would then have a say, although in practice a candidate "approved by the masses" was never vetoed.[31]

> Candidates who have graduated from junior or senior middle school and who have at least two years of "practical experience" are then invited to register with their units (brigades or factories). The units organize a mass meeting, which is attended by some members of the enrolment team in the course of which candidates are selected. Those candidates who are chosen must then present themselves to the commune authorities where again some will be rejected. The remaining candidates will finally go to the capital of the *hsien* where the enrolment team will interview them and select those who will go on to the university. The ratio of rejection is high: out of 9 candidates selected by the brigade, 6 will be eliminated at the commune level and 2 at the *hsien* level. Thus the ratio of elimination at the *hsien* level . . . is two out of three, and eight out of nine at the brigade level. . . .[32]

The selection system was not the only part of the educational system that changed. Curricula were simplified and made more "relevant." Many courses in the hard and social sciences—including statistics, finance, management, and history—were dropped or shortened. Political education received much more emphasis (the study of Leninism and Mao Tse-tung's thought was lengthened considerably). Students now spent much of their "classroom time" in the field or factory or working on problems submitted by the factories or communes with which they were connected.[33] Undergraduate work now took three to four years instead of the usual four to five.

In 1966–67, all Chinese universities closed their doors as the new curricula and admissions criteria were devised. Revolutionary committees took over university administration; "enrollment teams," also consisting of "three-in-one combinations" of cadres, workers, and students, made the final admissions decisions.

Entrance examinations were eliminated. The arguments for doing this involved the dimensions of efficiency, representation, and incentives.

Efficiency

According to the architects of the new selection policy, the old educational system simply was not efficient. It created narrow technicians, pointy-headed intellectuals, and theorists who could not tackle China's development problems. In the words of a Western scholar, the situation

> could be summed up thus: the old system turns out an elite which is incompetent and useless. Peasants say: "The more they go to school, the more stupid they become." There is a whole folklore of racy anecdotes featuring the palefaced, thin, dogmatic, dissatisfied graduate versus the quick-minded, efficient, hard-toiling . . . "local expert" who spent a short time in a less sophisticated school. . . .
>
> Peasants and workers mentioned hundreds of cases where highly trained personnel stumbled over technical problems which they themselves finally succeeded in solving by discarding the blind worship to dogmatic rules and principles. Besides . . . "if young people cannot, and above all will not, do jobs which do not fall exactly in their special domain the economic balance and progress might be endangered. Without a doubt too many academic scientists and technicians have been trained in recent years."[34]

For the sake of educational efficiency, work should be combined with study—so argued several studies presented at the National Conference on Urban Part-Work, Part-Study Education in 1965:

> Facts produced at the conference had shown that, though students in work-study schools spent only half of their time in classroom studies, what they learnt was not less than those studying at full-time schools. Sometimes their knowledge had proved to be even more closely related to life. Participation in labour had much improved the students' physique also. The consensus among workers was that this new system was satisfactory in four respects: the factory was pleased because such students helped production; the school was pleased because through linking theory with practice, the quality of teaching was raised; the parents were pleased because they needed to spend little or no money for their children to obtain a good education; the student was pleased because he could both study and do manual work.[35]

A corollary to this argument was that students should be selected from among the workers. Those with prior work experience would learn the most and the fastest. In 1966 an important piece of policy-relevant research was published concerning productivity at the No. 1 Shanghai Machine Tools Plant. According to the New China News Agency, "engineers and technicians directly promoted from among the workers with practical experience were more effective than university graduates. The training was faster and . . . [therefore] cost less."[36]

For Mao Tse-tung, the lesson from this particular study was clear. In 1968 he issued his "July 21 Directive": "It is still necessary to have universities, here I refer mainly to colleges of science and engineering. However, it is essential to shorten the length of schooling, revolutionize education, put proletarian policies in command and follow the road of the Shanghai Machine Tools Plant in training technicians from the workers."[37] Instead of using examinations, "putting politics in command" was thought to be a more efficient way to select the best students and future technicians and leaders.

Representation

Proponents of the new selection policy argued that higher education had remained the preserve of the old, urban-based, intellectual elite. Quite apart from the efficiency of selection, equity also mattered, and it was argued that examinations reinforced social stratification. This occurred in two ways.

First, since the children of poor people and rural people did worse on the examinations, they were underrepresented. The tests themselves may have been biased, or they may simply have reflected in an unbiased way inequalities that the new Chinese leadership did not wish to reinforce. Second, tests rewarded intellectual excellence. Book learning was apparently thought to be only weakly correlated with ideological purity. And the intellectually superior might unfortunately conclude that they should be socially superior. As a report in the New China News Agency argued:

> China is a state where the working people are the masters, it is inconceivable that the working class should run colleges to turn out people who look down upon physical labour and the labouring people . . . schools and colleges should turn out revolutionaries who are faithful to the cause of the working class. . . .
>
> The Soviet Union provides a lesson: its universities produce a privileged stratum of bourgeois intellectuals who are the "elite" of society sitting on the backs of the working people.[38]

In July 1966, seven students at the China People's University declared: "[Under the old system, college students] live in tall buildings, eat polished rice and fine flour, read ancient and foreign masterpieces, and with ideas of seeking fame instilled in their minds, they think of gaining individual distinctions."[39] Presumably, these inequities would be reduced by abolishing examinations, selecting along political criteria, and putting education in the hands of the Communist Party.

Incentives

It was argued that the new system also created the right incentives. Because those admitted would be designated by the masses on the basis of their political commitment, they would have tremendous motivation. They would not study for

POLITICS AND PROMOTION IN THE CHINESE ARMY

In 1964 a spate of articles appeared in the Chinese press clearly depicting the widespread concern over selecting, indoctrinating, and promoting the future leadership of the nation. The following is an excerpt from one article in the *Peking Review.*

Keeping Power in Proletarian Hands

An anti-chemical company of the Chinese People's Liberation Army (PLA) forces stationed in Canton has distinguished itself for its good work in promoting soldiers to be officers. Of the company's nine officers, several have come from its own rank and file. In the last few years, it has altogether promoted 23 men to officer rank. Many of them have been sent to reinforce the leading cadres of other PLA companies.

The Party branch of this company bases its work on a series of directives issued by the Military Committee of the CCP Central Committee and the General Political Department of the PLA concerning the training of young revolutionaries and on the idea of upholding the "four firsts," which are the PLA's basic experiences in political work. A deep understanding of the great significance of paying attention to the human factor has enabled it to see that this work concerns the big question of fostering and maintaining the revolutionary spirit of the PLA and insuring that the power is always in proletarian revolutionary hands. Consequently, the entire Party branch has taken up this work most seriously and worked out a concrete plan for fostering young revolutionary officers.

The company keeps two sets of records, one for picking squad commanders from the ranks and the other, higher officers from among the squad commanders. The Party branch examines every rank-and-filer who has completed one year's service, picks out those who have a good class origin, and are politically progressive, conscientious in work, capable and close to the masses, and then re-examines the selected ones, one by one in detailed discussions. Detailed personal accounts of candidates so chosen are then entered into the records.

Private Wei Kuang-chai was selected in this way. Of poor peasant origin,

---

personal fame or fortune or to become specialists. As some college students told a Western visitor during the Cultural Revolution: "We bring to the University the aspirations of millions of workers, peasants, and soldiers to study in the University. . . . Now students study for the people for revolution."[40] A professor in the Nanking Normal College noted, "Since most students are selected from among workers and peasants, they are highly motivated and concentrate on their studies. Very few fail."[41] With examinations gone, secondary school teachers would lose their authoritarian control over students. Instead of cramming for examinations, students would now have the incentive to work hard at a factory or farm.

Thus, proponents of the new selection policy maintained that it would combine the best of several worlds. It would be more *efficient* in both selecting and training technicians, scientists, and leaders. It would grant more *representa-*

he became a squad commander in 1961. Wei's records, put briefly, are: Accepted as a member of the Communist Youth League before completing one year's service; accepted as a Communist Party member in September 1960; elected a "5-good" soldier over a number of years and twice elected the company's "Good Party Member." In 1961, he became a "Good Squad Commander" and in January this year was promoted a platoon commander with the rank of second lieutenant.

Officers above the rank of squad leader are chosen with even greater care. The Party branch first examines one by one those squad commanders who have served two years, selects those who are the firmest in their revolutionary stand and are exemplary in all respects, and then submits the name list for the higher authorities' approval before the names are entered into the record. Second Lieutenant Chu Kuang-shou, who was promoted a platoon commander in May last year, was one such good squad leader. Under his leadership, his platoon got excellent marks twice in marksmanship tests, and won a place on the "4-good" platoon list at first-round choosing.

The two records keep detailed accounts of every trainee, including, among other things, his class background, political ideology, military training and knowledge, organizing ability and state of health. The Party branch takes this task of training new revolutionary cadres as a part of its regular work and links this with the work of developing "5-good" soldiers and "4-good" platoons.

All candidates are given guidance in studying Chairman Mao Tse-tung's works so that they are armed with Mao Tse-tung's thinking and can become Party members, proletarian fighters and all-round developed "5-good" soldiers before they are promoted to be officers. They are given ample opportunities to do political and ideological work and to master military techniques so that once they become officers they can carry out their duties loyally with confidence and efficiency.

Source: Excerpted from "Bringing up Heirs for the Revolution," Peking Review, No. 30 (1964), reprinted in The Great Cultural Revolution in China, ed. and trans. Asia Research Centre (Tokyo: Charles E. Tuttle Co., 1970), pp. 87–88.

tion to peasants and workers. And it would create *incentives* for productivity and revolutionary zeal.

BRINGING BACK ENTRANCE EXAMINATIONS

As early as 1972, Chou En-lai warned against placing excessive emphasis on productive labor by students while in school. A number of only partially implemented steps were taken to improve the universities after 1972, including an effort to strengthen research work and teaching in the natural sciences, the enrollment of at least some students directly out of secondary school (instead of requiring them to work in communes or factories first), and the reimposition of entrance examinations.

The new entrance examinations, which the State Council tried to install in 1973, were called "cultural examinations," even though they covered such fields as mathematics and the sciences. Immediate opposition to the tests arose. In particular, students of worker, peasant, or soldier backgrounds fought against the new selection procedure, and they fought successfully.

> The best known act of opposition to the system was that of *Zhang Tiesheng* who, having graduated from middle school, sat for a "cultural examination" for college entrance in July, 1973. He refused to answer the questions, handed in blank papers in physics and chemistry, and on top of this, criticized the enrollment system in a note to the leadership. The whole affair was publicized in the *People's Daily* along with demands for the abolition of entrance examinations, and Zhang was made a hero by the Left.[42]

The cultural examinations were discontinued almost immediately.

If the Cultural Revolution's reforms in selection and higher education were characterized by the elimination of the examination system, changes after the overthrow of the "Gang of Four" have been epitomized by the reintroduction of testing. At the end of 1977 the Ministry of Education announced: "An all-round appraisal will be made of the applicants morally, intellectually, and physically. Entrance examinations will be restored and admittance based on their results."[43]

A cartoon from that same time illustrates a new view of the policy changes promulgated in education during the Cultural Revolution (figure 1). Chang Hsue-hsin of the Higher Education Bureau declared: "The entrance examination . . . was suspended. This interference of the Gang of Four in education was one of their greatest crimes."[44] And the *Peking Review* was now full of scathing rebukes:

> Serious sabotage by the "gang of four" wrought havoc with China's science and education. Large numbers of universities, colleges and scientific research institutes were disbanded. The gap between China's level of science and technology and the world's advanced levels has widened. Quite a number of key scientific and technological problems in our national economy remain unsolved. And basic scientific and theoretical research in particular has been virtually done away with. The quality of education has declined sharply. Sabotage by the "gang of four" in educational work has not only caused a decline in the level of knowledge and education. Worse still, it has led to the corruption of our teenagers and other young people politically and ideologically, and has retarded the development of a whole generation of young people. Various fields of work are keenly feeling the shortage of successors for scientific and technical endeavours. Science and education are lagging so far behind that they are seriously hindering the realization of the modernization of agriculture, industry, national defense and science and technology.[45]

And so it was that national entrance examinations were reinstituted and the selection policy overhauled. In 1977, the Ministry announced that 20 to 30 percent of college students would be enrolled directly from secondary school.[46] Thereafter the percentage of such students rose rapidly. By 1979, the require-

FIGURE 1. Cartoon Criticizing the Educational Policy of the "Gang of Four"

Our revolution in education—

The Four took the lead in encouraging anarchy in the schools. Chiang shouts, "We'd rather have ignorant workers!" (than educated exploiters); Chang Chun-Chiao says, "I don't want any know-it-alls"; Yao and Wang scream, "So much for knowledge above all else! We'd rather have the weeds of socialism than the seeds of capitalism!"

Chi Hsin, 1977

Source: Jan-Ingvar Löfstedt, *Chinese Educational Policy: Changes and Contradictions 1949–1979* (Atlantic Highlands, N.J.: Humanities Press, 1980), p. 144. Reprinted by permission of the publisher.

ment of prior work in the factory or fields was repealed. The admissions system of recommendation by the masses and screening by the Revolutionary Committees was abandoned.

By 1981, all the open-door policies of education—taking the classroom to the factory or field, part-work/part-study schooling, changed teaching steps— had been slammed shut. In 1978, the key school concept was reintroduced. Traditional subjects in the social and natural sciences were reemphasized, with special attention to theory. More years of study were required for degrees. And intellectuals, no longer denigrated as "rightist revisionists," were redefined as "workers engaged in mental labor."[47]

College selection was highly competitive. Only about 5 percent of those eligible and registered to take the examination were admitted in the early 1980s.[48] To be eligible to take entrance examinations, one had to be an unmarried senior middle school graduate under twenty-five years of age or have an equivalent amount of education. If the candidate were working, his or her unit had to verify the equivalent qualifications. Those with outstanding qualifications who were attending part-time schools or vocational institutes could also apply. Candidates registered for the exams in the counties or districts where they resided. If the number registered was very large, the provinces, municipalities, and autonomous regions could use preliminary examinations or some other screening device (such as outstanding secondary school grades).[49] The Ministry allocated a certain number of university places to each province, large municipality, and autonomous region.

In 1981, the examination system worked as follows. Candidates could take the examinations in either science or liberal arts. They were examined in six subjects. Science candidates took tests in mathematics, physics, chemistry, Chinese language and literature, politics, and a foreign language (a choice of Spanish, English, Russian, Japanese, or Arabic). Liberal arts candidates substituted history and geography for chemistry and physics. Unless the examinee planned to continue studying a foreign language, that part was graded on a 30-point scale. The other five subject tests were graded on a 100-point scale. Thus, the maximum score was 530. For foreign language students, the language exam counted 100 points and the mathematics section was graded on a 30-point scale.

The national entrance examinations took place every year around mid-July for enrollment on September 1 of that same year. They lasted three days. Each subject test required about two and a half hours, and candidates took two tests a day. After the examinations were graded, the Ministry of Education set minimum scores for each department in each national key university. (In the case of provincial and regular universities and colleges, the minimum was set by the provincial level education office.) The minimum varied according to the enrollment plans, students' stated institutional preferences, and the distribution of scores that year. A score of 300 was needed to gain admission into a regular college. At the more competitive key universities, which enroll students from all over China, the minimum was at least 380. There was no minimum passing score on the individual subject exams.[50]

Candidates scoring above the minimum then underwent two more screenings: "political assessment" and "physical examination." Workers, peasants, and soldiers were apparently given some preferential treatment if their scores were comparable. Information on student behavior, participation in political activities in school, and on-the-job performance was also used. The basic unit to which the prospective student was attached prepared a written report on the candidate's attitude toward work, relationship with peers, and attitude toward the struggle, criticism, and the Revolution.[51] It is not clear how many candidates "failed" at this point, or how they did so.

Members of minority groups were given a considerable edge. (National minorities made up 5.7 percent of the Chinese population.) In 1980, the Ministry described the policy of preferential treatment: "In selecting new students, the minimum score requirements will be lowered for minority applicants from border areas, mountain regions, pastoral areas and other areas populated by minority peoples. . . . Minority national applicants who are not from areas populated by minority people will be selected first if they possess the same qualifications as Han nationals."[52] There was, however, no affirmative action for women. Only about 24 percent of those enrolled in higher education in 1979 were women, compared with 41 percent in secondary education and 45 percent in primary schools.

WHY CHANGE?

The Cultural Revolution had changed many things besides admissions. Curricula had been altered. Time to degree had been shortened. Work and schooling had been integrated. Enrollments had dropped, and so had academic quality.

The results had been disastrous, or so the authorities argued in 1977. Deng Xiaoping did not mince words in his negative appraisal of what had happened to Chinese higher education:

> Since the Cultural Revolution, schools have not paid attention to educational standards and instead overemphasized practical work; students' knowledge of theory and basic skills in their area of specialization have been disregarded. The deterioration of academic standards will have the long term effect of leaving fields such as the sciences without completely trained workers. . . . Since the Cultural Revolution, teachers have been afraid to take firm charge of their students. . . . There has been no examination system, and no fixed rewards or punishment. . . . This has resulted in widespread student anarchy. . . . Can such a generation become capable successors in the Chinese Revolution?[53]
>
> On the question of talented people, we must particularly stress the need to break with the convention in the discovery, selection and training of those with outstanding talent. . . . We must thoroughly eliminate the pernicious influence of the Gang of Four and take up the important task . . . of training in the shortest time a group of experts . . . who are first rate by world standards.[54]

On what basis did Deng Xiaoping and other leading Chinese officials and educators justify the reintroduction of selection by examination? Some foreign scholars have explained the change solely in terms of a shift in objectives or values. The new people in charge in China had a different "taste" for academic values versus "revolutionary education." There is a point to this explanation, but for our purposes I wish to emphasize factual issues rather than normative issues.

A 1979 EXAMINATION QUESTION

The following amusing question illustrates what is asked of aspiring university students on the Chinese language and literature examination. It also incidentally conveys a certain ideology of merit and testing.

Question 6. *Composition (Write it on the examination paper) (40 points)*

Read the following article carefully and rewrite it with the title "Chen Yiling's Story." The requirements are:

1. In accordance with the contents of the original article, write a narrative with Chen Yiling as the central figure. Do not concoct other details, and do not write it into a summary of "The Second Examination"; otherwise, points will be forfeited. No points will be given if it is written as a poem or "thoughts after reading it."

2. It should have a clear central idea, with attention given to tailoring and arranging the material.

3. It should have unity and coherence and be structurally complete.

4. It should read smoothly, be correctly punctuated, and have no incorrectly written characters.

5. It is best to write 600–700 words, no more than 800 words (including punctuation marks), otherwise points will be forfeited.

6. Pay attention to the writing form: each character should occupy one space on the manuscript paper; each punctuation mark should also occupy one space.

The Second Examination

Points	Grader

(Written by He Wei, with some revisions.)

Professor Su Lin, a vocal music specialist, encountered a very unusual situation. Among the more than two hundred examinees who took part in an entrance examination was a 20-year-old girl named Chen Yiling. She achieved excellent scores on the preliminary examination. Her performances in vocal music, sightsinging, ear-training and music theory were all graded excellent. In particular she had beautiful tone color and a wide vocal range, which was highly praised by everyone. However, her performance was extremely disappointing at the second examination. All his life Professor Su Lin had taught pupils throughout the country, but this was the first time he had come across a student so talented for her age. This was also the first time he had encountered such a thing.

The open examination was held in a beautiful traditional hall. When Chen Yiling stood composed in front of the several vocal music specialists of the examination committee and finished the famous song "In February" by Xi Xinghai, the specialists could not help exchanging looks of appreciation. According to stipulation, the examinee should also sing a foreign song. She sang the aria "One Fine Day" from the Italian opera Madame Butterfly. Her brilliant tone color and deep feeling amazed everyone present. Even Professor Su Lin, who has always been strict in his demands, nodded his approval. In his stern look was hidden the trace of a smile. Everybody gazed at Chen Yiling: in a woolen sweater of tender green and a pair of trousers of coffee brown, she looked as if she were a slim and erect small tree on a spring morning. With everyone's eyes fixed on her, this girl who normally was composed and at ease could not help feeling a bit embarrassed.

The second examination was held a week later. It determined whether one would be accepted. It could determine a person's lifetime career. After the strict preliminary examination, very few people remained; the reexamination would have even stricter demands. All well-known figures in music circles in this city were in attendance. Members of the examination committee and auditors almost all had severe and critical expressions at judging time. Nonetheless, everyone agreed that should there be only one person suitable for selection, that person, without doubt, would be Chen Yiling.

Who could have known that things would happen contrary to expectation. Chen Yiling was the last one to take the second examination. She sang the same two songs as before, but her voice became uneven and lost all tonal color. It was as if different people had been heard on the two occasions. Was it because she had stage fright and became nervous, or because she was not feeling well that her voice was adversely affected? Some even suspected that she might not be prudent in her life style. Those present gazed at each other in speechless dismay and turned inquiring and puzzled eyes on her. Though she was unable to conceal the fatigue on her face, her bright eyes having lost their luster and the mischievous corners of her mouth showing an anxiety beyond words, she still appeared, on the whole, forthright and candid, and thus trustworthy. Apologetically she smiled at everyone and then left the room as if she were a floating cloud.

Apparently Professor Su Lin was very angry. He always held that for one to become an artist beloved by the people, one should first of all be a noble-minded person, a person who could be a model for others in every respect. A girl like this who gave herself up as hopeless could never become an accomplished vocalist. Furiously he turned to look out the window. The city recently had been hit by a severe typhoon. Outside the window, broken twigs and fallen leaves were scattered about in a mess. An entire bamboo fence had fallen on the ground and was covered with puddles. What a dismal sight!

The examination committee was divided in its opinion on Chen Yiling. One group thought Chen's voice was extremely unstable and inconsistent, and that it would be difficult to make anything of it; the other group felt that she should have another try. Professor Su Lin had his own idea. He thought the important thing was to find out the root cause of the great vocal disparity in her two performances. If the problem involved her attitude toward life and career, she should not be accepted no matter how gifted she was. This was the primary requirement of all!

But what was the cause?

Professor Su Lin took from the secretary Chen Yiling's application form, and marked with a red pencil a thin line under her address. The photo attached to the application form showed a vigorous and cute face, with a small and beautiful mouth, a pair of sprightly, pure eyes, and a nose that puckered a bit at both corners when she smiled, all of which seemed to remind the vocalist that you can not use over-simplified methods to deal with a person—a person with vitality, thought and emotion. At least certain things about this girl in *front of him could not be learned from the simple application form. Should she be turned down this time, probably she would have to bid farewell to music forever. Her talent might thus be stifled. If such were the case, he would never forgive himself.*

On the next day, Professor Su Lin set out on the first tram car in the morning. Using the address on the application form, he searched with great difficulty and finally found the remote road in Yangshupu.* As soon as he entered the lane, he could not help being startled.

Some of the walls in the lane had toppled. Scorched beams and pillars presented a horrible scene of black. Among the broken roof tiles and debris one could occasionally see smashed fragments and burned rags. It was clear not only that the lane had been hit by a typhoon, but that it had also been ravaged by fire. Among the rubble, people were already busy sorting out things in the early morning.

Professor Su Lin, holding the slip of paper, did not know where to begin looking. Suddenly he heard from an upper window now opposite him a boy casually singing:

"Mi - i - i - i, m - a - a - a," as if he were a vocalist practicing his voice. Professor Su couldn't help smiling; "This must be her home!" He guessed right; the boy was probably Chen Yiling's little brother.

From the boy he learned that the sister was a demobilized army-woman. Having returned from an art troupe in the army, she was transferred to do administrative work in a factory. She was a member of the Communist League, enthusiastic and warmhearted. If any problem came up, whether in the factory or in the neighborhood, one would not go wrong by contacting Chen Yiling. Two or three days ago, a typhoon caused electric wires to spark and quite a few houses were burned down. To help find a place for the victims, Chen Yiling was busy all night without going to bed, which had a detrimental effect on her voice. It happened that the second examination fell on the next day. She just said: "Too bad!" And still went to take the examination.

That was how things had happened.

"Look, she is still busy over there," said the boy, waving his hand toward the window. "I'll call her. "I'll go and call her."

"No need to. Please tell your sister she has passed the second examination."

Coming from Chen Yiling's house, Professor Su Lin walked at a brisk pace. He thought to himself: "This girl has all the necessary requirements to become an outstanding vocalist. I almost committed a grave mistake!" On this fine morning, his mind was bursting with excitement. He wanted to hurry home to tell everyone the story about Chen Yiling.

Source: The examination question and the story "The Second Examination," by He Wei, appeared in translation in "1979 National Unified Entrance Examinations for Institutions of Higher Education," *Chinese Education* 12, no. 3 (1979).

* A district in urban Shanghai, known for its concentrated factories and workers' residences.— Trans.

I will use the three categories of arguments for the 1966 change—efficiency, representation and bias, and incentives—to assemble the new arguments used in 1977 to justify the reintroduction of examinations. It was now contended that the 1966 reforms simply had not worked, in terms of attaining the objectives sought. Instead, the 1966 reforms had led to less efficiency, few gains in representation, and a great distortion of educational incentives.

Efficiency

It is difficult to tell how much academic standards had fallen in the Cultural Revolution and how much worker productivity and intellectual work were affected. There is some evidence, however:

- In 1977, the Shanghai Revolutionary Committee administered middle-school-level tests to the 1976–77 college graduates who were about to assume management and technical positions in the province's scientific and technological units. The results were startling and gloomy: 68 percent of the graduates failed the mathematics examination, 70 percent failed the physics, and 76 percent failed the chemistry test.[55]

- In 1981, similar basic knowledge tests were given nationwide to middle-level science and technology engineers and workers who had graduated in 1975. Just under 50 percent failed. (Apparently, Chinese leaders were expecting much worse, for they expressed relief over these results.)[56]

- In 1979, the Shanghai Commission of Science and Technology surveyed those who graduated from technical schools and universities between 1972 and 1976. The commission estimated how many graduates were qualified by standards from before the Cultural Revolution. It judged that only about 20 percent were qualified at the university level and about 60 percent at the standard of technical secondary education. The other 20 percent were not qualified by either standard.

- In 1979, a group of American educators compared the 1978 national entrance examination outlines to those published for the 1959 exams. The educators assessed the depth and breadth of the knowledge expected from the candidates in chemistry, physics, mathematics, history, politics, Chinese language and literature, and English. They found evidence of backsliding in the 1979 academic standards, particularly in the hard sciences. The 1959 outlines expected students to be familiar with material that was much more sophisticated as well as broader in scope.[57]

The new Chinese leadership has argued that the educational policies of the Cultural Revolution did not lead to more and better technicians, scientists, and leaders for the next generation, but actually produced a smaller educational elite, whose skills were less relevant to Chinese needs. Abolishing the examinations, it was maintained, had played a key role in an educational debacle. The new conventional wisdom stated that tests lead to efficient selection,[58] and good incentives:

> First, the quality of the students enrolled has been generally improved, and this is a fact generally acknowledged by all institutions of higher learning. Second, the new students enrolled by universities are those who are morally, intellectually and physically sounder than others. . . . In other words, it is relatively accurate to select talented students through college entrance examinations. Third, college entrance examinations have brought into play the enthusiasm of large numbers of young people for study and have promoted the improvement of teaching in middle schools.[59]

Even if tests lead to more efficient selection and allocation, these benefits must be weighed against the costs. Not least is the financial burden of managing a nationwide system of examinations with over 6 million students. Examinations are administered in July; colleges begin in September. The Ministry has less than two months to correct them, establish minimum scores, receive political assessments, and match scores with institutions, departmental requirements, and student preferences. This is one reason why preliminary examinations are being suggested: "The workload is heavy and time is pressing. It is difficult to do this work meticulously. As a result, mistakes are likely, which will affect selection of the best qualified students."[60]

Representation

In other dimensions, the changes of the Cultural Revolution had probably been more successful. Data about the ethnic and class composition of higher education for the past fifteen years are scanty. It is likely that students of worker or peasant backgrounds are still underrepresented in higher education. For example, it has been reported that in Gansu province 86 percent of the population are peasants. In junior secondary schools, pupils of peasant background make up 84 percent of the student body, but the corresponding figures are 66 percent in senior secondary schools and 53 percent in higher education.

But the proportion of students from worker or peasant backgrounds probably increased during the Cultural Revolution. A study of a sample of emigrants from the Mainland to Hong Kong is suggestive. Two groups of "economically active nonfarm" Chinese—one group educated before the Cultural Revolution, and one during—were compared. In the latter group, the father's social class had a much weaker, although still positive, effect on the offspring's educational attainments and later occupation (however, the effect of the child's educational attainments on his or her later occupational income was also lower in the group educated during the Cultural Revolution).[61] Nonetheless, during the Cultural Revolution the representation of students from worker or peasant origins was not improved as much as some crude statistics might lead one to conclude:

> On paper, 70 percent of the students at Kwangchow Teachers' College come from the countryside and 30 percent from the cities. However, a large percent-

age of the students recruited in the countryside are actually former city-bred youth who moved to the rural areas to perform manual labour rather than children of rural origin. Thus, the bias in favour of city-bred students still exists. . . . Middle school education in the cities still remains overall at a higher level.[62]

Restoring the examination system was immediately criticized as adversely affecting the disadvantaged: "Reflecting a segment of opinion in many provinces, 'some people' at the 1978 National Conference on College Enrolment—most notably members of the Anhui delegation—challenged the examinations for favouring the urban areas over the rural, the minority over the majority, and students from exploiting or intellectual families rather than workers and peasants."[63] Data are not available for enrollment rates of minority groups during the Cultural Revolution, but as noted earlier, preference is still given to minorities in university admissions. On this score, there appears to have been little change.[64] According to one source, in some fields women must obtain higher scores to be admitted than men.[65]

Incentive Effects

According to many Chinese, the end of examinations was the beginning of educational corruption. During the Cultural Revolution, "entering through the back door" was prevalent—the use of personal or political influence, or bribes, to secure college admission for one's son or daughter. As a report from students at Peking University put it, "Everyone knows that the system of recommendation by the masses had a very bad influence at the grass-roots level. . . . The best way to get to the university was still to have a well placed father; lots of young people lost all motivation to study."[66] Admission by objective examinations after 1977 reduced the possibility of, and therefore the incentives to engage in, corruption and coercion.[67]

Examinations remove some incentives and create others. They are said to motivate students to study harder, at least to study what the exams test.[68] One may approve of this: "College entrance examinations have brought into play the enthusiasm of large numbers of young people for study and have promoted the improvement of teaching in school."[69] Or one may disapprove, especially if competitiveness and bookishness reach extreme proportions. A number of Chinese newspapers and magazines have lamented some of the ill-effects: despair, nervous breakdowns, and even suicides among anxious students and failed examinees. Cheating has been reported—occasionally involving the collaboration of teachers. Curricula and personal habits are said to be distorted by the exams.[70]

Only one in twenty examinees is admitted. "Failure" is the fate of the overwhelming majority, with all the ensuing problems of morale. This is not a problem with examinations per se: no matter how students are chosen, there are far fewer slots than aspirants (and as total tertiary enrollments have increased since the Cultural Revolution, more people now have the chance at higher education). But the Chinese government nonetheless has a difficult problem in mollifying those who are unable to pursue their studies. "The broad masses of applicants," writes one official, "must be educated to take into consideration the overall situation, make 'two preparations with one Red heart,' subordinate themselves to the needs of the state and correctly deal with the issue of college admissions."[71]

As academic criteria grow in importance, political criteria shrink. This too has incentive effects. Some Chinese officials worry that political education is being neglected and revolutionary zeal diminished. A May 7, 1981, circular from the Ministry of Education implied that recent university graduates had not expressed much political dedication. The Ministry was upset at the large proportion of graduates who seemed reluctant to obey the State and Party and take the job assignments given them upon termination of their studies. The circular stated: "The ideological confusion caused by the 10 year catastrophe has undermined the good practice of graduates accepting job assignments by the state."[72] It went on to say that universities should place more stress on political education.

Next Steps

In both quantity and quality, Chinese higher education lags far behind the industrialized West, Japan, and the Soviet Union. The country is said to be ten years behind its development needs, in terms of university-trained personnel. The government sees this shortage as the major constraint on its development plan. The expansion and improvement of higher education is said to be China's top educational priority for the 1980s.[73]

Current plans call for more and better universities. By 1990, the number of universities and colleges should grow to 1,100 (from about 633 in 1980) and the number of students to about 2.2 million (from about 1 million). A huge World Bank loan will aid this expansion.

In all of this the Chinese seem intent on more and better examinations. And not only for university admissions: even in factories, tests are being used in personnel selection. According to several Chinese pronouncements, "examinations are now being promoted as the preferred means of allocating factory jobs."[74] For example, in the selection of 8,000 new workers for the city of Sian, candidates had to take tests in politics, Chinese language, and junior secondary level mathematics, physics, and chemistry. And in 1981, four top officials from the Educational Testing Service in Princeton, New Jersey, conferred with educational policy makers in China, with reports of possible collaboration in standardized testing.

2

SELECTION POLICIES IN
DEVELOPING COUNTRIES

"The entrance examination . . . was suspended," said Chang Hsue-hsin of the Higher Education Bureau of the People's Republic of China in 1977. "This interference of the Gang of Four in education was one of their greatest crimes."

After eleven years of selecting university students without standard tests, China brought back entrance examinations in 1977. As much as any other step taken after the overthrow of the Gang of Four, this symbolized a new departure in public policy. It also underscored the importance to developing countries of policies for choosing the elite.

Many scholars have studied elites in developing countries, but rarely as a policy problem. Sociologists, political scientists, historians, and others have been interested in elites as a key to a nation's identity, historical evolution, and prospects for economic and social health. Regarding the system for selecting the Chinese literati, Max Weber wrote: "It has been of immeasurable importance for the way in which Chinese culture has developed that this leading stratum of intellectuals has never had the character of the clerics of Christianity or of Islam, or of Jewish rabbis, or Indian Brahmins, or Ancient Egyptian priests, or Egyptian or Indian scribes."[1] More recently, scores of studies have appeared on the backgrounds of high political figures in developing nations, patterns in the upbringing and attitudes of the upper classes, and ways that patronage and sponsorship enable elites to designate their successors.[2]

But how *should* future elites be selected? If civil service jobs are scarce, who should get them? If university slots experience excess demand, how should they be allocated? How should policy-makers in China think about the pros and cons of various selection systems? Most of the literature offers no specific advice. Most authors set themselves a different task. They aim to *describe* regularities among existing elites, or they want to *explain* why restrictive selection policies exist, often exploring the quite general hypothesis that elites try to perpetuate themselves. As the author of a recent study put it, "We start from the premise that every aristocratic group's adjustment to change is limited by its wish to maintain some kind of overall superiority over other groups, nonaristocratic elements in society."[3] In short, most studies of elites in developing countries are not policy-oriented.

Apart from the predilections of scholars and academic disciplines, this omission may result in part from the fact that societies do not announce policies for selecting future elites. Hereditary advantages of property, culture, and genes are not distributed according to social choice. Many governmental actions do affect the distribution of wealth and power, but there are no "Directors General for Elites"—or at least none that admit to it.

There are, however, a few well-accepted, conscious policies for choosing the elite. One is the selection of those who will receive higher education and professional training at public institutions. Who is chosen matters to the life of a nation, to the prospects for development, and to the perception and the reality of fairness and social mobility. True, the highly educated and the socioeconomic elite are not coextensive groups. A university degree is neither necessary nor sufficient for becoming rich and powerful.[4] But income and years of education are strongly correlated. In one African university, no matter what his social background, ethnic group, or political philosophy, it is said that "the student knows that the university degree is his passport to elite status. . . . Thus, the student, while often from a background of poverty or near poverty and frequently in severe financial straights during his stay at the university, is also an heir presumptive to elite status. He knows that only three years and his final examinations stand between him and lifelong security and comfort."[5] In much of Latin America, wrote another author in 1962, university graduates almost automatically "become part of the elite. It matters little whether a student is the son of a minister or the son of a workman. His mere enrollment in the university makes him one of the two per thousand most privileged in the land."[6] (The use of the male pronoun is telling, as we shall see below.)

It is easy to overstate this point, particularly in countries where the expansion of higher education has been rapid. But it remains true that doctors, engineers, and other university graduates usually occupy high positions on the socioeconomic scale. Therefore, admissions policies have an important, if not exclusive, effect on the allocation of human resources, and in turn on the allocation of status and wealth in the society.

In most developing countries, admissions policy is public policy; private universities and professional schools are relatively scarce. And in most countries the policy must be very selective. Selectivity is necessitated by the large number of candidates for a few educational slots: often only one in ten or twenty applicants can be accepted. The demand for higher education and professional training is large and growing throughout the developing world.[7]

The social costs of selecting the wrong students are high. The government typically pays more than 90 percent of the cost of a student's higher education. One year of higher education may cost twenty times more than a year of primary schooling. Failure rates are high in most developing countries, typically in the range of 30 to 70 percent. Moreover, the need for well-trained graduates is great: the social benefits of competent leadership are large. The state thus has an important stake in which and how many students complete their training.

But if there are strong efficiency arguments for using admissions policies to reduce the probability of failure and to raise the quality of eventual graduates, there are also important concerns about exclusionary effects. Will the future elite be chosen disproportionately from certain ethnic groups, regions, native languages, or socioeconomic classes? Do university admissions policies simply reinforce existing structures of privilege?

The study of elites in developing countries has many interesting and important aspects. In this book the task is not descriptive or explanatory—not what elites look like or how they arise or even what role they play in these societies. It is policy-analytic. What should one be trying to do with a selection policy? What are the key factual and normative questions, and how might they be addressed in a particular case? To enter the spirit of this task, imagine that you were in charge of the admissions system for public universities in a developing country. If you could design a selection policy, how would you go about doing so?

These generic questions are not limited to higher education. Most countries have important selection systems for employment in the civil service, in which similar issues arise. The private sector also has analogues to admissions policies in firms' entry-level hiring. At the broadest level, the problem of choosing the elite is how to set up an efficient, fair, and open system for selecting only a few among many aspirants for desired positions. The analysis here of admissions policies generalizes to the organization of nonmarket allocation systems; it involves a prescriptive look at the fundamental tension between meritocracy and elitism.

MERIT AND MARKETS

Why do I say "nonmarket allocation systems"? It is worth pausing to notice why the selection problem arises—or, put another way, to notice when the problem does not arise. Consider a stylized version of the labor market. In simple microeconomic models, there is no need for selection systems for employees. Workers are hired according to their easily measured marginal products and paid exactly that. If some workers turn out to be unsatisfactory, they can be fired without cost, or their wages can be instantaneously adjusted according to output. In such a situation there is no selection problem.

Reality presents a different picture. An individual's productivity is usually difficult to measure in the short run. Hiring and firing can be far from costless. It may be hard to vary wages according to different productivities. Under such conditions, it becomes economically rational to select future employees by *predicting* their marginal products. This is done by observing certain characteristics of the candidates and selecting a few among the many aspirants.

Admission to higher education is similar. The analogy to the simple microeconomic model for hiring would have students pay tuition according to their willingness to pay for the product the university provides and their contributions to the university's objectives. The tuition price would be set high enough for the market to clear. If students' willingness to pay and contributions to the university could be easily assessed and charged and unsatisfactory students could be expelled without cost, there would be little need for preselection.

But for a variety of good and bad reasons, real universities do not work this way. There are subsidized tuitions for the education received; willingness to pay is rarely considered. Students usually pay the same tuition regardless of their contributions to the university's objectives (an exception here is a merit scholarship). Flunking out large numbers of students is politically difficult, perhaps especially so in the developing countries. Consequently, universities solve the problem of excess demand through selection policies, not an untrammeled market.

If an auction were used to allocate university slots or civil service openings, the selection problem would disappear.[8] The problem exists because for political or other reasons we refuse to let the selection of future elites be subject entirely to market forces or because transactions costs are so high that it is uneconomical for us to do so.

HOW IMPORTANT IS THE SELECTION PROBLEM?

Higher education plays an important economic and political role in most poor countries. Governmental expenditures on higher education average about 4 percent of the gross national product in the developing countries (as opposed to 5.7 percent in the developed countries). This percentage is roughly constant across the continents—Africa 4.2 percent, Latin America 4.3 percent, and Asia 4.0 percent—although, of course, countries differ. We can generalize roughly and say that higher education takes up about 20 percent of a country's educational budget, secondary education about 25 percent, and primary education some 40 to 50 percent. Here again individual countries vary.[9]

Higher education has been growing fast in the developing world. For example, in black Africa in 1960 there were six universities; in 1977 there were 80, with Nigeria possessing 20. This rapid growth has led some critics to accuse Africa and other developing areas of having too many small universities of substandard quality. (Several larger, regional universities—Dakar; the University of Botswana, Lesutho, and Swaziland; and the University of East Africa— eventually disintegrated.)

Across developing countries from 1965 to 1975, enrollments in higher education grew at an annual rate of 10 percent. This was more than the annual rate of growth of secondary education (7 percent) or primary education (4.5 percent). On the other hand, most developing countries were beginning with extremely low enrollments at the tertiary level. By 1975 the less developed countries enrolled 4.4 percent of the relevant age in higher education, compared with 23 percent in the developed countries. In 1975 the percentage of 20 to 24-

year-olds enrolled in higher education was 48 percent in North America, 17 percent in Europe, 14 percent in Oceania, 6 percent in both Latin America and Asia, and 1.5 percent in Africa.[10]

Higher education is much more expensive than secondary or primary education; each additional student enrolled in higher education takes up resources that could be devoted to many students enrolled at the primary or secondary levels. The exact cost multipliers vary by country, and here there is a systematic pattern by per capita gross national product (GNP).

For example, the poorest group of developing countries (with per capita GNPs of less than $265 per year) have a per pupil higher education cost about seven times that for secondary schools in the same countries and twenty times the per pupil cost for primary education. These ratios decline as per capita GNPs are larger. For example, in the middle-income countries (with GNP per capita between $1,075 and $2,500 a year), the per pupil cost in higher education is four times that of secondary education and seven times that of primary education. In the developed countries, the corresponding figures are 2.5 and 3.5.[11]

These figures show that the poorer the developing country, the more higher education tends to be confined and exclusive, and the more expensive it is compared with lower educational levels. Thus, the distributional consequences of selection systems are more severe in the developing countries than in the industrialized West.

Numerous estimates of the importance of higher education for the development process have been attempted. In an old study for the Organization for Economic Cooperation and Development, three researchers found that the correlations between enrollment rates and GNP growth were significant, and the highest of these correlations was that for enrollment rate in the oldest age-group being studied.[12] A recent study of the World Bank estimated the social rate of return of higher education at 15 percent, with a lower rate of about 8 percent for higher education in agricultural subjects.[13] Of course, measuring the benefits of higher education is a difficult problem. Gains in earnings over time are the most widely used measure, but many people would not wish to rely solely on such data, particularly in developing countries, where labor markets are not known for their smooth and accurate reflection of social marginal products.

The private rates of return from higher education are likely to be even larger than the social rates of return. If good jobs and political offices have rents attached to them, we expect that individuals may extract more private gains from those positions than society will obtain public gains. Moreover, people value the positions opened to them by higher education for nonmonetary reasons, such as prestige or power. In a sense, these are also "private returns" that affect the demand for higher education.

Since higher education is subsidized, it is not surprising that it experiences excess demand. Many more people want to gain entrance to universities than can be accepted (or should be accepted, in terms of social benefits and costs). The

TABLE 2. Percentage of Students in Fields of Study (Mid-1970s)

Subject	Developed Countries	Developing Countries	World
Humanities	17%	19%	19%
Social sciences	19	19	19
Sciences	10	10	10
Law	6	9	8
Education	15	12	12
Engineering	11	11	11
Agriculture	2	4	4
Medicine	12	9	10

Source: George Psacharopoulos, *Higher Education in Developing Countries: A Cost-Benefit Analysis* (Washington, D.C.: World Bank, November 1980), p. 7.
Note: "World" includes oil-producing countries. Figures do not add vertically to 100 because of "other" subject categories.

extent of excess demand varies by the field of study; medicine and engineering are generally the most oversubscribed.

It is interesting to note that the pattern of subjects taken in universities in the developing countries is roughly the same as the pattern in the developed countries (table 2). This is again a generalization across many different kinds of countries, but it is still surprising that the developing countries have about the same percentages of students enrolled in engineering, arts, the sciences, and so forth as the developed countries do. Nonetheless, in the developing countries, studies indicate that the costs and benefits of higher education differ considerably by field. One estimate says that agriculture has the highest costs and the lowest benefits in terms of later earnings streams.[14]

Higher education may be a mixed blessing. One recent study showed that a significant predictor of political instability in developing countries is rapid growth in enrollment rates in higher education.[15] Moreover, educated unemployment is an increasing phenomenon in many developing countries, and some observers find it to be not only economically unproductive but also socially harmful.

In most developing countries, however, the benefits are perceived to outweigh the costs. In Indonesia and China, for example, the expansion and improvement of higher education has received the highest priority for the decade ahead. It is widely asserted that shortages of highly trained personnel are a constraint in the development process. It is difficult to be precise on this score. One may easily confuse different things under the label of "a need for more educated people." For example, a system may not reward capable managers. If so there may be a "shortage of trained managers," but it does not follow that by training more managers the system would suddenly benefit from trained managerial behavior. It is dangerous to presume that a lack of high-level skills will be remedied by education alone.

Nonetheless, it is impossible to deny that in the developing countries trained personnel is a crucial ingredient for efficient growth and effective governance. Tanzanian President Julius K. Nyerere states the usual argument with his unique eloquence:

> There is, in fact, only one reason why underdeveloped societies like ours establish and maintain universities. We do so as an investment in our future. We are spending large and disproportionate amounts of money on a few individuals so that they should, in the future, make a disproportionate return to the society. We are investing in a man's brain in just the same way as we invest in a tractor; and just as we expect the tractor to do many times as much work for us as a hand-hoe, so we expect the student we have trained to make many times as great a contribution to our well-being as the man who has not had this good fortune. We are giving to the student while he is at the university, so that we may receive more from him afterwards.[16]

THE EFFICIENCY OF SELECTION

A theme in many historical studies is the efficiency gained through a more "rational" allocation of people to scarce positions. "Efficiency" here refers to the quality of those selected in terms of their performance on the job or at the university. A more efficient selection procedure leads to better-quality choices.

Max Weber referred to the tendency of democracy and bureaucracy to "rationalize" procedures for selection and promotion. Rational selection means efficient selection: instead of using subjective or ascriptive criteria, a rational system chooses on the basis of objective measures. These measures are themselves chosen precisely because they are able to predict, albeit imperfectly, the later performance of interest.

Around the world, in countries as different as China and Chile and Chad, the "rationality" of university admission is defined in terms of academic criteria. One might even refer to an ideology of academic merit. The smartest and best-prepared students, academically speaking, are thought of as having the most merit. If everyone cannot be chosen, those who are selected should be the best; those with merit should be the next generation's elite.

The argument for this ideology is rarely made explicit. Perhaps the argument is thought to be obvious; if "merit" is defined flexibly enough, the argument may even become a tautology. "At any good university," said President Nyerere, "some of the best brains of the day should be living together."[17] But why? Some might say by a matter of right.[18] Others might point to the ideal of an open, meritocratic system as a guarantor of equal opportunity and social mobility. Others would make a Weberian argument, based on the efficiency of selection on the basis of merit.[19]

THE IMPORTANCE OF EFFICIENT SELECTION

When Professor Walter Kamba became principal and vice-chancellor of the University of Zimbabwe in 1981, one of the first problems he faced was an alarmingly high rate of academic failures at the university. He commissioned a study of the matter.

The study's findings highlighted the importance of efficient policies for selecting students. If students were admitted and flunked out, it had high costs—for them and for the country.

The admission of a student into the University raises high expectations of him as well as in his friends and relatives. Failure constitutes a traumatic experience for him. It damages his conception of himself and causes frustration and despair. . . .

The University is the highest national institution of learning. Over 90 per cent of its financial needs are provided for by the government of Zimbabwe. This large investment does require a correspondingly significant output of manpower. It is from this point of view that the high failure rate becomes a national concern.

Moreover, the quality and not just the numbers of graduates mattered to the newly independent nation. Prime Minister Robert G. Mugabe emphasized that the university should not be seen "merely as a training institution or a diploma factory." The few chosen for the university had to be the best the country could muster. University students are "a very privileged minority," Mugabe said. "They are also the intelligentsia and as such are of vital importance to Zimbabwe. Much has been given to the students, and an equal measure will be expected of them in return."

The study commissioned by Professor Kamba criticized the university's admissions system, which took one in six applicants solely on the basis of A-level examination results and school reports. The examinations, written in Great Britain, were said not to be "relevant to the needs of Zimbabwe." School reports could be misleading, since secondary schools encouraged rote learning rather than the problem-solving skills that were essential for the science-based professions. And it was precisely in those professions that the failure rates at the university were highest.

But the study offered little to replace the existing system. It recommended better orientations for aspiring students and more faculty counseling for students with problems. It did not provide the analytical and statistical basis for improving selection policies. Without such improvements, it is possible that, as a foreign observer notes, "the Zimbabwe government could find itself reevaluating the problem of educational expansion, or face the prospect of spending ever-increasing amounts of the national treasury on education at the expense of investment in job creation."

Source: Quotations are from Avery Russell, "Education in Zimbabwe: The Struggle Between Opportunity and Resources," *Carnegie Quarterly* 29, no. 3 (1984): 7.

It is this dimension of efficiency that I want to stress first. In this context "efficiency" refers to the quality of those selected, in terms of later performance, compared with the costs of selecting them. One selection system is more efficient in this sense than another, when the benefits in terms of the productivity of those selected minus the costs of using the selection system is greater. We might think of this as "static efficiency," since the idea leaves out the incentives that a selection system creates, which themselves have implications for efficiency. It will be convenient to treat incentive effects, or "dynamic efficiency," separately.

The gains in efficiency from one selection system to another can be large. For example, a careful study of the implementation from 1899 to 1945 of the Japanese examination system for choosing civil servants concluded:

> The connection between the Higher Examinations and civil service effectiveness was fundamental and manifold. Requiring rigorous verification of superior scholastic achievement provided the civil service with a continuing but controlled infusion of young men of proven intellectual capacity. Substituting education for class, regional, and family ties as the indispensable qualification for the inner elite made recruitment much more impersonal than ever before and therefore less vulnerable to favoritism and corruption.[20]

This is not to say that the Japanese examination system did not also have its costs and disadvantages, or perhaps additional benefits of a dynamic sort.

Little is known about the potential gains from more efficient selection systems in developing countries. In an interesting, alternative approach to the one taken in this book, Marcelo Selowsky of the World Bank, and his associates, attempted rough estimates of the gains in social efficiency from better selection systems. The authors assumed a single, perfectly measured dimension of "ability," which they identified with "IQ" and labeled as "early traits or innate ability." Following others in the human capital literature, they posited that ability and years of education were complementary. The social gain from an additional year of education was higher for the more able. Like many economists, they measured the social gain by comparing later earnings with the costs of providing the education.

For example, the authors assumed that if two students differ in IQ by one point, the value in terms of later earnings for an additional year of education would be 1 percent higher for the higher-IQ student than for the lower-IQ student. They based this estimate on studies done in the United States. As a rough guess, then, if a selection system raised the average IQ of those admitted by 5 points, it would lead to a 5 percent increase in the later earnings of those admitted.

These are simplifying and perhaps troubling assumptions, but they are probably no worse than similarly speculative and theoretical estimates made by economists of the putative benefits of efficient allocation in other contexts. Selowsky and his colleagues concluded that if students in developing countries were allocated to educational opportunities strictly according to their ability, the result would be about a 5 percent increase in GNP. The 5 percent figure held for developing countries across various continents and levels of GNP. Compared with economists' guesses about other sorts of "misallocation," efficiently selecting students would be worth more than twice as much to the GNP of developing nations as correctly allocating workers to sectors of the economy—and about twice as much as correcting the welfare losses due to trade protection.[21]

I will develop other methods of estimating the gains in efficiency due to better selection systems. For now, I wish only to leave open the possibility that the gains may be substantial.

THE REPRESENTATION OF GROUPS

Because selection systems allocate goods in excess demand, distributional considerations as well as efficiency matter. Opportunities for higher education are often distributed unequally among social classes, regions of the country, ethnic and communal groups, or sexes. And this may matter for public policy.

Let us call this the problem of group representation. I wish to distinguish the under- or overrepresentation of certain groups among those selected from "bias" in the criteria used for selecting. "Bias" occurs when a certain admissions criterion systematically misrepresents the later performance of one group compared with another group. In a biased test, for example, the later performance of one group will be systematically underpredicted (or overpredicted). "Underrepresentation" means that one group has proportionally fewer members among those selected than among those in the relevant population. Usually bias in the selection system will lead to underrepresentation, but underrepresentation may occur even with an unbiased selection process. We shall discuss these concepts in chapter 4.

To some observers it is a truism that selection systems will maximize the chances of the current elite to perpetuate itself. In particular, "educational systems are a key instrument in ensuring the reproduction of the prevailing social structure and must necessarily adopt a social definition of talent or achievement that favors the maintenance of the power and prestige of the privileged groups."[22] According to this view, selection criteria that prima facie seem efficient and based on an individual's merit are systematically discriminatory to the poor, the rural, the minority groups, and (less often noted) women.

Others counter that selection systems not based on the supposedly discriminatory criterion of academic merit could be even less fair. The representation of groups is a matter of degree; so is "elite self-perpetuation." Historically, at least, has it not led to more representation of disadvantaged groups when substituted for selection by connections or bribery? The Japanese examination system enhanced the representation of the underprivileged in the civil service:

> Finally, the Higher Examinations sounded—however faintly—the unfamiliar theme of equal opportunity in a society of historic inequalities. They did not

make it easy for sons of tenant farmers to become chiefs of powerful bureaus, but at least they made it conceivable; and for society as a whole, they helped to erode the barriers of social and economic privilege.[23]

But still the Japanese system, like most others, led to the underrepresentation of certain groups.[24] Of course, critics respond, underrepresentation does not mean no representation. Most systems make room for the very able person of whatever sect, social background, or ethnic group; this very openness enhances the viability of an elitist system that systematically underrepresents the poor, minorities, and so forth.

> To change the metaphor, the school system is a filter, not a dam. It is therefore possible to maintain belief in the myth that education is a social leveler. Confidence in the system is not often shaken, partly because some poor do succeed in it, and partly because it has the outward trappings of an open, but tough, competition. . . . Indeed, it is precisely its selectivity that gives the system its durability.[25]

An elite that wishes to perpetuate itself may therefore install a selection system that is optimally but not completely exclusionary of the nonelite. At least, so goes the argument.

What are the facts in the developing countries? To what extent are certain groups disproportionately excluded by the educational system?

Perhaps the most glaring example, and one usually not emphasized in the literature, concerns women. In most developing countries, women are greatly underrepresented in educational systems. According to one estimate, only 52 females are enrolled in higher education in the Third World for every 100 males.[26] It is interesting to note that even in societies where more females drop out at each stage of the educational system, some universities may have high rates of female enrollment. It is possible that less academically able girls drop out sooner, so that only the abler women remain when selection for universities is made, and in that pool of applicants, women may end up well represented. Thus, as with other disadvantaged groups, the plight of women may be in part hidden if one looks only at the percentages of applicants admitted. This is a topic deserving much more research.[27]

There is also much evidence of the underrepresentation of the poor and the disadvantaged (see table 3). The children of government officials are heavily overrepresented in the educational systems of such countries as Bourkina Fasso (formerly Upper Volta), Indonesia, the Ivory Coast, Malaysia, and the Philippines.[28] Children from the middle and upper classes are usually overrepresented in the student bodies, compared with those from the working classes. Students from urban areas are more likely to be admitted to universities than those from rural areas.

In most countries of the developing world, selection systems tend to exclude members of certain ethnic groups. Within some African countries, certain tribes are more represented than others, and the overrepresented tend to be those that

TABLE 3. **Examples of Underrepresentation of the Poor and Disadvantaged in Educational Systems**

Country	Education Level	Description of Adverse Impact
Upper Volta, 1970	Secondary	Selectivity ratio: "primary sector," 0.6; "traditional secondary and tertiary sectors," 4; "modern secondary and tertiary," 8; "public administration," 36
Ghana, 1966	Secondary	Selectivity ratio: "agriculture, fishing," 0.66; "manual crafts, skilled and semi-skilled," 0.66; "all others including civil servants, teachers, professionals, and businessmen," 3.3
Ivory Coast, 1969–70	Secondary	Selectivity ratio: "primary sector," 0.67; "traditional sector (farmers, traders, handworkers)," 0.72; "modern sector," 3.0; "private and professional services and public administration," 9.1

Philippines, 1976 — University of Philippines — Family income of various groups:

Income	% Among Philippine Population, 1971	% Among Applicants, 1974	% Among Qualifiers, 1976
<P3,000	59	26	5
P3,000–6,000	25	29	8
P6,000–10,000	10	21	15
P10,000–20,000	5	18	29
>P20,000	1	7	42

Country	Education Level	Description of Adverse Impact
Indonesia, 1981	University of Indonesia	Percentage attending university who were offspring of: Farmers, fishermen, workers: 4% Private (self-employed, business, professional): 32% Military and government: 41% Retired and others: 24%

Sources: Charles Elliott, assisted by François de Morsier, *Patterns of Poverty in the Third World* (New York: Praeger, 1975), chap. 9. Calculations based on data from the University of the Philippines, Quezon City, March 1977, and computer printout from the Registrar's Office, University of Indonesia (January 1982).

Note: "Selectivity ratio" is the proportion of the *school* population from a particular group divided by the proportion of the *total* population from that group. Ratios less (greater) than 1 are under(over)-represented.

in the colonial days had the greatest access to Western education. Some studies indicate that not much progress has been made in Africa since independence, in terms of overcoming adverse impact by tribe and ethnic group.[29] In many other developing countries, from Mexico to India, disadvantaged ethnic groups are underrepresented in the higher-education system. According to the 1980 Brazilian census, 10 percent of white males over five years of age had finished at least eleven years of education and 3 percent had finished at least fifteen years. The corresponding percentages for "browns" were less than 3 percent and less than 0.4 percent, respectively; for "blacks" the percentages were less than 2 percent and less than 0.2 percent.[30]

There are many possible causes for underrepresentation. The particular criteria used in selection may be biased in the predictive sense discussed above. There may be overt, discriminatory quotas, as in some universities in Indonesia, Sri Lanka, Malaysia, and South Africa. Perhaps more pervasive is what might be called institutionalized discrimination, where the structure of the socioeconomic system—its incentives and prior injustices—lead predictively unbiased selection policies to produce the underrepresentation of particular groups.[31]

Selection policies can be designed to counter these problems and increase representation. If biased criteria were the cause of underrepresentation, they could be replaced by unbiased criteria, and the result could well be a selection system that was both more efficient and more representative. On the other hand, if the criteria for selection were unbiased and underrepresentation still ensued, then policy-makers would face a trade-off between efficiency and representation. They might be willing to select a somewhat less capable elite in order to achieve the greater representation of important groups. If so, the selection system might use quotas for groups, or add points to the ratings of group members, or expend more resources in search of capable applicants from underrepresented constituencies. Structuring this trade-off is the subject of chapter 4.

INCENTIVES CREATED BY ADMISSIONS SYSTEMS

Selection policies create incentives of several kinds. These incentives—or aspects of dynamic efficiency—should be considered along with static efficiency and group representation in the design of selection policies.

One category of incentives concerns high-school students and teachers. The incentives created by admissions policies may be good or bad—perhaps good *and* bad. Three years after entrance examinations were restored in China, one official noted that high-school students were studying harder and learning more. "College entrance examinations have brought into play the enthusiasm of large numbers of young people for study and have promoted the improvement of teaching in school."[32] But too much bookishness can result, as the Chinese press occasionally highlights. If examinations are poorly designed and emphasize rote learning, they may induce high-school students to learn the wrong things the wrong way. Standardized achievement tests may inhibit local choice of subject matter and pedagogy, as a 1956 report by the Board of Secondary Education in Lahore, Pakistan, stated: "The dead weight of the examination has tended to curb the teachers' initiative, to stereotype the curriculum, to promote mechanical and lifeless methods of teaching, to discourage all spirit of experimentation and to place stress on wrong or unimportant things in education."[33]

AVOIDING ADVERSE INCENTIVES IN ZAMBIA

At the entrance to the Department of Technical Education and Vocational Training, in Lusaka, Zambia, one encounters a sign:

NOTICE

ADMISSION TO COLLEGES OR INSTITUTES
IS ON MERIT ONLY. DON'T NEGOTIATE
WITH INDIVIDUAL OFFICERS. THIS LEADS
TO CORRUPTION.

DIRECTOR.

I asked the director, Mr. R. Lubasi, about the sign. "Even with it," he said, "we are still besieged by requests from politicians and officials and VIPs to secure admission for their children or friends. We are trying to resist these forces with a strict policy of admission by examination. Then we can tell the VIPs that we would love to be able to help them, but we have no choice."

Later in our interview, Mr. Lubasi received a telephone call from a Zambian politician. At the end of the call, Mr. Lubasi told me he had just put into practice the philosophy he had explained. "Admission by merit only, helps to avoid corruption."

The choice of selection policies creates another sort of incentive, namely for those who can affect the selections made. A mechanical process based solely on objective criteria leaves no discretion for admissions committees, policy-makers, or others with interests in specific outcomes. Alternatively, if criteria for admission remain vague and subjective, all sorts of influences and judgments may be brought to bear—for both good and bad reasons. In the developing countries especially, one must consider how alternative selection systems will fare against the forces of corruption and nepotism.

Some criteria, such as standardized tests, put the power to select in the hands of educators at the center, who design the examinations. Other criteria give power to local officials, as when high-school grades and the recommendations of principals are heavily weighted. Still others try to circumvent the educational establishment altogether, as in the Cultural Revolution, when selection for universities was carried out by local cadres of the Communist Party.

Alternative selection policies thus create a variety of *incentives*, which may be overlooked, at great risk, if policy-makers confine their attention to static *efficiency* and *representation*.

POLICIES USED FOR SELECTION

Selection policies differ across the developing nations, but several generalizations may be advanced. Screening devices for higher education tend to be academic in nature, although many countries have quotas for particular ethnic groups. Academic standards have become progressively less stringent over the past two decades. In part this is the result of expanded enrollments and higher selection ratios, which (other things being equal) implies that the marginal student accepted is less qualified. In countries like Mexico, Morocco, and Ecuador, there have been successful campaigns for virtually open admissions.

Lower academic standards have many other causes. Conceptions of higher education are changing. Even in the industrialized countries, there is less confidence in the strictly academic nature of entrance requirements and indeed of the educational mission. As David Riesman has written about a selective American university: "The older convictions about what Harvard should be doing have unevenly lost their assurance; we live within the secular cathedrals of higher learning in the absence of the convictions which built the cathedrals."[34] Some of the loss in "quality" may be a gain in "relevance."

Nonetheless, educators and policy-makers worry increasingly about the dynamics of mediocrity. Enrollments expand, standards contract, and the system of higher education is said to be in peril. Evidence on this score is usually anecdotal. In my own recent work at universities in Indonesia, Pakistan, Thailand, Mexico, and the Philippines, I repeatedly heard reports of the costs of academic decline.[35] I was a member of a team of Harvard professors, chaired by President Derek Bok, which recently completed a lengthy analysis of the problems of higher education in Asia and Africa. We kept receiving overwhelmingly negative appraisals of both the academic standards and the practical utility of universities.[36] Without implicating my colleagues, let me state several of my own conclusions from the evidence we reviewed.

First, higher education in many developing nations has not lived up to its intellectual or developmental promise, in large part because of remarkably low standards. Second, there are many causes for the low and often declining levels of academic and practical quality. Among these causes are political instability and pressure, poor teachers, insufficient funds, rapid expansion, poor high schools, a lack of intellectual capital and traditions, and the pressure to strive for something immediate. Third, among the causes of low quality must be listed the failures of systems for the selection, examination, and promotion of students (and faculty). Admissions policies are not the sole cause or cure, but they do play a role in the dynamics of educational quality and relevance.

Entrance standards may be declining in many developing countries, but admissions decisions are still based primarily on academic criteria. Many universities have tried to take nonacademic factors into account in admissions, but in most countries these factors remain secondary. Table 4 summarizes some of the criteria used in selection.

A SPIRAL OF DECLINE IN ECUADOR

Osvaldo Hurtado, the former president of Ecuador, describes a sequence of events also found in other countries in the 1960s and 1970s:

These developments, which led to repeated crises in established universities, were compounded by two additional factors: the proliferation of new universities in the country, and the elimination of entrance examinations in 1968. Today there are seventeen universities in the country, several of which do not possess the human, technical, and educational resources required to provide meaningful university-level education. And the suppression of entrance exams meant that between the 1968–69 and 1969–70 school years, the university population grew by 43 percent, leveling off to slightly more than 10 percent annually during subsequent years. If the Central University—clearly the best-endowed in the country—was as early as 1964 plagued by an instructional staff whose "level of competence and ability to fulfill professional obligations was less than satisfactory," and with science departments that were "more than fifty years behind the times relative to other American universities," one can only imagine what has happened to the university as a result of the recent explosion of the student population. The rapid decline in academic levels has passed critical limits, to the extent that, according to some professors, new professionals being graduated from the university are totally unqualified to work in their areas of specialization. Given this situation, it is unlikely in the near future that the university can satisfactorily assume its proper scientific and academic roles at a time when the cultural and technological dependence of the country is rapidly increasing.
The objective of the elimination of entrance examinations was ostensibly the democratization of the university, making university education accessible to the Ecuadorean masses. It was in these terms that the measure was explained by university authorities, student federations, and nearly all the political parties operating on university campuses. But the thesis that the elimination of entrance exams would permit the children of the worker to receive a university education had no basis whatsoever in reality, given the fact that the nature of the country's economic structure works to deprive many young people of a high-school education; and in the case of the rural sector, many are the children who are denied even elementary-level schooling. This observation is confirmed by statistics published by the Central University's Institute

VALUES AND FACTS

The diversity of possible selection policies is a reminder that designing systems involves fundamental questions of value. Recall the Chinese case. The graduates of the No. 1 Girls' Middle School in Peking who wrote the letter to Chairman Mao asking for the abolishment of entrance exams based their case on the values that exams had traditionally served in China:

We hold that the existing system of admittance to higher schools is a continuation of the old feudal examination system dating back thousands of years. It is a most backward and reactionary educational system. . . .
Many young people are led not to study for the revolution but to immerse themselves in books for the university entrance examination and to pay no heed to politics. Quite a number of students have been indoctrinated with such gravely reactionary ideas of the exploiting classes as that "book learning stands above all.". . .

for Economic Studies. These data indicate that only 7.2 percent of the children of worker and artisan fathers were enrolled in the seventh grade (the first secondary-school grade in the Ecuadorean system) in the 1968–69 school year; the figures for 1969–70 and 1971–72 were 7.2 percent and 8.7 percent respectively. As is clear from these statistics, even without entrance exams, Ecuadorean universities are still necessarily characterized by traditional social stratification patterns, meaning that they are dominated by students from the middle and upper classes and possess at best a minority representation by students from the popular classes.

If the democratization of the university has not been accomplished, what, then, have been the political consequences of the elimination of entrance exams? As far as can be determined at this point, the principal outcomes have been, on the one hand, the appearance of two nominally revolutionary ultraleftist tendencies, the "violentists" and the "populists," and, on the other hand, the depoliticization of important sectors of the student population. In Guayaquil, the "Atlas" group has transformed the university into a military fortress, and its "guerrilla actions" have been responsible for the deaths of several students. In order to satisfy the needs of students enrolling in the university without proper qualifications, student political groups have pressured for a lowering of academic criteria in specific courses and for more permissive standards in degree programs and in granting diplomas. In certain cases, a major inducement for student political participation is the possibility of an appointment to administrative or instructorship positions, a trend resulting in a significant increase in the number of new university jobs created. Demagogic tactics have increased in direct proportion to the declining importance of ideas, leading to a style of Marxism that amounts to little more than the spouting of revolutionary slogans. This situation has inspired a general apathy among ever-growing numbers of students, a trend observed in recent FEUE elections, in which, at best, no more than 50 percent of the electorate participated. And it remains to be seen what the political repurcussions will be of the stampede of professionals entering the job market after 1976.

Source: Osvaldo Hurtado, *Political Power in Ecuador,* trans. Nick D. Mills, Jr. (Albuquerque: University of New Mexico Press, 1980), pp. 252–54.

The use of religious criteria in Iran, class background in Poland, performance in field work in Algeria and Tanzania, or for that matter measures of academic ability in most countries of the world—these choices contain value judgments. If one wanted to put it that way, one could say that selection policies are *political* in the sense that they involve fundamental questions of who should get what for which legitimate reasons. Such questions as "What kind of education for what kind of society?" and "What kind of students for what kind of development?" are of central importance.

With this in mind, let us compare the state of analytical work on the selection problem—and our specific case of university admissions—with the way we tend to think about economic policies. In the latter case too the core of most issues involves value judgments. Who should be paid how much for what sorts of work? What prices should be charged? How should various forms of property be held? These questions about wages and prices and property are fundamentally

TABLE 4. Higher Education Admissions Criteria (Worldwide)

Criteria	Comments
Selection by "merit"	

A. Test scores
  1. College entrance test
    a. Aptitude
    b. Achievement
  2. Secondary school completion test
	Sometimes administered by individual universities, usually by the state; in the U.S., by private corporations. The required minimum score usually varies by field of study and campus.

B. High-school grades
  1. Graduation sufficient
  2. Admission an increasing function of grade average
	Grades are usually determined by individual high schools, through the averaging of teachers' evaluations of students.

C. Other factors
  1. Group membership
    a. Quotas
    b. "Bonus points"
    c. Financial aid
	Exact quotas and bonus points are seldom made public; sometimes the existence of discrimination in favor of certain groups is kept secret.

2. Political beliefs
    a. Tested
    b. Determined by class background, etc.
	Political beliefs and class background are used primarily in "revolutionary" situations.

3. Personal qualities (leadership, personality, etc.)	Personal qualities are discerned through biodata, recommendations, interviews, etc.
Sponsorship	
A. Nomination by group (commune, cadre, party, etc.) B. Recommendations from individuals	Often used to ensure representation, also to give the power of selection to particular people. Predictive power of recommendations is demonstrably low. Abuses are frequent.
"Trial by ordeal"	
A. Open admissions, then pass/flunk B. Must perform national service first, with admission predicated on performance	Difficult to flunk students. Examples of point B: Algeria's Agricultural Institute of Technology and Tanzania's National Service. Applicants spend three months in a field workshop, then are selected on their adaptability to rural tasks.
Auction-like mechanisms	
A. Private institutions B. Scholarships by merit or need	Some examples in Indonesia of accepting according to willingness to pay. Need has replaced merit as the primary consideration in granting financial aid (=lower price).

political, just as selection policies are. But notice that we have a well-developed set of analytical tools to apply to the economic questions, tools that do not remove the normative heart of the problems but that may, when used properly, help us identify where and how values enter in the choice of practical policies. We have a tradition of thinking hard about economic policies, of not short-circuiting analysis and debate with the stopper "Ah, well, that's a political issue," as if this meant that nothing further could be said.

But in the case of selection policies and the design of merit systems, we have few tools and little of an analytical tradition, especially in the study of developing countries. Too often hard thinking is short-circuited by the valid reminder that values are at the heart of the problem. There is almost no literature with a policy orientation that one might consult concerning the question of who among the many who aspire to a cherished position should be chosen. Consequently, I believe, decision-making has suffered.

It is a thesis of this book that selection policies, such as university admissions, involve difficult factual questions as well as normative ones—questions where analytical tools and the marshaling of data can help us make better decisions, whatever our values. The techniques presented in the chapters that follow involve both statistics and economics; there are qualitative lessons as well as quantitative methods; case studies show both the uses and the limitations of these tools for real decisions. We will move step by step through the three principal dimensions of the selection problem:

- *Efficiency.* How well does the selection policy pick those who will do the best job? At what cost?
- *Representation and bias.* Does the selection policy lead to the over- or underrepresentation of certain social groups? Is this because the selection criteria are biased?
- *Incentives.* What good and bad incentives does the selection policy create—for potential candidates, for other institutions (such as high schools), for selectors, and for those who wish to influence selectors?

Analyzing these dimensions carefully does not mean that selection problems are any less value-laden; indeed, analysis can help decision-makers focus on how and where values should enter. But certain factual questions also matter, although in different ways, whether one is attempting to create a Muslim society or a Communist revolution or an ivory tower world of academic excellence, and we might as well address these questions as systematically as we can.

At the same time that I argue that selection policies deserve more policy analysis than they have received, I will also try to show the limitations of available analytical tools and data. Presumably we would like to know the long-run benefits to society from alternative policies for assigning individuals to various sorts of training and education. Imagine what a study of this would look like. We would need a longitudinal framework to see what happened to people many years after obtaining their training and education. We would need to control statistically for many variables. And even if we had such a study in a developing country—which we do not—would it be useful as a guide to present policy? Since the developing countries are changing so fast, the longitudinal results we would have on a cohort trained many years ago might not apply to the present. The research dilemma is fundamental:

> The uncertainty is rooted, not in the inadequacy of social scientific methods to locate the relative areas of research, but in the fact that the effects of education become apparent within a time span exceeding in duration the life of the generation that implemented any specific educational policies. The dynamic evolution of interconnected social phenomena prevents us from isolating variables for the purpose of establishing unambiguous causal relationships.[37]

The social sciences are limited in what they can say about the effects of alternative policies. This is the case even in the United States, where thirty years of research on the economics of higher education have failed to turn up more than classification systems:

> Most of what has been gained in the last three decades relates more to taxonomic than theoretical clarification. Economists and their fellow social scientists have devised several alternative classifications to explain the phenomenon of correlation but empirical research has done little to clarify even the relative importance of the various explanations. The major contribution of this research has been to convince nearly all scholars that the causal process which transforms education into higher income is a complex one and that simple ideological or methodological explanations will no longer suffice.[38]

This does not imply that analysis and evidence are not needed; it does remind us that, in this as in other policy areas, a humble stance is proper. Research and argument will seldom be conclusive on matters as broad, important, and politically loaded as choosing elites, but it is remarkable how little practical help on this issue researchers and scholars have provided to policymakers. Can we not do better? How might we combine concerns for efficiency, representation, and incentives in the improvement of selection policies?

3

THE EFFICIENCY OF SELECTION

In the mid-1970s at the University of Karachi, Pakistan, admissions policies at the School of Pharmacy came under attack. The demand for admission was fierce, partly because graduates of the School of Pharmacy could easily obtain visas to work in the Middle East and the United States. The dean was under great pressure to change the school's policy of choosing students on the basis of examination scores.

The issue was hardly academic, although it was partly that. Applicants turned down by the School of Pharmacy staged demonstrations. Enrollments were expanded in an effort to ease the pressure, but this led to overcrowded classrooms and unhappy professors, and the demand for admission still greatly outstripped the supply. Politicians and VIPs got into the act. One afternoon, in my presence a government minister ordered the dean to admit a certain applicant despite low examination scores. The dean said later, "I had no choice but to do so." Then came the academic side of the problem. A statistical study showed that scores on the examination used to admit students explained only 15 percent of the variance in final academic performance at the School of Pharmacy. The inference was drawn that therefore the examination was virtually worthless. To rejected applicants this meant that they had been kept out of their chosen profession by an inefficient and arbitrary policy.

How might the dean have assessed this evidence about the School of Pharmacy's admissions policy? How might he have evaluated the efficiency of the existing policy and alternatives to it, measured in terms of the later performance of the group selected? These queries lead to others that might be asked of any selection system:

- How should we measure the later performance of those selected?
- What information or criteria should we include in the selection process? Should we use an aptitude test, high-school grades, or an achievement test? What about interviews, recommendations, various measures of personality and character, and essays by students?
- If there are more candidates than positions, perhaps we should simply draw lots. How much would be lost if we selected randomly among applicants instead of using the current selection system?
- How much difference would it make if we lowered the current minimum standards for selection?

APPROACHES TO EFFICIENCY IN EDUCATION

The above queries pertain to the efficiency of a selection system. They are not questions that have preoccupied most students of the economics of education and training. Research on the efficiency of educational systems has tended to emphasize other, admittedly important issues, thereby ignoring the selection problem.

One approach is that of manpower planning. Estimates are made of the prospective demand in the country for trained personnel of various types—where the types correspond to fields like agriculture, economics, accounting, science, and so forth, as well as to levels of training, such as bachelor's, master's, and doctoral degrees. Implicitly, all graduates in a field and level are counted as equally valuable. What matters is not the selection of students but the "efficient" allocation of educational spending to fields most in need.

Another approach to efficiency looks at educational inputs. Given the need, say, for so many agriculturists at such-and-such a level, what is the best way to train them? What curricula are most efficient, given financial constraints and the characteristics of the teachers, the students, and the nation? And what pedagogical techniques, including various ways of measuring students' achievement, are to be preferred?

Rarely does either of these approaches to efficiency in education take account of the selection problem. Yet it is clear that these questions interact with the choice of admissions policies. When one contemplates the needed numbers of engineers or scientists, their *quality* as well as their quantity matters, and as quantity expands, quality in general will decline. The efficiency of various pedagogical techniques and "educational production functions" also depends on the academic characteristics of the students to be taught.

In the ideal case, these various considerations would be combined. The policy-maker would define an objective function. (The manpower planner's assessment of needs by field and level is a crude proxy for this.) He would then *simultaneously* choose educational inputs, curricula, and selection policies, making these choices so as to maximize the value-added of the education, measured in terms of the objective function.

In theory, then, admissions policies should not be considered separately from all the other educational policies. Put another way, no one admissions policy is likely to be right for all circumstances. The criteria for selecting the best research physician will probably differ from the criteria best suited for choosing barefoot doctors. And when we ask about the "efficiency" of a selection system, the prior question is always "Efficiency for what objectives?"

Educators and economists have standard tricks to simplify such problems. Instead of pretending that all educational policies are or could be chosen simultaneously, they accept that for practical purposes many of the policies are givens. For example, they may take as given the number of students to be enrolled in various fields and levels, and the current curricula and levels of educational inputs. Then, instead of attempting the impossible—specifying an objective function for society—they rely on proxies to answer the question "Efficient for what?" Educators often prefer academic objectives as measures of efficiency, using data such as grades in the university or graduation rates. Economists are fond of wages, which are presumed (with caveats) to reflect the social productivity of people upon graduation. (Economists may be uncomfortable when reminded that, as in Indonesia, a new Ph.D. in economics is paid less than a nongraduate, apprentice accountant; here, their caveats come in handy.)

These simplifications contain dangers. By presuming that other policies remain constant, the policymaker may prematurely rule out radical or systematic change. (We have seen an example of such radical shifts in selection and other policies in chapter 1.) There are limitations to measuring efficiency in terms of either academic performance or later wage earnings; we shall discuss these problems below. On the other hand, it is important to see that these simplifications also have a point. In utopia it may be possible to specify a social objective function, but we have no operational examples of such a function in the real world of imperfect measures and diverse opinions. Nor are we able to estimate all the interactions among choices of admissions policies and the whole range of other educational policies we might adopt. And yet decisions must be made. To inform decisions in the real world we must ask less grand and more constrained questions, recognizing fully that we run risks by doing so. Alas, we often have to take many features of the educational system as given. Even so, we may wish to assess the efficiency of various systems for selecting students for the education now provided. We want to know how well alternative selection policies will identify students who will do well later on, both at the university and in their later contributions to society. How well do various possible admissions criteria predict later performance?

MEASURES AND OBJECTIVES

The first step concerns our objectives in selection. What do we mean by "later performance"? What *measure* (or, better, several measures) might we use to gauge that performance? As we think about this issue we will almost surely realize that we cannot measure the later performance we really care about, at least not with precision. Widely used measures, such as grades earned at the university or salaries earned in later life, are incomplete and imperfect. They are only proxies for what we value.

Several possible outcome measures might be studied, and they can be usefully placed in two groups:

1. *Measures of academic performance*
   a. *Short-term*. Examples: First-year grade point average. Probability that a student has a grade average above a threshold of "competent" perfor-

mance (e.g., GPA $\geq$ 2.0). Probability that a student has a grade average above some threshold of "excellent" performance (e.g., GPA $\geq$ 3.5).

b. *Long-term.* Examples: Probability of graduating. Time to degree. Cost per successful graduate. Overall grade point average. Overall probability of achieving above a threshold of "competent" performance or above a threshold of "excellent" performance.

2. *Measures of later-life contributions to society*

a. *Short-term.* Examples: Probability of being employed within x months of graduating. Starting salary. Some index that attempts to gauge the short-term social contribution: for example, sector in which one works, geographical area in which one works, performance rating on the job, and dedication to national goals.

b. *Long-term.* Examples: Discounted income streams. Social status achieved after n years. A measure of professional competence as a doctor, economist, public manager, teacher, and so forth. Some index that attempts to gauge the long-term social contribution (similar to 2a).

As we move down this list of performance measures, it is clear that they become more important, but also more difficult to obtain and analyze. Indeed, to obtain measures for 2b we would need to wait for many years. And by then, with the fast pace of change in developing countries, the admissions system and curriculum would probably have changed, making the results of our study difficult to apply. Similarly, if we studied people who were now in mid- and late-career in a developing country and asked what predicted their success, we would be looking at a population whose selection, training, and available predictors would be quite different from those of today's cohort.

Consequently, we cannot have all the studies we would like to have. Instead, in order to speculate about the predictors of long-term, later-life contributions, we rely on a combination of impressionistic science, ideology, and hope.

We do know a little from the experience of other countries. In my research on selection and testing in the United States, I examined what has been learned about the predictors of various kinds of later-life contributions.[1] I discovered an interesting divergence between what people *thought* predicted various kinds of "success" and what studies had *shown* to predict success.

People *think* that successful people are intelligent and well-educated, and also have good interpersonal skills, are creative, are honest, work diligently, have "good character," and so forth. People *think* they can predict who will be successful in later life.

Studies *show* that intelligent and well-educated people achieve more "success," measured in various ways. (Adolescent IQ correlates between 0.2 and 0.4 with measures like later income, social status, publication rates for academics, etc.—this correlation is not corrected for restriction of range or criterion unreliability. Years of education correlates about 0.4 with earnings and slightly higher with social status.) But regarding the other characteristics people think are associated with success, the evidence is much weaker. In part, of course, this is because it is so difficult to measure interpersonal skills, honesty, good character, diligence, and the rest. People *think* they can identify such traits, but studies *show* that people disagree a lot in their judgments of these characteristics in particular young people. Consequently, in the United States, given that you know a young person's IQ and years of education, there is almost no evidence that measures of interpersonal skills, honesty, good character, diligence, and so forth, improve the prediction of any measure of later-life contributions.

This conclusion troubles me. I think that I can tell you which of two equally smart young people is likely to "go further in life," depending on my impression of their personalities, character, diligence, and so forth. But perhaps each of us thinks so—"*I* can tell"—and yet the evidence shows that on average we as a group cannot. It may assuage your and my troubles over this nonintuitive conclusion by wording it as follows: "Even though you and I can tell, a *system* designed to make such predictions for thousands of young people cannot, given existing measures, tell on average which of them will be more successful in later life, after controlling for academic ability and achievement."

Perhaps progress with psychological measures and other ways of assessing character will cause us to change this view in the years to come. I hope so. But for now, I believe that, for the United States at least, it is the correct view.

Who knows whether it is also the correct view for developing nations? I would bet that in most developing countries the social class of a young person's parents would help predict the young person's success in later life, so that between two young people with equal academic ability, the one with the more advantaged parents will be more successful by almost any measure. I would also bet that in most developing countries a man will turn out to do better in later life by many measures than an equally able woman. Perhaps you disagree. On the other hand, perhaps you would agree and would add other demographic variables that lamentably forecast success (region of residence? race? urban background?). Suppose for the sake of the argument that my bets are correct. Should we therefore admit *more* of those from advantaged families, and *more* men, than their academic ability and preparation alone would warrant?

Most of us would avoid this conclusion, even though it does follow from an intuitively appealing argument for educating those who will be "successful." Suppose we went further. Suppose we had *perfect* predictions not just of success but also of the "social value-added" of higher education for each applicant. Suppose social class or sex, in a given society, turned out to affect "social value-added" significantly. We still might decide not to use selection criteria like social class or sex. We might say that the selection system should be sex-blind, because we aspire to a just society in which equally able men and women *would* have equally successful careers. Then again we might not say this.

My point is that we are clearly in an area where ideology and ethics, and not just the prediction of later success, matter a great deal. Whatever we find in a study of the efficiency of prediction, a critic may say that he or she disagrees with the performance measure, or believes that we should select as if we had a better university system or a more ideal society, or wants us to select people with certain characteristics simply because those characteristics are good in themselves. The critic would have a point. Much of the problem of defining measures and assigning utility functions resides in the domain of philosophy.

Once we have a measure and a utility function, statistical questions take center stage. Let us now turn to some techniques of general applicability, using data from the University of Karachi's School of Pharmacy at the time the dean was having his troubles.

ASSESSING PREDICTIVE POWER IN THE
CONTEXT OF SELECTION

When selecting university students, we do not know for certain how well various candidates will perform later on if they are chosen. All we can do is *predict* how well they may do. Thus, the name of the game we are about to play is prediction. Alternative selection criteria can be statistically analyzed in terms of how efficiently they forecast later success, and the results can be applied to the particular selection problem faced by the institution or country.

The University of Karachi's School of Pharmacy selected only about one in eight applicants. The principal criterion was the candidate's score on the Intermediate (Inter) exam taken after twelfth grade. A few seats were reserved for students from far-flung regions, from scheduled castes, or with a parent on the university's faculty. Increasingly, political pressures led to the admission of students who on other grounds would not have qualified.

I collected data on 110 graduates of the School of Pharmacy in the Class of 1974. For each student, I obtained the final pharmacy marks—a measure of how much students had learned in their years at the School of Pharmacy—and scores on the Inter exam. I also obtained each student's score on the Matriculate exam, taken at the end of the tenth grade.

These data are limited in several ways. No other predictors were available. The only performance measure was academic in nature. Notice too that the sample included only those who ended up graduating from the School of Pharmacy. Along the way, some students had dropped out, so they do not appear in the sample. As we shall see, this affects the interpretation of our statistical results.

How well do students' scores on the Inter exam, which is used to admit them, predict their final pharmacy marks? Let us abbreviate Inter with I and final pharmacy marks with P. If I predicts P, we expect the correlation between them to be positive and significant, and we might intuitively feel that if I is to be the sole criterion for admission, I should explain much of the variance observed in P.

What was the actual relationship in this sample? The correlation between I

and P was 0.39. This means that I explained $(0.39)^2$ or about 15 percent of the variance in P. This result was statistically significant: if there were in fact no correlation between I and P, we would observe a correlation of 0.39 or larger less than 1 percent of the time. But what about that figure of 15 percent of the variance explained? This means that 85 percent of the variance in pharmacy marks among graduates was *not* explained by the main criterion for admitting those students. To many people who learned of this study's results, this fact implied that the Inter exams were almost worthless as a criterion for selecting students.

This is a tempting leap of logic, but we should be wary of making it just yet. It is true that in many other areas of statistical analysis we would say that 15 percent of the variance explained was a sign of poor prediction. In the context of selection, however, correlation coefficients are biased downward in several ways.

One has to do with unreliability in the measure of later performance. Unreliability in this context means that the measure contains random errors of measurement. In Pakistan most examinations are not "objective," in the sense of multiple-choice or true-false questions; they are of the essay variety. Several colleagues and I did a small study at the University of Karachi that showed that different teachers grading exactly the same answer sheets often disagreed markedly in the scores they awarded. This study did not involve the School of Pharmacy, but it did confirm a general finding in other countries. In the words of a British scholar, "There is abundant evidence that examinations of the so-called *essay type,* used in this country and elsewhere, tend to be intrinsically unreliable."[2] If the measure of performance is unreliable, this means that it contains random error that no predictor can be expected to forecast.

Fortunately, if the extent of this unreliability of measurement is known, we can adjust the observed correlation coefficient to take it into account. In the case of the School of Pharmacy, this adjustment led to an increase of the correlation coefficient from 0.39 to 0.47.

Another way that correlation coefficients are biased toward zero relates to what psychometricians call "restriction of range." We would like to know the correlation between I and P among all applicants to the School of Pharmacy. In our sample, we can observe only the correlation among those who were actually admitted and eventually graduated. The variance in Inter scores in our sample is much less than the variance among all applicants. Since selection was based on the predictor we are analyzing, the range of that predictor is restricted in the sample of those admitted. Consequently, the correlation between I and P is *lower* than it would be for the population we are interested in, namely, the applicant pool.

Again there are ways to correct correlation coefficients to take this problem into account. In the case of the School of Pharmacy, one way of correcting for restriction of range raised the correlation from 0.39 to a much more impressive 0.65. There are many ways to correct for this problem, and scholars disagree

CORRECTING CORRELATIONS FOR UNRELIABILITY AND RESTRICTION OF RANGE

A variety of techniques for correcting correlations for unreliability and restriction of range exist. Here are two classical methods, based on certain simplifying assumptions.

Unreliability. Divide the observed correlation coefficient by the square root of the reliability coefficient. The reliability coefficient can be thought of as the correlation between two measurements of the same individual. In the case of well-devised standardized tests, the reliability coefficient can reach 0.9. For grade averages in a given semester, it might be 0.7. My estimate of the reliability of marks given at the University of Karachi, based on a small study of agreement among graders, is 0.7.

Thus, the 0.39 correlation observed at the School of Pharmacy should be divided by the square root of 0.7. The result is a correlation corrected for unreliability of the performance measure, and its value in this case was 0.47.

Restriction of range. The choice of methods for correcting for restriction of range depends on assumptions about the way selection took place and the nature of the predictive relationship beyond the bounds of the already selected sample. One widely used formula is:

$$r_{adj} = \frac{r^*(\sigma/\sigma^*)}{\sqrt{1 - r^{*2} + r^{*2}(\sigma^2/\sigma^{*2})}}$$

where r_{adj} is the adjusted correlation coefficient, r^* is the correlation observed within the selected sample, σ is the standard deviation of the predictor in the applicant pool, and σ^* is the standard deviation of the predictor within the selected sample.

If $\sigma/\sigma^* = 2$, as it may well in the highly selective universities of many developing nations, then a correlation of 0.39 becomes an adjusted correlation of 0.65.

In the case of the School of Pharmacy, after correcting for both unreliability and restriction of range, the correlation between Inter scores and pharmacy marks was 0.73. This means that $(0.73)^2$ or 53 percent of the variance in performance among pharmacy graduates was statistically explained by their Inter scores.

Source: For the assumptions underlying these corrections, see Frederic M. Lord and Melvin R. Novick, *Statistical Theories of Mental Test Scores* (Reading, Mass.: Addison-Wesley, 1968), esp. chap. 6 and pp. 140–48.

about which is preferable. But amid the statistical complexities, a qualitative point should not be lost. *We must be careful in extrapolating statistical findings from a sample of people who have been selected on the basis of a predictor to the entire population of applicants.*

ASSESSING EFFICIENCY OF SELECTION

How much value do Inter scores have in selecting a subset of applicants who will do well in the School of Pharmacy? We cannot tell simply from the size of a correlation coefficient or the percentage of variance explained. The answer depends on a number of specific features of the particular selection problem under consideration.

The appendix to this chapter develops this point further. A major qualitative finding is this: In a situation where only a few of many applicants can be selected, a selection criterion that leads to only a "small" increase in predictive power can lead to large gains in the quality of those selected.

Consider a few hypothetical but realistic examples. Suppose a School of Pharmacy admits 10 percent of its applicants, and suppose 80 percent of that applicant pool would pass if admitted. Suppose that over the entire applicant pool, an admissions test is correlated 0.4 with passing. If we admitted students randomly, 80 percent would pass and 20 percent would fail. If instead we used the test and chose those with the highest scores, 95 percent of those admitted would pass and only 5 percent would fail. This seems to be a substantial improvement, even with what in other contexts might be considered a "small" correlation coefficient.

Here is a second example. Suppose the school also cares about the number of students who achieve some level of superb academic performance. Let us assume that "superb performance" is correlated 0.5 with the admissions test across the entire applicant pool. And assume also that 5 percent of the applicant pool would be capable of achieving that level of performance if admitted. As before, 10 percent of the applicants are accepted. With random selection, 5 percent of the admitted class will perform superbly. Using the test as the basis for admission, this figure rises to 19 percent of the class. Again, this looks like an important gain.

As a final supposition, imagine that we knew what the distribution of grades in the School of Pharmacy would be if applicants were randomly admitted: a normal distribution with an average grade of C and a standard deviation equal to one grade. Suppose the admissions test correlates 0.4 with grades in pharmacy school and 10 percent of applicants are admitted. With random selection, the average grade would be C. Using the test for admissions decisions, the average grade would be B−. (If we had perfect foresight and admitted the 10 percent who would have the highest grades in pharmacy school, the average grade would be A−.) Table 5 summarizes the results.

TABLE 5. Illustration of the Value of a Predictor

Method of Selection	% Failing	% Performing Superbly	Grade Point Average
Random	20	5	2.00 (C)
Test score	5	19	2.70 (B−)
Perfect prediction	0	50	3.76 (A−)

Note: The table assumes correlations of 0.4 between the test score and passing, 0.5 between the test scores and superb performance, and 0.4 with average grade; that 80 percent of applicants could pass if admitted, 5 percent would perform superbly, and the expected distribution of grades among all applicants would be normally distributed with a mean of 2 and a standard deviation of 1; and a ratio of admissions to applicants of 1 to 10.

These calculations were based on the psychometric work of H. C. Taylor and J. T. Russell, and C. W. Brown and E. E. Ghiselli, in classic articles.[3] Their work depends on certain simplifying assumptions—not only those I made explicitly about the applicant pool but also the assumption of linear, homoscedastic predictive relationships. The qualitative point is that in a highly selective situation a predictor may have a "low" correlation coefficient and still be highly useful.

How "useful" are such gains? The answer depends on the utility function we apply to these measures of later performance. Perhaps the best we can do in practice is ask policy-makers how much it is worth to them to improve expected performance of those admitted by such-and-such an amount. Let me illustrate how such an analysis might proceed, again using the example of the School of Pharmacy.

The appendix to this chapter derives a mathematical expression for the utility gained from an increase in the correlation between admissions criteria and later performance. That expression says that the gain in average performance is equal to the gain in the correlation coefficient times the average score on the predictor of those admitted times the utility of a one standard deviation increase in later performance.

It is the last part of that expression that I wish to focus upon here. A conservative estimate of the utility of a one standard deviation increase in performance would be obtained as follows. Look at the current graduating class at the School of Pharmacy. How much is a one standard deviation increase in pharmacy marks worth to society, in rupees? If you could magically improve a pharmacy student's marks from the 50th percentile of the class to the 85th percentile—which is about a one standard deviation increase in a normal distribution—how much would this be worth to society?

We might put this question to policy-makers, or to ourselves. You might try a number or two of your choice. Indeed, a valuable part of the exercise is to see how the answer changes depending on various value judgments about the utility of that one standard deviation change.

Let me illustrate the methodology by arbitrarily giving the number Rs. 20,000, or about U.S.$2,000 in the mid-1970s. The utility of a one standard deviation increase in academic performance at the pharmacy school might be even higher, but I don't know how I could prove this. If we use this figure, we can calculate the efficiency of using the Inter test to admit students instead of admitting students by random selection. The answer, as shown in the appendix to this chapter, turns out to be over Rs. 6 million per year, for a total of 200 pharmacy students admitted annually.

What we have done contains a number of simplifying assumptions, and so the rupee figures should not be taken as firm findings. But two qualitative findings shine through. First, even with a relatively modest correlation coefficient, a selection criterion may lead to important gains in efficiency. Second, analysis is helpful for showing where and how value judgments, and facts about the particular selection problem, interact.

The kinds of tools illustrated here could be used to address other questions of interest to the dean of the School of Pharmacy and other educational policy-makers. Suppose that by adding other information besides the Inter score the correlation could be raised from 0.39 to 0.50. How much would that be worth? (Answer: Rs. 4,360 per selected student, or Rs. 872,000 for 200 admittees per year.) What if enrollments were increased at the School of Pharmacy so that 20 percent of applicants got in. In such a case, how much would be gained by using the Inter exam instead of random selection of students? (Answer: Rs. 20,440 per selected student, or Rs. 4,088,000 for 200 admittees per year. Note that this is less than the figure of more than Rs. 6 million derived for the current situation. This shows again that improvements in selection criteria are more valuable the more selective we are, if costs are held constant.)

LOOKING AT THE COSTS OF SELECTION SYSTEMS

The discussion so far has centered on increases in the quality of those selected. No analysis of efficiency would be complete without also looking at the cost side. How much does it cost to use or improve various predictors?

The costs are of several kinds. Let us use the case of a test as the example. (Throughout this chapter, the methodology applies to other predictors besides tests; we have focused on tests not because they are necessarily the best selection criteria but because the example at hand involves them.)

Costs of Preparation

Tests must be designed and printed. Design often involves the collaboration of educators, test experts, and government officials. The selection of questions may

A DOLLAR VALUE FOR A STANDARD DEVIATION?

It seems unusual, if not unnatural, to ascribe a monetary value to measures of academic achievement. If we take the exercise of doing so in the right spirit, however, it may help us understand the implications of alternative selection policies.

An idea advanced by John E. Hunter, Frank L. Schmidt, and others is to put a dollar value on a one standard deviation increment in performance. For the formula defined in the Appendix to this chapter, what one wants, strictly speaking, is an estimate of the dollar value of a one standard deviation change measured among all those who apply, not just those who are admitted or those who graduate. What one wants is, however, difficult to get; and what one has, in most cases, is an idea of how big a one standard deviation increment in performance is among those admitted or among those who graduate. These standard deviations will be smaller than the standard deviation among all applicants; estimates based on them will be conservative.

Hunter and Schmidt reviewed studies that gave dollar values to the difference between two workers in the same job, one at the 50th percentile of performance and the other at the 85th percentile—a difference of about one standard deviation. They estimated that this value is about 40 to 70 percent of the average salary in that job.

How much is it worth to a developing country to have an engineer, say, who is at the 85th percentile of his college class as opposed to one at the 50th percentile? This question has seldom been asked, and no doubt the answer depends on the stage of economic development of the nation, the mission of the particular university, and our assessment of the reliability and validity of available measures of "performance" at the university.

I have found it useful to put the question directly to policy-makers. Let them try different answers and see what the implications are. By forcing policy-makers and ourselves to put dollar values on such objectives, it helps us think harder about those objectives, as well as about selection policies.

Source: John E. Hunter and Frank L. Schmidt, "Fitting People to Jobs: The Impact of Personnel Selection on National Productivity," in *Human Performance and Productivity,* ed. E. A. Fleishman (Hillsdale, N.J.: Erlbaum, 1982).

---

involve both technical considerations and quasi-political negotiations over who gets to make the test; both have costs.

Costs of Administration (or Gathering the Information)

The actual taking of the tests involves direct costs for the facilities, test monitors, and publicity. Those taking tests also incur costs, including traveling to the test site and the opportunity costs of taking the exam. Notice that these costs involve all test-takers, not just those who end up being selected. Thus, in a very selective system, the costs per person actually chosen will be higher than in a less selective situation.

Costs of Utilizing Results in the Decision Process

Tests must be graded, which is expensive. Essay examinations are usually more costly than multiple-choice and other "objective" tests. Another cost is often overlooked: students must wait to learn of their exam results before taking a job, pursuing their education, and so forth. In the 1970s in Pakistan, it took six months for the essay examinations to be graded and the results compiled and announced. During this time, many students paid an opportunity cost of waiting. The exams took place after students finished the twelfth grade, so they were not enrolled in school in the meantime. Finally, different criteria impose different degrees of cost in the decision-making process itself. "Objective" measures may involve less time and discussion than "subjective" criteria.

Estimates of these costs are difficult to make, especially in developing countries. Few data on them were available for Pakistan. In the absence of detailed research on the costs, the judgments of educators and students may be tapped for rough but useful estimates.

LESSONS ABOUT THE EFFICIENCY OF SELECTION

The example of the School of Pharmacy at the University of Karachi illustrates some lessons about estimating the efficiency of different selection systems. We saw how a combination of statistical analysis and value judgments about the utility of a gain in academic performance could be combined to estimate the benefits from using a test to admit students instead of admitting them randomly. But the analysis was better for helping us see the structure of the problem than it was for deriving an exact answer. Indeed, in this as in most other public policy problems, exactitude is an illusion. (This is not an excuse for sloppy thinking.) We also saw that in a highly selective situation, even though a predictor explains a "small" percentage of the variance in later performance, using that predictor in admissions may nonetheless be valuable.

More broadly, we reviewed several steps that might usefully be followed to analyze the efficiency of alternative selection policies. With appropriate changes in language, the methodology can be applied to all sorts of selection policies, such as the design of hiring and screening systems, the awarding of research grants, the allocation of scarce import permits, or the choice of contractors.

First, we need a *measure of performance* (or several measures). In the example of the School of Pharmacy, we used a measure of final academic performance. Ideally, we might have preferred some measures of the social value-added of the education to each student, in terms of how much the student would contribute to society as a result of the education received. That ideal is seldom attainable. In practice, the analyst of selection problems has to use short-run proxies for long-run objectives. Analysts should experiment with a variety of such proxies, remembering that in most social research there is no one right way to measure results.

Second, we require a *utility function* defined across the measure or measures of performance. How much do various-sized increases in the later performance of those selected matter to us (or to society)? This may sound dauntingly theoretical, and indeed the specification of utility functions is a thorny problem, both in theory and in practice. One practical technique is to translate gains in proxies into money terms, as we did by asking how much a one standard deviation gain in academic performance at the School of Pharmacy was worth in rupees. This question by its nature transcends statistics. Policy-makers, technical experts, and citizens should be consulted about the "worth" of gains in later performance. The analysis should display the results under a range of possible answers to the value question. The methodology leads to interaction between analyst and policy-maker, which can be the most useful part of policy research, leading to the clarification of both values and facts.

Third, we need to assess how well various criteria for selection *predict* later performance. Through regression and correlation analysis we obtain a (multiple) correlation. Various statistical pitfalls must be kept in mind. We need to check whether a linear model is appropriate; if it is not, we may be able to reexpress the predictors to obtain linearity in the predictive relationship. We need to correct correlation coefficients for unreliability in the performance measure (but not in the predictors) and for restriction of range. We can then assess, for a given selection ratio and utility function, how gains in the correlation between the (combination of) predictor(s) and the measure of later performance translate into rupees.

Finally, we need to assess the *costs* of alternative selection criteria. These costs are of several kinds. Only if the benefits of using a predictor outweight its costs do we decide to go ahead and use it.

Value judgments permeate the analysis. Especially in the selection of performance measures and utility functions, reasonable people may well disagree. Most of us will be uncomfortably faced with a classic dilemma in policy-making: the need to use partial, incomplete, imperfect proxies for what we really care about. We may have only imperfect data on academic outcomes or short-run wages and employment, and nothing on how well the student or graduate achieves socially useful ends. By using the proxies we may endorse a myopic and incrementalist perspective and distort the true objectives of the system. If we fastidiously spurn the proxies—saying that one cannot measure the kinds of later performance that really matter—we may risk a solipsistic irrelevance to the world as we find it, and we may forgo the real benefits to society that improved, if still imperfect, selection systems can bring.

Who should be selected if only a few can be? What concept of "efficiency" is right for a particular society at a particular point in history? Such questions transcend statistical analysis. But whatever our answers to such questions, it is likely that we will create better selection policies with the help of analytical tools like the ones we have been developing.

APPENDIX: THE USEFULNESS OF IMPROVED SELECTION

This appendix derives an expression for the gain in utility associated with an increase in predictive power, in the context of selection. The derivation shows how the utility of improved prediction depends on specific features of the particular institution in question, such as the ratio of students accepted to applicants, and on value judgments about the utility of gains in performance.

Consider once more chapter 3's example of the School of Pharmacy at the University of Karachi. Let us begin with the regression equation relating an individual's performance in pharmacy school (P) to the individual's score on the Inter Exam:

(1) $\quad P = \mu_p + \beta Z_I = e,$

where μ_p is the mean later performance of a *randomly selected* group of applicants, Z_I is the student's Inter score expressed in standardized scores (or z-scores), and e is the error term. The standardized Z_I is calculated by subtracting the average Inter score in the applicant pool and dividing by the standard deviation of Inter scores in the applicant pool: $Z_I = (I - \mu_I)/\sigma_I$. The mean of the standardized score is 0 and the standard deviation is 1.

What is the average performance *of the selected group* of applicants? It is:

(2) $\quad E(P_s) = E(\mu_p) + E(\beta Z_{Is}) + E(e),$

where the subscript s means "in the selected group." Since $E(e) = 0$ and μ_p and β are constants, this becomes:

(3) $\quad \overline{P}_s = \mu_p + \beta \overline{Z}_{Is}$

Since $\beta = r(\sigma_p/\sigma_I)$, where σ_p is the standard deviation in later performance in pharmacy school of a *randomly selected* group of applicants, and since we have standardized the Inter scores so that $\sigma_I = \sigma_{z_I} = 1$, then $\beta = r\sigma_p$. We thereby obtain:

(4) $\quad \overline{P}_s = \mu_p + r\sigma_p \overline{Z}_{Is}.$

How can we use this formula to assess the efficiency of selection with the Inter examination?

One way is to compare the average performance of the selected fraction of applicants in two situations: first, where the *Inter exam* is used to do the choosing and, second, where students are instead selected *randomly* from the applicant pool. The first case is described by equation (4). In the second case, the expected performance in pharmacy school $\overline{P}_s$ is just μ_p. Therefore, the *gain* in expected performance in the selected group from using the examination is:

(5) $\Delta \overline{P}$ per selectee $= r\sigma_p \overline{Z}_{Is}$.

Let us examine equation (5) term by term.

Notice that the r here is the correlation between the Inter score and later performance in pharmacy school computed for *the entire applicant pool*. It is the r_{adj} *after* correcting for restriction of range. As shown above, for the pharmacy school, this $r_{adj} = 0.65$. If we also adjust for unreliability, $r_{adj} = 0.73$.

What is $\overline{Z}_{Is}$? That is the expected Inter score of a selected student. If Inter scores are normally distributed and the proportion selected is π, then it can be shown that

(6) $\overline{Z}_{Is} = \phi/\pi$,

where ϕ is the ordinate of the standard normal distribution corresponding to a π chance of being selected. For example, if one in five applicants is selected, $\pi = 0.20$. We look in statistical tables to find the value of ϕ, namely, the ordinate of the standard normal distribution (or, equivalently, the probability density of a standardized normal random variate), corresponding to a standard score of X such that 0.20 of the distribution is above X. X here equals 0.84, meaning that in a normal distribution 20 percent of the population have standardized scores above 0.84. The corresponding ϕ is 0.280. So $\phi/\pi = 0.28/0.20 = 1.4$, meaning that the *average* Z_I in the selected group is 1.4.

What about σ_p? Recall that this is the standard deviation in pharmacy school performance of a *randomly selected* group of students. The standard deviation in performance that we actually observe among the students selected via the Inter exam will be smaller than σ_p. Alas, in the absence of an experiment, we cannot observe σ_p, but we can make a few assumptions about it, do some sensitivity analysis, and obtain some useful results.

For example, let us be conservative and set σ_p to the standard deviation in P that we now observe among selected students. (It must be at least this large.) Ask yourself, How much is a one standard deviation increase in performance in pharmacy school worth to society, in rupees? If you could magically improve a pharmacy student's final performance from the 50th percentile to the 85th percentile—this is about one standard deviation in a normal distribution—how much would this be worth to society?

You can use a number or two of your choice. Let me arbitrarily give the number Rs. 20,000 per student. Using this as the value in rupees of σ_p, we can calculate the efficiency (in rupee terms per student) of using the examination to select pharmacy students as opposed to selecting students randomly. We do so as follows:

$r = 0.39 \rightarrow r_{adj} = 0.73$

$\pi = 0.125$; here we suppose that one in eight students is selected

ϕ corresponding to $(\pi = 0.125) = 0.272$

$\overline{Z}_{Is} = \phi/\pi = 0.272/0.125 = 2.18$

$\sigma_p = $ Rs. 20,000

Then $r\sigma_p\phi/\pi = 0.73 \times 20,000 \times 2.18 = $ Rs. 31,828 is the gain per student that is obtained by selecting with the examination as opposed to selecting randomly. If we have 200 students, the gain is $200 \times 31,828 = $ Rs. 6,365,600 per year.

A number of simplifying statistical assumptions are embedded in this analysis, including linearity, homoscedasticity, and normality. But the general idea shines through. *Even with its relatively low R^2, the use of the Inter exam leads to sizable improvements in the efficiency of selection.*

The same statistical methodology could be used to address other questions. For example, how much would it be worth to improve the test, so that the unadjusted correlation would go from 0.39 to, say, 0.50? (Answer: Rs. 4,360 per selected student.) How much would it be worth to use additional information that would increase the multiple correlation R by a certain amount? If enrollments were increased so that the selection ratio π were 1 in 5, how much would then be gained by using the examinations instead of selecting randomly? (Answer: Rs. 20,440 per selected student.) Using a range of values for σ_p would be advisable in presenting the analysis to policy-makers.

4

REPRESENTATION AND BIAS
The Case of the Philippines

In the spring of 1976, Philippines' President Ferdinand Marcos spoke at the commencement exercises of the main campus of the University of the Philippines, near Manila. His theme was equality of opportunity for admission to the university. He asked the officers of the university "to institute early reforms that will democratize its admission system. These reforms must ensure that there be an increasing participation by our poorer young men and women in the life of the mind that the University now promotes so well."[1]

As the nation's premier institution of higher education, the main campus of the University of the Philippines (U.P.) enjoyed a great surplus of applicants. Out of 18,205 candidates in the previous year, only 4,669 were admitted—about 26 percent. The applicant pool itself was highly qualified. All had passed the country's standardized National College Entrance Examination. Over half the applicants were estimated by the university to be capable of satisfactory work at U.P. Many of those rejected were valedictorians and salutatorians in their high school classes.

But it was not the selectivity per se that caused President Marcos to worry. Indeed, he and others recognized that the excellence of the University of the Philippines was in part due to the excellence of its entering students. As one dean told me in 1979, "Educating students is like cutting diamonds. We need pedagogical excellence in order to make each facet shine. This is what makes the finished product worthwhile. But the raw material has to be a diamond." The problem was that the students being admitted were disproportionately members of the upper classes. The probability of being admitted increased with the income of one's family (see table 6). Moreover, it was felt that too few of the students were from the outlying provinces and that too many were from Manila. President Marcos raised a fundamental question: Was it right for a public institution, heavily subsidized by the state, to educate disproportionate numbers of already privileged groups of the society?

President Marcos challenged the university to do better. In doing so, he opened up related questions. Was the university's selection process "biased" against the poor and those from outside Manila? What does "bias" mean in this context? If one wished to admit more members of the poorer classes, how could

TABLE 6. Family Income and Admissions to U.P., 1976

	Percentage with This Income or Less Among		
Family Income (P000)	Philippines Population, 1971	UPCAT Applicants, 1976	U.P. Admissions, 1976
0–2.5	50.9%	12.6%	4.2%
2.6–5.0	79.0	25.1	10.7
5.1–10.0	94.0	48.9	28.5
10.1–20.0	98.8	74.5	58.0

Source: Program Development Staff, *Democratization of Admissions* (Office of the President, University of the Philippines, March 1977), p. 13.

one gauge the trade-off in terms of foregone academic excellence? What would be the costs and benefits of "democratizing" admissions to various degrees?

HIGHER EDUCATION IN THE PHILIPPINES

By Asian standards, the Philippines is an educational outlier. Literacy is high— 75 percent in 1980, which compares favorably with estimates of 24 percent in Pakistan, 62 percent in Indonesia, and 69 percent in the People's Republic of China.[2] About two-thirds of enrollment in high schools is in private schools. Even at the university level, many institutions are privately run. Enrollment rates are high (see table 7). In some respects, the educational system in the Philippines resembles that of the middle and higher income countries of the world.

Students who want to attend college in the Philippines must take the National College Entrance Examination (NCEE) upon leaving high school. This standardized test includes a series of subtests in such subjects as English, mathematics, and science; it also includes aptitude tests, with scores calculated for "symbolic and verbal relations" and "abstract reasoning." A composite of these various subtests is the General Scholastic Aptitude Test. The top 75 percent of those who take this test are considered to have passed it and to be qualified for college study.

The University of the Philippines is more exacting. It requires its students to take a College Admission Test (CAT), which includes subtests in nonverbal reasoning, English, reading, mathematics, and science. Then the university creates its own index, a weighted sum of these test scores and high-school grades (the exact equation is discussed below).

Because of the U.P.'s stringent admission policies, not all students who pass the NCEE take the CAT. Of those who did and who applied to the U.P. in 1976, only about the top 25 percent were admitted. About one-third of these students turned out not to pass their courses.

Thus, as in many other countries, the selection takes place in several stages.

TABLE 7. Gross Enrollment Rates in the Philippines
and Selected Asian Countries (1980–82)

Country	Primary Level	Secondary Level	Higher Education
Philippines, 1980	110%	63%	26%
Indonesia, 1981	117	30	3
Pakistan, 1980	56	17	2[a]
People's Republic of China, 1981	118	44	1
Malaysia, 1982	92	55	2[a]

Source: UNESCO, Statistical Yearbook (Paris: UNESCO, 1983).

Note: Figures are rounded to the nearest percent. Gross enrollment rates are ratios of those enrolled to the number of young people in various age-ranges considered, in that country, to be "eligible" for that level of schooling. For all countries in the table, the age-range for higher education was twenty to twenty-four years old, but the "eligible" age-ranges for the primary and secondary levels were different:

Country	Primary Level	Secondary Level
Philippines	7–12	13–16
Indonesia	7–12	13–18
Pakistan	5–9	10–16
People's Republic of China	7–11	12–16
Malaysia	6–12	12–18

[a]Based on data from the mid-1970s.

One must do well in high school, one must do well in two standard entrance examinations, and then one must do well once at the university.

THE CORRELATES OF SCHOLASTIC APTITUDE

Throughout the world, it is a well-documented fact that children of wealthier families tend to do better on scholastic aptitude tests than children of poorer families. It is also true that, on average, members of some ethnic groups do better on these tests than members of other ethnic groups.[3] In most countries, children of urban and suburban backgrounds do better than children raised in rural areas. What causes these differences, however, remains a matter of controversy. Most authorities agree that several factors are at work; the disagreement is over the relative weight of each cause.

The first category of possible causes is *educational*. The schools attended by lower-scoring groups are often of lower quality in terms of teachers' qualifications, class size, physical facilities, and so forth. Improvement in these features of schools may lead to gains in students' test scores and academic achievement. These last two sentences seem indisputable, but the evidence to support them is not always strong. Many studies in the United States have been interpreted as showing that school policy variables have only modest effects on academic outcomes. In my own work on unusually effective high schools, I estimated that the best schools raise their students' achievement scores by at most half a standard deviation.[4] This is a difference worth working for, but it is consistent with the view that only a small fraction of differences between groups in academic achievement can be explained by differences in the quality of their schools. In the developing countries, more research is needed on these matters, as the evidence is mixed. For example, research on secondary schools in Pakistan showed (1) that the schools of poorer students were not appreciably worse along the usual measures of school quality than the schools of richer students and (2) that variations in school quality were not statistically associated with gains in student achievement.[5] But researchers at the World Bank have recently uncovered evidence that in some developing countries, better schools will lead to statistically significant improvements in students' test scores.[6]

Second, there may be a number of directly *economic* causes for lower academic achievement. For example, by dint of their lower incomes, poor families may offer a less academically enriching environment than rich families.

Third, there are *social* variables. For example, the poor and the rural may tend to have families that value education less than the rich and the urban. Students from poor homes may do poorly in school or drop out more often for this reason, among others. Perhaps this lower evaluation of the benefits of education is "rational" in some cases, in the sense that it correctly reflects the differences in socioeconomic benefits accompanying education for different groups and individuals. In other cases, it may be "irrational," the residue of conservative or uninformed attitudes in a world where education does in fact have a high value for most poor and rural students.

Other causes may stem from what we might call the *"intimate background"* of an individual. By this, I refer to those "cultural" and possibly innate factors that do not seem to be affected in the short run by improvements in gross indices of economic and social well-being but which still may affect academic achievement. According to most psychologists, a considerable body of research *among whites* has established that scores on IQ tests and other measures of academic aptitude are partially "heritable."[7] Moreover, it has been argued that in the United States and in England some of the differences among social classes in scholastic aptitude are the result of different gene pools.[8] It is not worthwhile for us to enter deeply into the smoldering and politically loaded debate in the West over these issues. We must simply note that, apart from educational, economic, and social differences among groups, there *may* be other factors operating that affect differences in scholastic aptitude among those groups.

A fifth category of possible causes is worth mentioning, though to some people it may seem quaint. Some students may try harder and thereby raise their test scores and other measures of academic achievement. It is fashionable to assume that *"effort"* is the product of social and economic backgrounds or of cultural/innate endowments. But at least at the level of individuals, and some-times at the level of schools and broader groupings, it is clear that higher levels of effort can be generated, which in turn result in higher levels of scholastic achievement.

Finally, there may be differences among groups in test scores because of *biases in the tests* themselves. If the measuring instruments are socially or cultur-ally biased, students from poor or rural backgrounds may tend to score lower, even if their distributions of academic ability are the same as the distributions for students from wealthy or urban backgrounds. If such bias exists, it means that a rural student, for example, will on average receive a lower score than an urban student of equal academic promise. Of course, tests are not the only measures that may exhibit bias: so may interviews, measures of personality, high-school grades, work experience, and so forth.

It is difficult to disentangle these six possible explanations of observed dif-ferences in academic aptitude among groups. It is difficult even to imagine a study that would assign each factor its proper weight and assess the possible interactions among factors. With real data, and in the politically understandable absence of controlled experiments, the methodological issues approach the intractable.

As mentioned in chapter 2, it is worthwhile to distinguish "bias" from "underrepresentation." I will use "bias" in the predictive sense: a test or predic-tor is biased if people from different groups who have the same score do not, on average, perform equally well later on. For example, if rural students with a score of 60 consistently do better in their university studies, or in their later lives, than urban students who also score 60, then the test *underpredicts* the rural students' later performance. It is therefore biased against the rural students.

Notice that a group may score below another group, even on an unbiased test. In other words, *differences between groups do not imply biased measure-ments or biased predictions.* As an analogy, imagine weighing children from two groups, one group from desperately poor families and the other from middle-class families. Children from poor families would probably weigh less, but this would not mean that the weighing scales were biased against them.

I will use "underrepresentation" to refer to disparities among groups on the predictors themselves. If one group tends to score lower on a predictor than another group, then using that predictor to select people will have adverse im-pact on the lower-scoring group, who will be underrepresented compared with their proportion of the relevant population. If we selected children for some health program based on their weight, then we could say that this procedure would have an adverse impact on poor children, in the sense that proportionally fewer poor children would be selected. However, whether this procedure would be biased against the poor children would depend on additional information about whether and how well a child's weight predicted success in the program for the children from the two groups.

When faced with group differences in academic qualifications, what should the university do? Evidently, if the university chooses those with the best academic credentials, it will reward those whose educational experiences, socioeconomic environments, genes and cultural backgrounds, and hard work have resulted in higher scores. Such a policy would often lead to the underrepresentation of the poor, rural, and members of certain ethnic groups. Should the university follow such a policy anyway, perhaps in the name of efficient selection? Or should weight also be given to the representation of these various groups?

We have talked about the efficiency of selection policies. In this chapter a new set of issues arises:

- How can we assess the extent to which measures of scholastic achievement are biased?

- What changes in admissions practices would lead to more members of underrepresented groups being selected?

- How much would these changed policies "cost" in terms of foregone academic performance?

We shall address these questions in the context of the case of the University of the Philippines. Among other things, we shall analyze a fascinating social experiment, where less academically qualified poor and rural students were admitted to U.P., given special tutoring and counseling, and evaluated after four to six years. Along the way, we shall develop and apply tools for analyzing representation and bias in selection policies.

HOW THE U.P. ADMISSIONS SYSTEM WORKS

The evolution of selection policies at the University of the Philippines followed a pattern not unlike that found in many other developing countries—and many years before in the United States as well. In earlier years all that was needed for admissions was excellent performance in high school. As the number of high-school graduates with good grades increased, the university was forced to use other mechanisms for selection. Admissions tests were developed; they proved valid in the sense that they effectively predicted academic success. Finally, there arose pressure to overcome the adverse impact of the admissions system by admitting more people from disadvantaged backgrounds.

The university had a relatively open admissions policy before 1971. Students who graduated with honors from high school, or whose four-year high-school grade point average (HSGPA) was 90 percent or better, or who graduated from high schools administered by the University of the Philippines—all were automatically admitted to the university. This policy was workable because the number of high-school graduates with such characteristics who sought admission was relatively small. But by the late 1960s, many at the university began to

TABLE 8. Effect of the College Admission Test on Academic Prediction at U.P. (early 1970s)

Predictor	Correlations with Grades in First Year	Correlations with Cumulative College Grades
Three-year high-school GPA	0.38	0.32
CAT Score	0.50	0.42
Three-year HSGPA + CAT	0.63	0.53

Source: Calculations based on "The Effectiveness of Certain Selective Admissions Criteria at the University of the Philippines" (n.d., Mimeographed, available at the U.P. Registrar's Office).
Note: Based on 1,493 U.P. students.

question this policy on academic grounds. There were two reasons for their misgivings:

> For one thing, quite a number of students admitted, among them valedictorians, salutatorians, and other high school honors graduates, did not have the requisite skills in English and mathematics, and were therefore dropping out, for scholastic delinquency reasons, from the university at alarming rates. For another, the number of high school graduates seeking admission into the University had begun increasing steadily from year to year, and it was becoming more and more difficult to admit all those who "qualified" on the basis of the 90%—or better—automatic admission policy.[9]

So the university's leadership studied the feasibility of a selective admissions policy that would use high-school grades *and* a student's score on a College Admission Test. This study emerged with a number of findings. By using the CAT in addition to high-school grades, the percentage of students who successfully completed their studies could be raised from 70 percent to 90 percent.[10] Table 8 shows the correlations of these predictors with first-year grades and with cumulative grade point average at the university. Using the methods of chapter 3, it can easily be seen that adding the test score to high-school grades as a predictor led to significant increases in the academic performance of the entering class. Consequently, in the 1971–72 academic year the university formally adopted a selective admissions policy that used both test scores and high-school GPA—a combination called UPCAT—as a basis for selecting students.

But by 1976 the faculty and indeed President Marcos had become more and more sensitive to the underrepresentation of people from poor and rural backgrounds. As a result, the university initiated an experiment in the democratization of admissions.

Starting in 1977 about one hundred students a year who were below the usual admissions cutoff in academic terms but who were from poor and rural backgrounds were admitted. These students were given scholarships, careful remedial attention in English and mathematics, special counseling, and other services at the university. The university did not seem to stretch too far academically for this "experimental democratization sample" (XDS, as the group became known). Instead of the usual university cutoff of about a 2.5 predicted grade point average at the university, the cutoff for XDS students was a 2.785 predicted GPA (at U.P., grade point averages are computed in such a way that the lower the average the better, and a 3.0 or higher average is considered unsatisfactory). This 2.785 cutoff corresponded to a 60 percent chance of doing better than 3.0.

So the University of the Philippines has consistently stressed a policy that made predicted grades the sole criterion for admissions but has, over time, used different measures to make the predictions. (As we shall see in chapter 5, there was also a policy that gave the president of the university and certain other academic officials the ability to admit additional students at their discretion.) Academic merit was the sole basis for selection. The debate now taking place in the Philippines is not over the appropriateness of this criterion but over whether, on academic measures such as the UPCAT, the academic potential of rural and poor students is understated systematically.

ADVERSE IMPACT

There is no question that poor and rural students do worse in their high-school grades and especially the standardized tests than rich and urban students do. Take regional differences, for example. Table 9 shows results based on the National College Entrance Examination in 1973. This test has a broader clientele than the U.P. College Admission Test. It is taken by almost all high-school seniors who wish to go on to any college. Notice that on this test Manila students tended to do about half a standard deviation better than non-Manila students. The top 75 percent of NCEE test-takers were considered to have passed. Students from Manila made up about 19 percent of those who took the NCEE and 22 percent of those who passed. If the top 25 percent of that top 75 percent were admitted to the University of the Philippines, this would correspond to the top 20 percent of all those who took the test. And among this top 20 percent, the representation from Manila was about double that in the population of NCEE test-takers (38 percent vs. 19 percent). Thus, students from the provinces were disproportionately excluded.

These figures incidentally indicate a property of selective admissions. When the distributions of qualifications of two groups differ, as they do in the case of students from Manila and students not from Manila, these differences may seem inconsequential at the mean. After all, what is half a standard deviation? But as we move out to the right-hand tails of these distributions—as admissions committees at selective schools must do—the ratios between the high-scoring and lower-scoring groups grow larger and larger. If we take the top three-quarters of

TABLE 9. Performance of Manila and Non-Manila Students
on the National College Entrance Examination (1973)

	From Manila (19% of Test-takers)		From Provinces (81% of Test-takers)			% Students from Manila among:	
					Difference (σ Manila)	Top 75%	Top 20%
	μ	σ	μ	σ			
Overall test	513	74	473	60	0.54σ	22	38
Aptitude test							
Symbolic and verbal relations	513	82	479	73	0.41σ	23	31
Abstract reasoning	592	66	562	67	0.45σ	22	29
Achievement test							
English	492	101	447	86	0.45σ	21	33
Math	500	95	454	79	0.48σ	21	36
Science	469	90	426	76	0.47σ	21	34

Source: Calculations based on P. Richards and M. Leonor, *Education and Income Distribution in Asia* (London: Croom Helm, 1981), chap. 6.

Note: Based on high-school graduates taking the General Scholastic Aptitude Test of the NCEE in 1973. The overall test score was the average of scores on subtests in "symbolic and verbal relations," "abstract reasoning," English, mathematics, and science. The subtests originally were designed to have a mean of 500 and a standard deviation of 100. The lowest average scores for provinces were East Bisayas (461) and North Mindanao (463). The highest averages for provinces outside the Manila area were Central Bisayas (489) and Bicol (481).

students—namely, those who passed the NCEE—there is hardly any overrepresentation of people from Manila, but if we take the top 20 percent, then the overrepresentation becomes quite noticeable. And if, contrary to the situation in the Philippines, only the top 5 percent were being chosen, then 74 percent of those chosen would be from Manila. Differences in performance that may not seem to matter on average can loom large at the right-hand tail.

There are newer data about regional differences in performance. Table 10 shows the percentages from various provinces in the applicant pool and among those admitted. The ratio of admits to applicants gives some idea about the degree of differential representation of students from particular regions in the *admissions* process. Notice, however, that overrepresentation can also occur in the *application* process: almost half the applicants are from metropolitan Manila.

In unpublished analyses of the 1982 UPCAT results, a team from the University of the Philippines examined the way various regional and other background factors seemed to correspond to test scores and high-school grades. After controlling for the type of high school and the rural or urban location of the school,

TABLE 10. Regional Differences in UPCAT Scores (1983)

Region	Applicants		UPCAT Qualified		% Applicants Qualified
	N	%	N	%	
Ilocos	1,499	5.7	242	4.9	16.1
Cagayan Valley	837	3.2	69	1.4	8.2
Central Luzon	1,929	7.4	268	5.4	13.9
Southern Tagalog	4,017	15.4	541	10.9	13.5
Bicol	937	3.6	137	2.8	14.6
Western Bisayas	1,442	5.5	364	7.3	25.2
Central Bisayas	544	2.1	199	4.0	36.6
Eastern Bisayas	606	2.3	94	1.9	15.5
Western Mindanao	300	1.1	66	1.3	22.0
Northern Mindanao	538	2.1	138	2.8	25.7
Southern Mindanao	758	2.9	193	3.9	25.5
Southwestern Mindanao	390	1.5	78	1.6	20.0
Metropolitan Manila	12,355	47.2	2,580	51.9	20.9
Foreign	18	0.1	3	0.1	16.7
Totals	26,170		4,972		Average 19.0

Source: Calculations based on computer printout from the Registrar's Office, University of the Philippines (1983).

students from Manila scored about four-tenths of a standard deviation higher on the various components of the CAT. However, students from Manila scored significantly lower in their high-school grades than did students from other regions, which led their overall UPCAT scores to be about the same as those from other provinces. It is interesting to note that, contrary to the results of the 1973 NCEE, students from northern Mindanao did better on the standardized tests than did other students in the Philippines—on average across the tests, about four-tenths of a standard deviation better.[11]

Now consider income and its relationship to performance on the UPCAT. What were the differences in scores across income groups? Several studies have shown that annual family income is correlated between 0.25 to 0.42 with various CAT scores.[12]

A 1983 computer printout from the Office of the Registrar of the University of the Philippines shows that only 4,972 of 26,170 applicants were admitted (19 percent). But of the 12,456 applicants whose families had incomes under P30,000, only 13 percent were qualified. On the other hand, among the 13,714 students whose families had incomes above P30,000, 24 percent were admitted. I calculate that this difference corresponds to about a half a standard deviation difference in performance on the UPCAT between these two groups.

Several things should be noted about these differences. First, the actual

TABLE 11. "Mental Ability Scores" of Filipino Sixth-Graders at Different Kinds of Schools (1975)

	Rural Public School	Urban Public School	Private School
Average parental income	P394	P555	P705
Nonverbal mental ability score			
Average	48.9	52.6	61.5
Standard deviation	12.8	14.5	13.0

Source: Calculations based on P. Richards and M. Leonor, *Education and Income Distribution in Asia* (London: Croom Helm, 1981), chap. 6.

Note: The difference in these so-called "mental ability scores" in rural public ("barrio") and urban public ("central") schools was about 0.3 standard deviations (in σ units of the lower-scoring group). Differences between the other groups were: rural public and private, 1.0σ; urban public and private, 0.6σ.

differences in scores among the groups who took the test, or who applied to the University of the Philippines, probably *understates* the differences that exist between students from Manila and students from outside Manila, or between poorer and richer students.[13] Second, there is partial evidence that, as in many other countries, test score differences emerge at an early age. For example, table 11 shows data on Philippines sixth-graders from three different kinds of elementary schools. These elementary schools differed not only in their educational resources but also in the socioeconomic classes from which they drew. Already in the sixth grade, students from richer families had higher aptitude test scores than students from poorer families.[14]

ASSESSING BIAS

Group differences in measures of performance does not imply that those measures are biased predictively. Recall the definition of bias above, which focused on differential *prediction* across groups. How might we assess whether the later performance of a group is underpredicted (or overpredicted), compared with another group? There are several possibilities.

Construct a Prediction Equation with Additional Variables

One possibility is to construct a prediction equation as described in chapter 3. To the equation add variables for group membership. If these variables are statistically significant, then the group is significantly under- or overpredicted *after* statistically controlling for the academic predictors such as test scores and high-school grades.[15] For example, consider the following equation:

$$CGPA = \alpha_0 + \alpha_1 \, CAT + \alpha_2 \, HSGPA,$$

where *CGPA* stands for grades at college, α_0 is the intercept term, α_1 and α_2 are the regression coefficients, *CAT* is the score on the College Admission Test, and *HSGPA* is the high-school grade point average. Now suppose we added a term for whether the students were from Manila or not—let us call this dummy variable "*MANILA*"—and another variable for income. Thus we end up with a new equation:

$$CGPA = \beta_0 + \beta_1 CAT + \beta_2 HSGPA + \beta_3 MANILA + \beta_4 INCOME.$$

The βs will not in general be equal to the αs, since the second equation includes more independent variables than the first.

In this second equation, if the coefficients β_3 or β_4 are significant, this means that after controlling for the test score and high-school grades, students from Manila or from different income levels do better or worse (depending on the sign of the coefficients) than predicted.[16] In this sense, if β_3 or β_4 are significant, it may indicate that these academic predictors are biased.

Unfortunately, studies at the University of the Philippines have not focused on this question. Instead they have examined whether the test scores themselves, or high-school grade point averages, could be predicted by knowing a student's family income, region, and so forth. In other words, these regressions use a different dependent variable: instead of *CGPA*, variables like *CAT* or *HSGPA* or *UPCAT* are used on the left-hand side. As a result, the coefficients on the right-hand side do not indicate bias in the CAT or HSGPA. All they show is that different groups score differently on the tests and grades; this does not mean that these tests and grades are biased in the sense of systematically under- or over-predicting later performance at the university or elsewhere.[17]

Although our question has not been asked often at the University of the Philippines, in the course of one of the investigations of this topic, a few regressions like the ones we seek were actually run. The findings: once test scores and grades were statistically controlled for, neither regions nor parents' incomes had any significant relationship to grades at U.P. The admissions tests and high-school grades therefore do not appear to be biased against students from particular regions or income levels. We must be quite tentative on income, since the income data used in these regressions were highly imperfect.[18] With regard to the regions, we can be more confident: given a student's CAT score and high-school grade point average, being from one region or another did not make a difference in college grades. Ilocos was the exception. Students there did about 0.14 better in their college grade point averages than would have been predicted by their test scores and high-school grades. In this sense, the test scores and high-school grades were biased against students from Ilocos.

Analyze Predictive Relationships by Group

A second possibility is to analyze the predictive relationships separately for different groups. The method just described of using dummy variables for differ-

COMPUTER OVERKILL

The computer was allowed to run wild in a 1983–84 effort by a U.P. Faculty Study Group to predict academic performance.

Various grade averages were used to measure academic performance—grades in each year of college and cumulative GPAs over various years. For each such dependent variable, the Study Group used stepwise regression with a host of predictors—all components of the CAT, high-school grades, the thirteen regions, income, and sex . . . *and* quadratic and cubic transformations of many of these variables . . . *and* interaction terms (such as high-school grades times income). The results were nonsensical.

With stepwise regression, the computer chooses first the variable that correlates most highly with the dependent variable. The computer inserts this variable in a regression equation and computes the relevant coefficients. Then with that variable controlled for, the computer looks through the list of independent variables again and picks out the remaining variable with the highest correlation with the dependent variable. It adds this second variable to the regression equation and recomputes the relevant coefficients. This process continues. The computer keeps adding new independent variables until no more on the list enter at a prescribed level of statistical significance.

But for exploring data sets like these, stepwise regression with so many variables is not a good idea. The variables are highly collinear. The various components of the CAT, for instance, are correlated with each other around 0.6 to 0.8. This means that through minor variations in the sample, one or another variable will enter, and once it is controlled for, the other variables may not seem to be important. With multicollinear variables like these, it is often better to create in advance an amalgam of some of them—for example, by summing the components of the CAT into a single score or by combining the various socioeconomic measures into a single index.

However, the members of the Study Group did not do this, and as a result the regression equations they obtained for each dependent variable varied dramatically. Their predictions of first-year grades or second-year grades or

ent groups in a single equation detects differences in the *intercepts* among those groups, but it does not identify differences in the slopes or the standard errors of estimate that might hold across those groups. To check on these other possible sources of biased prediction, we need to run separate regressions for the different groups.

The idea here is to divide the data set into the various groups of interest. For example, one group might be the students from Manila and the other group might be the students from the provinces. Taking these groups separately, one would run two regressions using the academic predictors:

Manila: $CGPA = \gamma_0 + \gamma_1 CAT + \gamma_2 HSGPA$

Provinces: $CGPA = \lambda_0 + \lambda_1 CAT + \lambda_2 HSGPA$

third-year grades or various cumulative GPAs included a variety of different independent variables. Sometimes high-school grades would be very significant, sometimes not. Sometimes quadratic terms would enter. Sometimes bizarre interaction terms, like high-school grades times the English CAT score, would enter. The Study Group seems to have been puzzled by these divergences. They did not perceive that such odd findings could easily result as statistical artifacts of stepwise regression with multicollinear independent variables, applied to data sets that contained a good deal of sampling error.

Despite all the computer runs, the Study Group neglected to run linear regressions with the CAT score and high school grades as the two predictors.

Fortunately, from the various correlation matrices provided in the Study Group's working papers, I have been able to calculate a multiple correlation coefficient R of roughly 0.45 between four-year GPA at the university and a combination of the CAT and high school grades. The computation was as follows:

$$r_{CGPA, HSGPA} = r_{12} = 0.31$$
$$r_{CGPA, CAT} = r_{13} = \text{about } 0.4*$$
$$r_{CAT, HSGPA} = r_{23} = 0.27$$
$$R_{CGPA|HSGPA, CAT} = r_{1.23} = \sqrt{\frac{r_{12}^2 + r_{13}^2 - 2r_{12}r_{13}r_{23}}{1 - r_{23}^2}} = 0.45$$

*Calculated from correlations with the various components of the CAT.

This finding compares well with those of the study done in the early 1970s for two-year CGPA at U.P., where the multiple R was 0.53. And the R of 0.45 was not importantly lower than the best R achieved by the Study Group, with its most complicated stepwise regressions.

None of these correlations has been adjusted for unreliability or restriction of range.

If the γs and the λs differed significantly in size, this would indicate that the predictive relationships were different for the two groups. It would imply that using a single, combined equation for the two groups would tend to underestimate or overestimate the performance of one group or another, at least over certain regions of the prediction. There is another way that the results of these two regressions could demonstrate bias: if the standard errors of the estimate in the two equations were different. At this point, however, the statistical manipulations become complex, and the reader must turn to specialized monographs.[19]

Run an Experiment

A third possibility could be to run an experiment. For example, the university might admit more disadvantaged students, or students from rural areas, or

TABLE 12. Predictions of Four-Year Grade Averages (1978–82) for XDS and Non-XDS Students at U.P.

For XDS students ($N < 100$):

$CGPA = -1.54 + 1.60\ UPG$ $R^2 = 0.13$ $R = 0.36$

For non-XDS students (N not indicated):

$CGPA = 0.22 + 0.91\ UPG$ $R^2 = 0.20$ $R = 0.44$

Source: Unpublished statistical working documents from the Research Subcommittee on Freshman Admission at the University of the Philippines (1983).

Note: UPG is the predicted grade based on high-school GPA and the CAT, using weights derived from a 1973 study. The sample includes unspecified numbers of students who entered in 1978 and persisted through four years at U.P. Information was not available on sample means and standard deviations and standard errors of regression coefficients.

students from a particular minority group. The university could then evaluate how well these students did, compared with what was predicted for them.

There are few instances of such experiments anywhere in the world, which is understandable. It is politically difficult to experiment, and often there are powerful forces to maintain the status quo. Moreover, if students from certain backgrounds are in fact admitted with lower prior test scores and grades, the educational authorities may be reluctant to study carefully the performance of such students once admitted. It may simply be risky politically to do so.

The Philippines is an exception. The University of the Philippines ran the XDS experiment, and the performance of XDS students from 1977 to 1982 has been appraised by a faculty research committee.

The methodology was as follows. The committee computed university grades based on the 1973 UPCAT regression equation. Then it compared those predicted grades with the actual grades earned by students in the XDS program as well as by students not in the XDS program. For students admitted in 1978, the results are shown in table 12 and figure 2.

Notice that the 1973 equation (table 12) provides a slightly biased prediction of the four-year CGPA of non-XDS students.[20] But the point is to examine the regression equation for the XDS students and compare it with the equation for the rest of the students. Recall that XDS students were chosen with predicted grades between 2.5 and 2.8. Within this range, the XDS students did slightly *worse* than their 1978 classmates. For example, an XDS student with a predicted GPA of 2.7 in fact achieved an average of 2.79; a student not in the XDS program with a predicted GPA of 2.7 would be expected to end up with a GPA of about 2.68. Thus, the XDS student is estimated to do about 0.1 worse on four-year college grades than a similarly qualified non-XDS student.

The actual overprediction of the performance of XDS students was probably more severe. Disproportionate numbers of XDS students did not survive at the

**FIGURE 2. A Graphic Representation of Prediction Equations
for XDS and Non-XDS Students (1982)**

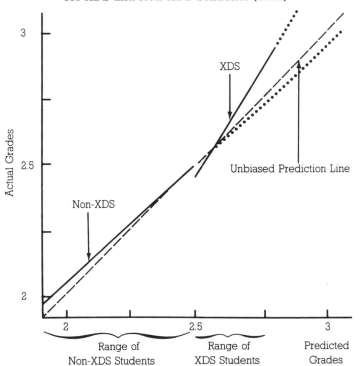

Source: Based on table 12.
Note: The dotted lines are extensions of the XDS and non-XDS regression lines beyond the
appropriate ranges of the data.

U.P. through four years. As an internal evaluation by the U.P. counseling office
concluded:

> The same data reveal that although the courses the students originally enrolled
> in were courses of their choice, rampant shifting from one course to another
> occurred. Statistical computations show that 42.10% of the total XDS students
> shifted from their original courses. Furthermore, approximately 24% to 75%
> [depending on their majors] of the students were disqualified on first count, with
> a few more incurring a second, third and fourth disqualification. Out of the
> original 209 students from Batch 1977 and Batch 1978, only 39 had successful-
> ly graduated from the University.[21]

In a sense, the regression study just cited examined only the best-performing
XDS students and left out those who fell by the wayside. The overprediction of

XDS students was therefore probably greater than the regression results indicated.[22]

The over- rather than underprediction of XDS students is contrary to what many people would have expected. One might have reasoned as follows: An XDS student is educationally deprived, perhaps not having enjoyed as high a level of school instruction in English and other subjects as non-XDS students. If so, the normal equation for predicted university grades would tend to *under-predict* the actual later performance of XDS students—especially if, as was the case in the XDS, the experimental students received the benefit of expensive tutoring and other help at U.P.

However, the actual result was *overprediction*. This is often found for disadvantaged groups in the United States. Contrary to many people's expectations, for example, the test scores and prior grades of blacks tend to overpredict, rather than underpredict, their later academic performance.[23] Why this should be so has received little investigation. There are technical, statistical reasons for expecting some overprediction when the top members of a lower-scoring group are selected.[24]

In any case, it is bad news that the evaluation of the XDS program did not find evidence of underprediction. I say "bad news," for if XDS students had done better than predicted there might have been an argument for admitting even more of them. As it was, the U.P. evaluation of the program led to a decision in February 1984 by the university board of regents to terminate the XDS program.

DEALING WITH PREDICTIVE BIAS

Suppose that such an analysis had found predictive bias against one of the groups. What should be done?

Several approaches are possible. Once there is evidence that a particular predictor is biased, we should analyze the sources of the bias. One method for doing so is called "item analysis," where particular questions on a test, say, are scrutinized to see whether some groups systematically miss the right answer, compared with the groups' relative performance on other questions.[25] If item bias is found, then such items may be deleted from the test, in effect remaking the predictor itself.

Sometimes it will not be feasible to reconstruct the predictors, but we can still correct for predictive bias. For example, by using the regression equations *for each group,* we can adjust the predictor to make predictions equally accurate for each group. Suppose we found that a test was predictively biased against rural students. If so, we could use the prediction equation based only on the rural students and calculate predicted grades for rural students. Then we could do the same for urban students, using the equation derived from the urban sample. We would then select students based on predicted grades thus calculated, rather than on predicted grades calculated from one equation for the entire applicant

SEXUAL BIAS?

A poor choice of statistical methodology can cause trouble. The faculty committee that in 1983 investigated admissions got into trouble over "sexual bias" in the UPCAT. Here's what happened.

1. As in most countries, males did better than females on the math and science admissions tests. Females did better in English and reading comprehension. (As we know, these results do not necessarily imply that the tests were biased predictively.)

2. The committee's stepwise regressions ended up with English and reading comprehension as the two components of the CAT in the prediction equation for four-year CGPA. But because of multicollinearity, virtually the same predictive power could have been obtained by instead using the entire CAT, or some other components of it. Without the math and science components included, though, fewer males than females would be admitted.

3. Alarmed, the committee decided to recommend a complicated formula, where males would automatically have points added to their UPCAT scores.

4. Female faculty members—of whom there are many, including many deans—gasped at this idea. One dean told me, "I cannot accept a system wherein a boy, just for that reason, has a better chance of being admitted than a girl with the same UPCAT score." Controversy flared.

At last report, the committee's recommendation had not been adopted. Notice that no one had shown that, given HSGPA and the complete CAT, males did better or worse at U.P. than females. That is, there was no evidence that these predictors were sexually biased in the predictive sense. But the story shows another way that adverse impact can enter. If a committee can choose among several *equally valid* predictors, it should consider which predictors show the least adverse impact. In this case, using the complete CAT in conjunction with high-school GPA probably would avoid adverse impact against either sex, with equal predictive efficiency.

---

pool. By using different equations for the rural and urban students, predictive bias may be avoided.

A common situation is when the dummy variable for group membership shows up as statistically significant, but regressions stratified by groups do not show significantly different slopes. In this case, there is a simple remedy to predictive bias: simply add the number of points to the predictor that exactly compensates for the underprediction of the group against which the test is biased.

For example, recall the case of students from Ilocos, who at U.P. performed 0.14 grade units better than their compatriots, even after controlling for the best predictive combination of test scores and high-school grades. To compensate for this bias, we might simply improve the predicted grades of every Ilocos student by 0.14.

Note that a result of correcting for biased prediction is a more efficient selection system. In effect, one is adjusting the measuring device, such as UPCAT, for predictive inaccuracies. In many cases, such adjustments will also lead to the greater representation of groups that have been hitherto disproportionately excluded.

THE TRADE-OFF BETWEEN EFFICIENCY AND REPRESENTATION

Suppose we now have unbiased predictions of later performance for the members of the different groups and suppose that nonetheless groups perform differently. If we select strictly according to predicted performance, we end up with what we may judge to be the underrepresentation of certain groups. If we wish to increase the representation of the group with lower predicted performance, but may only admit a fixed number of students, we must reject some students with higher predicted performance. To increase representation, we have to pay a price in later performance. How can we assess the costs, in terms of predicted performance, of various degrees of preferential treatment for particular groups?

It is important at the outset to separate different kinds of costs. Two distinctions are important. First, which measures of costs and benefits should we use? As discussed in chapter 3, there are many possible short-term and long-term measures of academic and later-life performance. For reasons of feasibility, we are only able to look at academic measures here. Longer-term success measures would be preferable, but apparently no studies exist in the Philippines that connect performance in high school or in the university to later-life success.

Second, costs may be reckoned as marginal, average, or total costs. For decision-making purposes, marginal costs are usually what matter.[26] The average cost of a certain degree of representation, and especially the total cost, may also be of interest. The point is to keep it clear which kind of cost we are talking about.

The *marginal cost* of achieving a certain degree of representation is the difference in predicted performance of the last (or marginal or lowest-scoring) person selected from the lower-scoring group, compared with the highest-scoring person rejected from the higher-scoring group. Consider figure 3. In this hypothetical but realistic example, it is assumed that on average students from families with P30,000 or more annual incomes score 0.5 standard deviations higher on the UPCAT, or predicted grades, than students from families with annual incomes below P30,000. If the university accepts the highest 20 percent of the total applicant pool—and two income groups are of equal size—about two-thirds of the students selected will be from the wealthier families.[27]

Suppose we wanted more poor students to attend. What would be the costs of increasing the percentage of students from poorer families? We might address this question as follows:

FIGURE 3. Approximate UPCAT Scores for Students from "Richer" and "Poorer" Families

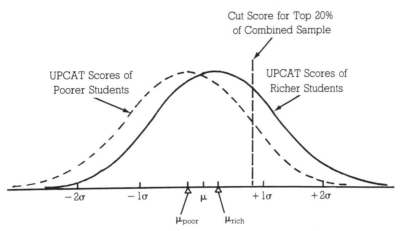

Standard Deviations in UPCAT for Combined Sample

Source: Calculations based on computer print-out from the Registrar's Office, University of the Philippines (1983).

Note: "Poorer families" are those with incomes < P30,000; "richer families" are those with incomes > P30,000. About half the U.P. applicant pool comes from poorer families, but because these poor students score about half a standard deviation lower on the UPCAT, they make up only about one-third of those selected (i.e., in the top 20 percent of the combined sample).

- Compute the distributions of predicted performance (e.g., predicted GPA, predicted number of promotions) for each group A and B.

- Combine the groups into a single pool, T. Given the number N and proportion π to be selected, calculate the cut score C_T (such that N candidates fall above C_T).

- For various desired proportions p of the group A among those selected, calculate the difference in cut scores for groups A and B.

  - What cut score yields $p \times N$ candidates from group A? Translate this into units of predicted performance.

  - What cut score yields $(1 - p)\, N$ candidates from group B? Translate this into units of predicted performance.

  - Plot the difference in performance on the vertical axis against p on the horizontal axis. The resulting curve describes the marginal costs (benefits), in terms of foregone (increased) predicted performance, of changing the proportion of As among those selected.

In most real applications, we will know the means and standard deviations of predicted performance in each group and across the entire applicant pool.[28] If

FIGURE 4. Marginal Costs of Admitting More Students from Poor Families

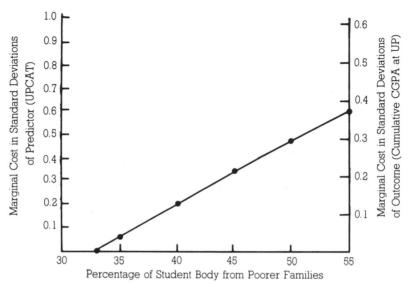

so, it is relatively easy to perform the calculations necessary for figure 4, which graphs the marginal costs of representation of students from poorer families.

Figure 4 is a complicated figure that conveys much useful information. The left-hand vertical axis portrays the marginal costs in terms of the predictor—in this case, UPCAT scores—of admitting various proportions of students from poorer families. For example, if we wanted 40 percent of the students to be from poorer families, it would "cost" about 0.2 standard deviations in scores on the UPCAT.[29] That is, to get a 40 percent representation from the poorer group, the difference in UPCAT scores between the lowest-scoring admit from the poorer group and the highest-scoring reject from the wealthier group would be about 0.2 standard deviations. (This is equivalent to the difference between the 77th and the 82nd percentile scores on the UPCAT.) For 50 percent representation of the poorer students—their actual proportion in the applicant pool—the marginal cost would be about 0.5 standard deviations in UPCAT scores (or the difference between the 72nd and the 86th percentile scores).

How much do such differences matter? This query leads us back to the problems of chapter 3: connecting predictors to outcomes and utility functions. Suppose the UPCAT correlates about 0.6 with first-year grades at U.P. and about 0.5 with cumulative four-year grades. Correcting these correlations for unreliability (but not for restriction of range) would probably raise these correlations to about 0.7 and 0.6, respectively.[30] Let us use the 0.6 figure. Recall that a correlation coefficient of 0.6 means that a one standard deviation change in the predictor (here, the UPCAT score) is associated with a 0.6 standard deviation change in the outcome (here, CGPA at U.P.). If the predictor is not biased for either group, then the cost in terms of the outcome will be on a scale that is 0.6 that of the predictor. The right-hand vertical axis in figure 4 shows the marginal costs, in terms of standard deviations of cumulative GPA, that correspond to various percentages of students from the poorer group. Having 40 percent of the students be from the poorer group has a marginal cost of about 0.12 standard deviations of GPA at U.P.—this is 0.2 × 0.6. For 50 percent representation of poorer students, the corresponding figure is about 0.3 standard deviations.

How would such a graph be useful? Using this information, it is easy to pose the decision problem to policy-makers: How much at the margin is it worth to have another student from one of the poorer families? The optimal degree of representation of the poorer students occurs at the point where the value of having one additional poorer student—perhaps measured in terms of some ultimate objectives of social mobility—is exactly equal to the value of the marginal cost in terms of foregone academic performance.

As in chapter 3, we could try to translate standard deviations of academic performance into money. Suppose one standard deviation of cumulative GPA had a utility of $1,000 per student per year. Then the marginal cost of having 40 percent of the students be from poorer families would be 0.12 × $1,000, or $120 per year. (Of course, it will be difficult for decision-makers to agree on the value of the standard deviation of performance, and the analyst is advised to use a range of possible values here.)

Is having one more student from a poorer family worth that much? If not, then fewer should be admitted; if it were worth more than that in the policy-maker's judgment, then the quota for poorer students should be raised higher than 40 percent of the student body. The marginal cost of having poorer students admitted in proportion to their numbers in the applicant pool (i.e., 50 percent) would be 0.3 × $1,000 = $300 per year.

One *average cost* of interest is the difference in expected performance between the *average* admits from each group, because of increased representation. Under the assumption of normality, which seems to work well for values above the mean in data like these, the average score of a person admitted in group A is:

$$\mu_{\underline{a}} = \mu_a + \sigma_a(\phi_a/\underline{P}_a)$$

where $\mu_{\underline{a}}$ is the average score on the predictor of those selected from group A, μ_a is the average score for all applicants from group A, σ_a is the standard deviation for that group, $\underline{P}_a$ is the selection ratio for members of group A in the quota we are analyzing, and ϕ_a is the ordinate of the standard normal distribution corresponding to $\underline{P}_a$. Then this average on the predictor would be translated into an expected grade point average by the regression equation for group A. A similar calculation is done for group B. Then the difference in average performance between the two groups is compared with the difference that would occur if a common cut score were used—that is, as if there were no quota for increased group representation.[31]

The *total cost* of the expected performance for the entire admitted group, given the representational quota, is simply the average cost times the number of students admitted from the lower-scoring group.

With no quota, the average admit from poorer families is 1.32 standard deviations (in σ_T, not σ_{PF}) above the mean UPCAT score in the applicant pool. The corresponding figure for the average admit from wealthier families is 1.43. So, with no preferential treatment for students from poorer families, among all students admitted there will be a difference of $1.43 - 1.32 = 0.11$ standard deviations in UPCAT. This results in a student body composed of 33 percent from poorer families. These are baselines from which to judge the average costs of quotas.

Take a 40 percent quota for students from poorer families. The average UPCAT score of the students selected from the poorer families would be about 1.23 standard deviations above the mean of the applicant pool. The average score of the richer students selected would be about 1.50 standard deviations above the same mean. So, the *average* cost would be $(1.50 - 1.23) - 0.11 = 0.16$ standard deviations in the UPCAT score. If the UPCAT correlates 0.6 with cumulative GPA, this becomes an average cost of $0.16 \times 0.6 = 0.1$ standard deviations of cumulative GPA. For a 50 percent quota, the average cost would be about 0.38 standard deviations in UPCAT, or about 0.23 standard deviations of cumulative GPA.[32]

The *total cost* is simply the average cost times the number of students from the lower-scoring group. Suppose 5,000 students are admitted each year. If 40 percent, or 2,000, are to be students from poorer families and the average cost is 0.1 standard deviations of GPA, then the total cost is 200 standard deviations. If one standard deviation of GPA is worth $1,000 per year, this comes to $200,000 per year. The decision-maker may ask: Is it worth $200,000 per year to increase the percentage of students from poorer families from 33 percent to 40 percent?

The total cost of a 50 percent quota for poorer families is $2,500 \times 0.23 = 575$ standard deviations of cumulative GPA, or $575,000 per year.

LESSONS FROM THE PHILIPPINES EXAMPLE

Several interesting findings emerge from our analysis of the case of the University of the Philippines.

First, the prediction of academic performance at the University of the Philippines is comparable to prediction at universities in the United States, with multiple *R*s of 0.45 to 0.65 (the latter for first-year grade point averages). A simple combination of high-school grades and the College Admission Test is a valuable way to select a class that will perform well at the University of the Philippines, although the predictions are hardly perfect. (The methods of chapter 3 can be applied to make this general statement precise.)

Second, groups often perform differently on measures of academic performance. In the Philippines, for example, it appears that students from families with incomes of less than P30,000 a year score about half a standard deviation lower on the UPCAT than students from families with incomes greater than P30,000 per year. (There are regional differences in performance on the College Admission Test; however, these differences are for the most part offset by opposite regional differences in high-school grade averages.)

A third lesson from the Philippine example is that these differences do not by themselves imply that high-school grades or the College Admission Test are biased, in the sense of systematically over- or underpredicting the later performance of certain groups. To address the question of bias, one needs to study differential prediction. Studies of bias often look in the wrong place. They tend to ask whether groups score differently *on the predictors,* when they should also ask whether, after controlling those predictors, some groups tend to do better in later performance.

Fourth, the University of the Philippines provides an almost unique example of an experiment to assess bias. It is surprising that the results of the XDS indicate that academic criteria used to select students at U.P. were *not* predictively biased against the disadvantaged students who participated in the experiment. In fact, if anything, these criteria favored the XDS students, in the sense of over- rather than underpredicting their performance at the university. This conclusion is supported by other evidence based on regression analysis.

Fifth, the University of the Philippines may have drawn the wrong policy conclusion from its study. Its faculty research committee seemed to conclude that since adjusting predicted performance for bias led to virtually no increase in the number of disadvantaged students admitted, there was no reason to give disadvantaged students preferential treatment. The board of regents considered this evidence and canceled the XDS program. But the policy problem raised by President Marcos in his 1976 commencement address went further than the correction of predictive bias in admissions criteria. Even if it cost something in terms of the university's academic standards, would it not be socially worthwhile to increase the proportion of disadvantaged, underrepresented groups at the university? If so, how far should such preferential treatment go? What is the optimal degree of representation?

The answer clearly depends on value judgments. But it also depends on certain facts, for example, what is the "trade-off surface" between greater representation and forgone academic performance? Figure 4 provides one way of answering this question. The total cost in terms of forgone academic performance of increasing the number of students from families with incomes below P30,000 from about 1,660 to about 2,500 (of the 5,000 students admitted each

WHAT THE COSTS OF REPRESENTATION DEPEND UPON

If we replace more-qualified students with less-qualified students from a disadvantaged group, it will probably cost us something in terms of later performance. How much it will cost us depends on several specific features of our situation. (All statements are *ceteris paribus*.)

- *Differences in groups' qualifications.* The greater the difference between groups, the greater the costs of preferential treatment.

- *Bias in the predictors.* If the qualifications are predictively biased against the disadvantaged group, then admitting more students from that group may not cost anything in forgone performance. If the bias is the other way, it will tend to cost us more.

- *The prediction equation.* The higher the correlation between the qualifications and the outcome we care about, the greater the costs of preferential treatment.

- *The selection ratio.* The more selective the university, the greater the costs of preferential treatment.

- *How much later performance matters.* The greater the utility of increases in later performance, the greater the costs of preferential treatment.

Since these specific features vary across institutions, it follows that there is no one "right" degree of preferential treatment for disadvantaged groups. Careful analysis is needed to determine the optimal extent of representation and "democratization of admissions" for each specific circumstance.

---

year) would be worth about $575,000 per year. This calculation is not exact, as it depends on a number of assumptions, for example, that one standard deviation in cumulative GPA at U.P. is worth $1,000 per year. But it does illustrate the kind of analysis that President Marcos's challenge to the university required.

CONCLUDING OBSERVATIONS ON REPRESENTATION AND BIAS

Building on the work of chapter 3, this chapter has added a second dimension of selection policies: the appropriate treatment of group differences. Several analyses should be carried out concerning bias and representation.

First, we need data on the differential performance of various groups of interest on the criteria used in selection. For example, it would be helpful to have the distributions of UPCAT scores for applicants from different regions, sexes, races, and so forth.

Second, through statistical analysis we must analyze the existence and extent of predictive bias in those criteria. "Bias" is defined in terms of systematic under- or overprediction of later performance. As chapter 3 emphasized, the choice of performance measures is crucial but complicated and value-laden. In this chapter, limitations of data forced us to look at short-run and long-run academic measures of performance; data were not available on performance after students left the university.

Third, we should try to correct biased measures. This can be done by reconstructing them, as when one drops or changes items on biased tests. Or we might change the scores of under- or overpredicted groups to correct for biased prediction.

Finally, whether predictive bias exists or not, we should analyze the costs and benefits of greater representation of disadvantaged groups. This chapter has developed and illustrated new techniques for doing this analysis. The basic idea is to balance the marginal benefits of greater group representation against the marginal costs. Obviously value judgments matter here, and people disagree about both the benefits and costs of representation. We have seen how to calculate and display the marginal costs in terms of selecting a group member with lower predicted performance instead of someone from another group who has a higher predicted performance. This tool is of relevance to a wide variety of selection problems, where we may prefer to give preferential treatment to members of a certain group or region or sex or race.

The point of this chapter has not been to derive the ideal admissions policy for the University of the Philippines. It is at once much less and considerably more. It is less because, as we have seen throughout, the "ideal" policy depends on value judgments, and these can be provided only by those empowered to make educational policy in the Philippines. It is more because a method of analysis has been demonstrated, a method with applications beyond Philippine borders and indeed beyond university admissions. Problems of group representation and bias—of affirmative action and reverse discrimination and preferential treatment and quotas—arise all over the world, in a variety of policy domains. The tools presented here—and illustrated again in chapter 6—may advance but will certainly not by themselves resolve discussions of how far to go in affirmative action.

5

THE INCENTIVES CREATED BY SELECTION POLICIES

The graduate students I taught during two years as a visiting professor of economics at the University of Karachi were extremely talented. Many compared well with my students at Harvard, in terms of ability. They also worked hard, at least in my courses, where I tried to provide them with detailed feedback. But I soon learned that in many of their other classes they were not thought diligent. Several colleagues and I did a survey of homework, library use, and assignments at the university. We found that most students, and I'm afraid most faculty, treated their work at the University of Karachi as a half-time occupation.[1] It still moves me to recall the emotional remark that one of my ablest students, a shy and traditional young woman, made one day: "Sir, why should we work hard? In Pakistan that's not the way you get ahead. That's not how it works over here."

I heard this sentiment elsewhere. In studies I was doing in a couple of Pakistani government agencies, I worked closely with many middle-level officials. Most were not paragons of the work ethic. After I earned their trust, they would tell me of their alienation from organizations that did not reward "merit." To them, promotions seemed to be based on connections more than on competence and hard work. I was distressed at the low level of energy and commitment many civil servants put into their responsibilities. Surely many factors were involved, but a primary cause seemed to be that selection for higher education or jobs or promotions did not, in many people's minds, depend enough on their achievements.

A selection system creates incentives. Being chosen—or admitted or promoted—is like a reward. The person selected gets access to benefits that are not available to those rejected. Consequently, people will compete to be chosen. They will tend to acquire or develop the characteristics that the selection system rewards. If admissions criteria put heavy emphasis on rote learning, applicants will have an incentive to memorize. If people are selected according to their family or political connections, they will pursue those connections rather than presumably more productive activities. And so forth. Notice that the incentives created by a selection system do not just affect the few students who end up being chosen; they also influence the behavior of the many more students who are rejected or who end up not applying. Incentive effects ripple back through the system of education.

That a reward system creates incentives is a foundation of the economic analyses of wage scales, tax and subsidy policies, pricing systems, and even tournaments. And yet in the literature on selection for higher education and the civil service, this dimension is usually left out. Policies are analyzed primarily with regard to what we called in chapter 3 "static efficiency": given a pool of applicants with certain characteristics, how do alternative selection systems affect the quality of the few who are chosen? This is an important question, but it is not the only one. Important aspects of what might be called "dynamic efficiency" should not be overlooked:

- How does the choice of selection policies affect who will apply, who will be in the pool of candidates?
- How do alternative policies affect what subjects pupils pursue in earlier levels of education? or how hard those pupils study? or the way they learn (e.g., rote learning versus synthetic learning)?
- What effects do alternative policies have on teachers and principals?
- What incentives do various selection policies create for those doing the selecting? In particular, what opportunities are opened up for corruption, nepotism, and discrimination?
- What incentives do alternative policies have for university professors and administrators?

Saying that such issues should be considered is easier than showing *how* to include them along with issues of static efficiency and representation, in the design of selection policies. As we shall see, here among the various dimensions of selection policy we must rely most on the judgments of experienced educators. The measurement of incentive effects is still in a rudimentary state, but this does not mean that the topic can be overlooked.

EFFECTS ON HIGH-SCHOOL STUDENTS AND CURRICULA

The most important of the incentive effects created by admissions policies, perhaps, concerns high schools. What colleges select upon, high schools tend to stress. The way high-school students study—what, how, and how much—is shaped by the criteria universities use in admissions.

An interesting example concerns the United States in the last two decades of the nineteenth century, when it was in many respects a developing country. Educators then had begun to worry about the "articulation" between universities and high schools. In those days, Harvard required applicants to take up to eleven specialized examinations designed by its own faculty. Other colleges designed their own exams, covering the classics as well as history, literature, mathematics, and other subjects. The multiplicity of standards for selection put secondary schools in a bind. An influential high-school headmaster of the day complained:

> [The] establishment by any college of a requirement not in harmony with those prevailing in other colleges, is a direct blow at the cause of sound education. . . . [No] college founded for the advancement of sound learning and devoted to the furtherance of education has any moral right to hamper the work of secondary education by thus laying down an arbitrary, individual requirement.[2]

It was not just the diversity of admissions standards that caused problems, but their content and rigor. In those days, only about 5 percent of the eligible cohort attended college; as in most developing countries today, the vast majority of high-school students did not. But high-school officials felt pressure to offer courses that would enable students to go to college, even if only a few. What colleges required therefore shaped what high schools offered, not just to the college-bound few but to all their students. Put bluntly, entrance examinations in classics led to high-school courses in classics, which ill suited the needs of most high-school students. The president of Columbia University wrote in 1898 that a secondary school

> cannot give its pupils the best possible secondary education, and at the same time have its efficiency judged by its ability to fit some or all of its graduates to pass the tests prescribed in a thousand forms for college entrance. My mind is perfectly clear that the relation usually existing hitherto between secondary school and college must be reversed; instead of the secondary-school programme having to conform to college entrance requirements, college entrance requirements must be brought into harmony with secondary-school programs.[3]

The president of Harvard concurred:

> The secondary schools of the United States, taken as a whole, do not exist for the purpose of preparing boys and girls for colleges. Only an insignificant percentage of the graduates of these schools go to colleges or scientific schools. . . . A secondary school program intended for national use must therefore be made for those children whose education is not to be pursued beyond secondary school.[4]

Recognizing these incentive effects led to the alteration of admissions requirements. First, not all college applicants should have to pass classics; a range of subjects should be considered acceptable. Second, colleges should combine forces in the design of entrance examinations. Thus the College Entrance Examination Board, which persists in greatly expanded form today, was founded in 1900. Third, perhaps examinations should put more emphasis on academic aptitude than on the mastery of particular subjects. *If* it could be shown that aptitude tests predicted success at the university as well as subject-matter tests, an argument based on incentives could be made in favor of the former. Aptitude tests would free the high schools to offer varying courses, depending on local needs and capabilities, without thereby sacrificing the chances for their college-bound graduates to be admitted to the best universities. Subject-matter tests, however, would tend to lock the high schools into those particular subjects.

The story is more roundabout than a brief description can convey. My point is simply that, at a crucial time in the history of higher education in one developing country, the incentive effects of admissions policies on secondary education were a crucial concern. And although the reforms of the late nineteenth century were not entirely successful,

> by 1910, the "newer" disciplines had been fully accepted in the list of college entrance subjects in all significant American colleges. Entrance requirements had been standardized within each discipline, and complaints of arbitrary grading or poor administration of entrance exams had practically ceased. The colleges had learned to cooperate with one another, and to an extent unthinkable a generation earlier. The quality of instruction in the secondary schools and the range of offerings vastly improved.[5]

INCENTIVE EFFECTS IN THE PEOPLE'S REPUBLIC OF CHINA

The case of China, presented in chapter 1, sharply displays the various dimensions of selection policies: static efficiency, representation, and incentive effects. I used those headings in chapter 1 to organize the arguments given in 1966 for abolishing entrance examinations for universities—and the arguments used in 1977 for bringing the examinations back. Questions of fact, not just of value judgments or objectives, were and are at issue in the choice of selection policies.

Incentive effects were crucial. The critics in 1966 focused on the bad incentives created by the examination system. It was argued that the examinations induced secondary school students to become narrow eggheads, to cram their brains with knowledge not useful to the people's revolution, to remain aloof from political activities and nonacademic pursuits. If the admissions process became politicized in the best sense, it was contended, students would have incentives to develop more desirable intellectual and personal traits. They would be selected by local cadres of workers, peasants, and soldiers; the criteria would be fitness for the revolution, being "the best from among the fine sons and daughters of the proletariat, young people who truly serve the broad masses."[6]

There would also be important incentive effects on the secondary schools and teachers. Teachers would lose their authoritarian control over the students. In 1974 a professor at Peking University told an American visitor that students and teachers were now "comrades-in-arms in the trenches. We changed the situation in which the teacher was superior. The 'dignity' and 'absolute authority' of teachers is an idea influenced by Confucius. Teachers should learn from the virtues and good ideas of students."[7] Confucius himself was not as rabidly pro-teacher as this professor implied,[8] but it is true that without examinations and grades, students had fewer incentives to follow their teachers' commands. The abolition of examinations greatly altered power relationships within Chinese academic institutions.

By 1977, those favoring the reestablishment of exams stressed the unfortunate incentives created by the new, political system of admissions. Students did not master their academic work; in terms of chapter 3, the distribution of performance shifted downward, not only among those selected for the university but also in the population of secondary school students. Apparently the efficiency losses that ensued when these academically less-prepared students took jobs were deemed large—larger, it would seem, than the purported benefits from having engineers, scientists, managers, and technicians with a more revolutionary outlook. Little hard evidence is available on these matters, but some data indicate that the hoped-for gains in revolutionary zeal from removing the entrance exams and instead using political criteria for selection were smaller than anticipated, because of corruption.

By corruption I mean the perversion of ostensible criteria such as "revolutionary fitness" toward more venal criteria like "offspring of a party official." Recall the report from students at Peking University, cited in chapter 1: "Everyone knows that the system of recommendation by the masses had a very bad influence at the grass-roots level. . . . The best way to get to the university was still to have a well placed father; lots of young people lost all motivation to study."[9] What the Chinese call "entering through the back door" became prevalent when examinations were abolished. Not only could subjective judgments about revolutionary zeal enter into the selection process, so could political pressures, bribery, favoritism, and whim.

Mechanical systems—such as centrally graded, standardized tests—are a guard against such abuses. They hamstring the selectors, reducing their freedom of movement and providing fewer incentives and opportunities for corruption and coercion.

In many countries these considerations are decisive. In theory, one may wish to select on a variety of subjective, hard-to-standardize, political and moral criteria. One may believe that, apart from academic variables, these further dimensions of character and motivation are crucial in selecting the ideal group of future leaders. And this may be correct in theory; the problem is practical. Can such attributes be reliably measured? If they are introduced into a system, can safeguards be administered to preclude "entering through the back door" and other abuses, which undercut the whole point of the enterprise?

In days of old, the Chinese system of sponsorship provided a partial solution to this dilemma. The Chinese recognized that the complicated and highly valued examination system was only a partial answer to choosing its administrative leadership. Examinations could measure intellectual power and cultural formation, but they did not purport to measure how well a person would meet the practical challenges that faced a high official of government. To augment the exams, an elaborate system of recommendations was instituted, but recommendations with safeguards against corruption and whim. The recommender was held responsible for the person he recommended. If you recommended someone for a job and he did well, you could receive "requitement and commendation" yourself, but if he did badly, you could be liable. Table 13 shows how the penalties to the recommender were related to the penalties incurred by the person recommended. This system was administered scrupulously, and the evi-

TABLE 13. Recommender's Liability in China (c. A.D. 1020)

If the person recommended was later punished with:	The recommender could be punished with:
Death	Deportation
Deportation	Forced labor
Forced labor	Beating with a heavy or light rod
Beating with a heavy rod	None
Beating with a light rod	None

Source: Based on Tables 7 and 8 in E. A. Kracke, Jr., Civil Service in Early Sung China, 960–1067 (Cambridge: Harvard University Press, 1953), chap. 10.

Note: The recommender's punishment depended in part on whether the principal's crime was "personal rapacity," "intentional," or "administrative delinquency" (in various combinations). Penalties were often commuted.

dence is that in early Sung China at least this method of incorporating subjective judgments about personal character into the selection process was relatively free from corruption and abuse.[10]

THE NEGATIVE EFFECTS OF DISCRETION IN THE PHILIPPINES

Such safeguards do not usually operate. In chapter 4 we examined the admissions system of the prestigious University of the Philippines. Admissions policy is based on "academic merit." Predicted university grades, with the predictions derived from high-school grades and an entrance examination, are the criterion for acceptance. But there is an exception to this academic meritocracy: "presidential discretion."

In 1970 the president of the University of the Philippines (U.P.) had a student whom he wished the university to admit. The registrar refused, noting that the student's predicted grades were not better than the cutoff. The president took the matter to the university's policy-making councils, and in October 1971 a resolution was passed that gave the president "the discretion to extend the privilege of admission to certain freshman applicants if, in his judgment, their cases are meritorious." Such students would be admitted beyond the fixed number of seats filled through the normal, merit-based admissions process.

The policy-making councils recognized that there could be good reasons for such discretion. For example, what should be done with students who had studied overseas, say as exchange students, and therefore had noncomparable high-school records? Were there not also exceptional cases, students with promise inappropriately gauged via predicted grades?

Over the next few years, admissions by discretion grew. Others besides the president wanted and received discretionary admits: the athletic department, the deans of regional branches of the university, the chancellor, and so forth. Only one student was admitted through such discretionary channels in 1971. The next year, forty-five students were, and the following year saw 221 discretionary admits. By 1981 the total had snowballed to 1,131. In other words, of the approximately 5,000 students admitted to U.P. in 1981, over 22 percent had been admitted outside the scope of the merit-based process.

"It should be emphasized," wrote the authors of a recent internal U.P. analysis of presidential discretion, "that the one single unique factor which accounts all too significantly for the exponential growth of presidential discretion is the very exercise itself. For the exercise of presidential discretion, like a chemical chain reaction, feeds on itself and creates its own momentum."[11]

There were powerful pressures on those having the discretion. The U.P. applicant pool grew from 9,164 in 1972 to 28,632 in 1982, while the number of admits stayed roughly constant. U.P.'s tuition was only about one-tenth of the tuition at private universities with comparable academic standards. The declaration of martial law in 1972, with the subsequent crackdown on leftist student groups of the university, made U.P. more attractive to well-off families. Many of the people who wanted to get into U.P. could not make it on strict academic grounds; they now had the incentive to pressure the university president to exercise his discretion. "Therefore, the 'powerful' and 'influential,' hearing that such things as presidential discretion do exist in the University, become all too eager to test whether they are indeed 'powerful' and 'influential' by seeking to become beneficiaries of its exercise."[12]

In March 1984, I interviewed a former U.P. president and asked him about this process. He said frankly that the political pressure was intense, frequently taking the form of a direct order. There was also pressure from powerful alumni and members of the university's governing board. He said that he tried to balance these claims by also using his discretion to admit needy students and valid "exceptional cases." Moreover, he would not stretch too far academically: most students admitted via presidential discretion were only slightly below the usual U.P. threshold of predicted grades. But he regretted presidential discretion. By the time he took office, he said, presidential discretion had a life of its own; it would have been too costly in political terms for him to abolish the procedure. (The president of U.P. is not tenured in that job; and indeed, this man was later removed from office for other political reasons.)

In practice, discretionary admissions favored the rich and powerful. Of those admitted to the College of Arts and Sciences through presidential discretion in 1981, about 78 percent were from families with incomes above P30,000. About 86 percent were from metropolitan Manila. The authors of the recent report on presidential discretion observed acidly: "This phenomenon is of course only to be expected. After all, does one really expect the disadvantaged to have access, in significant numbers, to the discretion wielders of the University? Who, other than the privileged, does one really expect to be able to whisper, all too audibly, 'I am a personal friend of VIP So-and-so?'"[13]

ANY MEASURE IS CORRUPTIBLE

Examination scores—particularly those from multiple-choice exams graded by computer—are less susceptible to abuse and corruption than most other criteria for selection. But they are not immune, as two African examples indicate.

In August 1984, teachers in Swaziland's districts of Mbabane and Hhohho were, in the words of *The Times of Swaziland,* "up in arms against an alleged junior certificates examination scandal." Teachers alleged that "corrupt methods were used by some teachers who mark the Standard Five and J.C. examination papers in order to get financial gain. They alleged that some of the markers took the children's scripts to their homes and asked friends who were not qualified in the subjects in question to use examination answer guides to mark the papers." Why? Because teachers were paid according to how many exams they graded. As a result of this practice, many examination scores were not a valid reflection of how much a student knew or how well he or she would perform in later studies.

The Swazi example involved essay exams. But even computerization does not remove all possibility of abuse. At about the same time that the Swazi teachers were up in arms, another testing scandal rocked the educational establishment in South Africa.

In the province of Transvaal, according to the *Sunday Express* of Johannesburg, "the Transvaal Education Department fiddled last year's matric results to give hundreds of additional distinctions to pupils who did not earn them."

"In just one case," the paper went on, "about 370 distinctions awarded by examiners for higher-grade Afrikaans were increased to 808 distinctions by TED computers. This meant that Afrikaans pupils earned 438 distinctions too many for the paper on their home language, with endless ramifications in terms of bursaries awarded, admissions to coveted courses at universities, and so forth."

A predictable result is that Transvaal students with such "distinctions" would not tend to do as well in the university as anticipated. "The Transvaal Teachers' Association recently questioned the quality of first-year students, saying it was disturbing that only 39% of 390 first-year diploma students at the Johannesburg College of Education obtained a clear pass. Was the matric examination at fault? asked the TTA."

Sources: "Teachers Want Exam Probe," *The Times of Swaziland,* August 6, 1984, pp. 1, 5; Kitt Katzin, "Matric Exam Results Were Fiddled," *Sunday Express* (Johannesburg), August 12, 1984, pp. 1–2.

What were the consequences of this explosion of discretionary admits? The faculty research committee reviewing the evidence was concerned about "discrimination" against students who scored higher than those admitted by presidential discretion but were rejected. For example, it was argued that admitting someone by presidential discretion who was only 0.05 units of predicted grades below the usual admissions cutoff discriminated against 626 applicants who scored higher but were not admitted. In most cases, those admitted by presidential discretion had better than 2.8 predicted GPAs, but occasional cases would be below 3.0, the threshold for satisfactory performance at the university.

Presidential discretion had academic costs. On average, those admitted by presidential discretion performed worse than the rest of the students. The faculty committee called it "lackluster performance."

> That the academic performance of the beneficiaries of presidential discretion is neither "good enough" nor "bad enough" is of course only to be expected. Their performance is not bad enough because these students generally belong (with some exceptions) to the group of UPCAT applicants whose [predicted GPA], though below the [usual cutoff], remains above 2.785. . . . Their performance is not good enough either because their [predicted grades] are in all cases lower than [the usual cutoff].[14]

But most important to the faculty research committee was the principle involved. The practice of presidential discretion had corrupted the university's values. Not only the presidential discretion students, but others at the university, might derive unfortunate lessons.

> What kind of values is the University then inculcating in students who, having been admitted through presidential discretion, continually invoke influence—with or without basis, with or without grounds—with this or that VIP, not only for admission. . . . Do not other students also somehow imbibe these values . . . simply from the knowledge that "influence" does have its own very visible rewards in the University?[15]

The committee recommended abolishing discretionary admission. Notice that their point was not theoretical: they did not say that discretion, properly employed, might not be beneficial. It was the practice in the Philippines that they lamented. In our terms, presidential discretion had created the wrong incentives; it had opened the door to the exercise of influence and various forms of corrupt behavior.

The faculty committee's report carried the day. On February 23, 1984, the U.P. board of regents and the university president issued a decision to abolish presidential and other forms of discretionary admission.

ECONOMIC ANALYSIS OF INCENTIVE EFFECTS

How might a decision-maker analyze incentive effects? Economics offers some guidance. In the past decade or so, a hot topic on economic theory has been the incentives created by selection systems. This work contributes qualitative insights, but as yet the research of economists has not reached a state where it can be applied quantitatively to our selection problem.

A trailblazing contribution was Michael Spence's 1974 book, *Market Signaling*. Spence showed that incentive effects from selection systems could lead students to overinvest, from a social point of view, in the criteria used for selection. "From reasonably early ages, students are guided through courses of study designed to make them look like good bets (lotteries) to colleges. The expenditure of student effort, and the concomitant anxiety over a prolonged period, may constitute a large diversion of human resources and energies away from relatively productive activities at early ages."[16] Students would "signal" their future productivity to colleges by investing in the predictors that colleges used. Spence's theoretical contribution was to show that a multitude of self-reinforcing signaling equilibriums might result from this process. Moreover, some of these equilibriums could be socially nonoptimal, in the sense that society would be better off if the incentive effects of selection systems were not so powerful. For each individual, investing in the signal might be economically rational, but for society the result over all individuals might well be irrational.

An educational credential—such as being above a certain GPA or having a certain undergraduate degree—is a signal. Spence's theoretical results were seized upon by critics of "the credential society"[17]—a society that hired or promoted those who had surpassed what the critics thought were arbitrary and unproductive educational hurdles. Critics analyzed credentialism as a way for elites to restrict competition. Apart from being a socially productive investment in "human capital," education could become another sort of conspicuous consumption, another mechanism for the perpetuation of the privileged class. Spence had produced models where educational credentials were socially unproductive—and yet this unsatisfactory outcome could be a self-sustaining equilibrium, not a temporary aberration. Some social critics found this result appealing.

A flurry of research followed. Some economists pointed out that signaling could be socially productive. In a society with imperfect information, applicants' investing in credentials could play a useful role in allocating their human capital efficiently. Joseph Stiglitz noted: "If, as we have suggested, education provides information [as a signal to employers] as well as skills, then it is providing a 'commodity' for which it is well known that the market 'fails.' "[18] So, the incentive effects could be positive as well as negative: admissions criteria could create productive as well as unproductive incentives for students back through the system, and the choice of criteria also influenced how efficiently applicants would be allocated to educational openings.

To my knowledge, no one has quantitatively assessed the incentive effects of various university admissions criteria on high schools and high-school students. Research has focused on educational credentials as signals to the job market—or, put the other way around, on how selection criteria for jobs create productive and unproductive incentives to invest in education. For example, a recent study of the returns to primary and secondary education in a sample of 384 wage laborers in Nairobi and Dar es Salaam concluded: "The direct returns to reasoning ability in the labor market are small, those to years of education [i.e., the credential itself] are moderate, and those to literacy and numeracy—dimensions of human capital [i.e., how much people had learned]—are large."[19] The credential effect did not seem large. But empirically, it has proved difficult to estimate these various effects.[20] Spence told me in an interview: "What we take to be the signal and later success are highly correlated, but the data don't tell you, and are not likely to tell you, whether this is because of a credential effect or a productive effect of the education. In principle, it could be tested, but in practice what we're left with is intuition." We seem to be a long way from being able to estimate statistically the magnitude of various incentives created by selection policies.

But theoretical work proceeds apace. For example, in a fascinating recent paper, Mary O'Keeffe, W. Kip Viscusi, and Richard J. Zeckhauser extend the literature on contests and tournaments in economic life. Contests are closely related to selection policies: individuals are rewarded (selected) on the basis of their performance relative to other applicants. This is different from the conventional microeconomic model, where individuals are rewarded for their own marginal productivity: now relative rather than absolute performance is what counts.

The authors show that contests may be desirable when contestants' outputs are affected by chance or cannot be reliably measured; when rewards are indivisible (an example is access to the university: you are either in or out); and when one wishes to allocate different groups of people to different contests. They go on to point out that, depending on the features just listed, the designer of a contest (or selection policy) may choose *not* to use the predictors that have the highest correlation with later performance.

A simple example conveys this surprising result. Suppose the top 20 percent of exam-takers will be admitted to the University of the Philippines. Suppose an applicant knows that he is in the top 1 percent of academic ability. He may not choose to study hard for the UPCAT, feeling quite confident that even with a middling effort he will score in the top 20 percent and be admitted. Similarly, a student who believes she is in the bottom half in academic ability may also not give her best effort, reckoning that no matter how hard she works she is unlikely to end up in the top 20 percent.

But suppose an admissions policy-maker decided to make the UPCAT a *less* precise measure of attainment. In effect, more random error might be introduced into the College Admission Test. Surprisingly, this might have beneficial effects on incentives. The top 1 percenter may realize he is not sure to get in, and so long as effort is still positively related to his score on the imprecise UPCAT, he may study harder than before. So may the woman in the bottom half, as she now figures she has a chance to get in.

"Appropriately imprecise monitoring," write O'Keeffe, Viscusi, and Zeckhauser, "may be particularly helpful in motivating the most able workers."[21] Such a result can never occur in the static setting of chapter 3. But when incentives are seen as part of the problem, it may be desirable to have a less perfect predictor. (Of course, one would have to trade off the improved incentives with the losses in the quality of the group selected with a less precise predictor.)

This is an interesting theoretical point. It reminds us that incentive effects may not adequately be addressed through the static considerations of chapter 3. Unfortunately, however, we are a long way from gauging in practice the magnitude of these effects. How much does the precision of prediction affect how and how hard potential applicants will study? All the theory tells us is to watch out for such effects: it does not yet provide us with methods for measuring them. Alas, here we do not now have quantitative techniques like those in the previous two chapters.

A QUALITATIVE ANALYSIS OF INCENTIVES

This does not mean that we can afford to ignore incentive effects, but it does imply that we have to rely on the subjective judgments of leading educators instead of statistical studies. Incentives affect students, teachers, those doing the selecting, the university, and the job market.

Tests and Other Academic Measures

Key questions here include the subjects covered, the type of learning being tested, proneness to coaching and cheating, and the degree to which the tests measure "aptitude" or "achievement."[22] In my experience, admissions tests in many developing countries do not provide incentives that are as beneficial as they might. They stress memorization instead of reasoning; they are too easily "mugged," in the sense that cramming rather than learning may be the best form of preparation; they do not cover the full range of subjects studied in high school; and they do not include a large enough component of "aptitude," thereby inhibiting local variations in curricula.

High-School Grades

Grades are good in the sense that they create incentives for students to study what high-school teachers want them to study. On the other hand, high schools in most countries differ greatly in their grading standards, making comparisons across schools and students difficult. It is interesting to note that in many countries the schools attended by groups that are underrepresented in the university—the poor, the rural, and so forth—tend to give higher grades. If so, using grades in selection has a redistributive effect.

Recommendations

With appropriate safeguards, recommendations may enable a selection system to take into account such "soft" but important variables as character, motivation, and personality. Unfortunately, such safeguards often do not exist, and recommendations tend to be inflated (everyone is "excellent") and are prone to influence. I once asked a provincial Minister of Education and Planning in Pakistan why he signed so many recommendations; he would sign hundreds a day, in audiences and visits, for people he presumably did not know well. "The people feel cared for when I do so. And," he added, "I have instructed all educational institutions and government offices to ignore my signature on any such recommendations."

Interviews

Evidence in the United States indicates that, perhaps surprisingly, interviews are poor predictors of any sort of later performance.[23] But interviews do create incentives. For example, they let the interviewer establish a power relationship over the person being interviewed. Like recommendations, they may create incentives for influence-peddling and other abuses.

Work Samples

A few countries require students to work for a period of time before applying to the university. Their record in such work is factored into the selection process. Apart from whatever predictive validity such policies have, they obviously also create incentives—both good and bad. A problem with lengthy work samples is their opportunity costs. During the Cultural Revolution, the Chinese sent aspiring students and also faculty members into the rural areas. Deng Xiaoping commented on the costs of doing so:

> When Deng visited the United States in early 1979, a dinner was given for him in Washington before he went out West, where he received a cowboy hat and a personal view of the bouncing rumps of Texas cheerleaders.
>   With exquisite diplomatic callousness, one of those invited to the dinner in honor of Deng, who himself had been one of Mao's victims, was an American who had written glowingly of Maoism. This guest happily told Deng that she had heard a Chinese physicist say that he had been sent to the farms, but that working with his hands there was as worthwhile and educational as anything he had ever done.
>   "He lied," Deng said.[24]

Quotas for Groups

Quotas may create positive and negative incentives. On the positive side, a quota *may* give members of lower-scoring groups a greater incentive to study hard, and in some theoretical models a quota may also induce greater effort within the higher-scoring group. But most people who comment on quotas point to unfavorable "incentives." People may be reinforced in thinking of society as composed of groups instead of individuals, thereby fostering divisiveness. Little hard evidence exists on these matters. In Malaysia it appears that remarkably pervasive quotas in favor of ethnic Malays did not lead to ethnic divisiveness; the quotas may even have calmed an explosive political and ethnic crisis.[25] On the other hand, some commentators attribute growing caste tension in India and ethnic violence in Sri Lanka to measures taken in the 1970s to provide group quotas for jobs and university admissions.[26] These are topics on which much more research is needed, and in any policy decision about quotas, the wisdom of local observers should be carefully tapped in an effort to estimate the possible incentive effects.

The theme that runs through our analysis of incentives is that they are important but difficult to specify empirically. Research will be helpful, and theoretical models such as those provided by economists contribute qualitative insights. But policy-makers will have to rely on the subjective judgments of educators, politicians, and ordinary citizens on these matters. At this point, perhaps all a policy analyst can do is make sure these dimensions are not overlooked. As the U.S., Chinese, and Philippine examples indicate, incentives can be an absolutely critical dimension in the choice of selection policies.

6

INTEGRATING THE ANALYSIS
The Case of Indonesia

In chapters 3, 4, and 5 we considered the three dimensions of policies for selecting elites: static efficiency, representation, and incentive effects. For each dimension, we saw how analytical techniques coupled with appropriate data may be used to improve policy-making. Now it is time to combine these dimensions. The medium for doing so is an analysis of admissions policies for higher education in Indonesia.

THE PROBLEM

Over the next decade, the government of Indonesia plans a rapid expansion of higher education. The wave of students that entered primary schools in the big expansion some years back will reach college age in the late 1980s, generating unprecedented demand for college entrance. And the nation needs more highly trained people. According to the World Bank:

> Given that skilled manpower has emerged as the primary constraint to the use of additional resources, expanded expenditures on education and training should have a high priority. Large, and in some areas growing gaps between supply and demand for technical and professional manpower justify substantial investments in education beyond the secondary level. . . . The success of development programs in the 1980's will depend heavily on progress made in alleviating the skilled manpower constraint.[1]

The Agency for International Development concurred:

> There is a dearth of professional and technical and, particularly, of administrative and managerial skills manpower in Indonesia. Of over 50,000 people in the Indonesian labor force, only 1.9% are classified as Administrative/Managerial. The limited number of trained manpower at all levels is generally recognized within the Government of Indonesia and among the donor community as the single most limiting factor on Indonesia's development.[2]

These shortages of highly trained personnel stem from low enrollment and low graduation rates. Although enrollments have increased more than twentyfold since 1950, only about 2 percent of the nineteen to twenty-five age-group were enrolled in institutions of higher education in the early 1980s. The Indonesian government hopes to raise this figure to 5 percent by the year 2000, which implies an annual growth rate of 5 to 6 percent.

As for low graduation rates, students who graduate take an average of eight years to complete a five-year degree program, and few actually graduate. Studies at the University of Andalas and Gadjah Madah University showed that, ten years after entering, only about one-fifth of the students had received degrees. Only 4.8 percent of those enrolled in 1978 at public institutions of higher education graduated that year. (If enrollments were stable, this figure would be 20 percent if every student enrolled graduated in five years.)

Is it a bad thing that graduation rates are low? To answer this question precisely, one would want to know the social value-added of a university degree for different kinds of students, compared with some university work and no university work. Such studies have not been carried out in Indonesia. It is presumed there that the actual social benefits of qualified graduates are considerable, but this question deserves additional study.

Why are graduation rates so low? For one thing, many admitted students are unable to pass their courses. Up to 50 percent fail their final examinations. Despite an extremely selective admissions system, which is described below, not all students selected are qualified.

Other factors are also important in explaining low graduation rates. The quality of instruction in universities is often poor. Teachers have too little time to spend on teaching, and fewer than 3 percent of the staffs of public universities have Ph.D. degrees. Books, especially in Bahasa Indonesia, the national language, are often scarce, and laboratories are frequently overcrowded or even unavailable. Indonesia's cumbersome *doctorandus* degree, with its thesis requirement and the need to pass all courses in a year to be promoted to the next, leads to delays; fortunately, reforms that will in time lead to a more flexible degree are under way. Students sometimes drop out for financial reasons. In 1982, student fees averaged about Rp. 85,000 a year, over one-third of the per capita income.[3] Some students drop out because they can get good jobs without a degree; this is apparently a frequent phenomenon for students of accounting. Finally, graduation rates depend on the quality of the secondary and primary school systems and on the academic ability and motivation of its young people.

Better admissions policies might help raise graduation rates. As one dean told me in an interview, "We need to expand our enrollments. However, we need to make sure we have students who can succeed. The education is heavily subsidized by the state, so failures are socially costly, especially for a poor country." Admissions policies are only part of the solution, and their effects will clearly depend on what is being taught, how well, and toward what purpose, as well as on the quality of the applicant pool. As the system of higher education expands, however, the importance of efficient selection procedures cannot be overlooked.[4]

Admissions policies entail costs, and this is an important part of the efficiency dimension in Indonesia. For example, Indonesia now has several examination systems. Twelfth-graders take one set of examinations to qualify for secondary school diplomas, but these exams are not part of the college admissions process. Instead, three other examinations are used in admissions:

- The two-day PP1 exam, in separate versions for science and nonscience students, which is used to select about 16,000 entrants to ten *major* universities, from about 200,000 test-takers. Examinees are allowed to rank three choices (by faculty and by university), and except for a bit of discretion at the margin, they are assigned to their choices depending on their test scores.

- The PP3 exam, used for entrance to *regional* universities and containing considerable material designed by each local university.

- The PP4 exam, used for entrance to *teacher-training* schools (IKIPs), administered nationally.

Students bear the direct costs of the examination system through a fee paid to take the exam, but there are other costs too. Many students take multiple examinations, entailing anxiety, travel, opportunity costs, and so forth. Would it be possible to reduce costs by combining examinations? One official asked: "Actually, we are at a crossroads. Can we somehow integrate the national final examination for secondary schools with the entrance examination?"

Beyond the efficiency of admissions policies, Indonesian officials are also worried about the representation of the poor and the rural. One top government policy-maker told me: "The first issue, nationally and politically, is how we can use intake policies to achieve a more representative student body. But this is now difficult to achieve, because of the heterogeneous population and the poor quality of schools on the outer islands." Several kinds of "representativeness" can be distinguished: by geographical region, ethnic origin, sex, socioeconomic class, rural or urban, and perhaps others.[5]

As we have seen elsewhere, a third dimension of admissions policy concerns the incentives created by selection criteria. The Indonesian college entrance examinations are designed with high-school curricula in mind, but unlike the certifying exams, they do not strictly test what students have learned in their particular courses. This may be a strength as well as a weakness. By trying to measure preparedness for college study, the entrance exams may enable better predictions of college success, increasing educational efficiency, but they may also reduce the incentives for students to master their high-school material. At least, so some critics complain. Said an official of the Directorate General of Higher Education, "There is always the question that the entrance examinations don't fit the SMA [secondary school] curriculum." For example, the IPS examination (the nonscience exam in PP1) tests only four of the seventeen subjects covered in the SMA curriculum.

Other incentive questions arise. Will multiple-choice examinations like the PP1, PP3, and PP4 properly encourage students to write better prose or master their laboratory exercises? Only examinations are used, not high-school grades.

Does this optimally motivate students to study hard in high school? Do alternative policies create incentives for abuse or corruption?

What were some of the policy alternatives? My discussions with Indonesian officials and academicians in 1982 suggested that several questions were under active consideration or debate and would benefit from policy research.

- *Combine the admissions tests.*   Might it make sense to combine the PP1 and PP4 examinations? What about the PP3 exam?

- *Add an aptitude test.*   In any of the entrance examinations, or in a combined test, would it be useful to have one portion try to measure "aptitudes," as distinct from "achievements"?

- *Give weight to the certification examination or to high-school grades.* One proposal was to allow only some high-school graduates to take the PP1 test, perhaps those scoring in the top one-third on their high-school certification examinations. A somewhat different idea would be to give the scores on the certification examination some weight in the admissions process. A still different proposal might be to use a measure of high-school rank in class, or high-school grade average, as part of the admissions process.

- *Give weight or use quotas to achieve a more representative student body.*   For example, would a quota for students from outside the main island, Java, make sense? Are the tests predictively biased against members of certain groups? Could this bias be corrected by adjusting the scores?

- *If the entrance examinations could be made more predictively accurate for a certain cost, would this be worthwhile?*

These alternatives are not mutually exclusive. As phrased, they are general. These alternatives should be compared across several dimensions. Ideally, we would have a matrix, with the dimensions of admissions policies on one axis and the various policy alternatives on the other. Then, the pros and cons—and the uncertainties—of each alternative could be compared.

STUDIES OF ACADEMIC PREDICTION

As discussed in chapter 3, the assessment of the efficiency of selection involves a number of steps. The first is to obtain appropriate measures of later performance. Even in the most developed countries, controversy is widespread over the appropriateness of criteria of performance such as academic achievement, earnings in later life, later socioeconomic status, and so forth. In Indonesia, as in many other developing countries, few relevant studies exist. Basic information about the later job prospects of young people with various degrees of academic accomplishment is unavailable. Many measures of successful academic performance, such as whether a student has graduated or not, have not been systematically related to various predictors. Some of the instruments used in Western countries, such as intelligence tests, personality profiles, letters of recommendation, and interviews, have not been validated for many developing countries. Indeed, in Indonesia information on the reliability and validity of college entrance examinations and high-school grades—to name only two of the predictors of interest—has never been compiled. Little is known about the efficiency of alternative selection systems in Indonesia.

As a consequence, the analyses presented here will inevitably be criticized, and correctly, as incomplete and inconclusive, and calls for more research are always to be expected. (By the way, such calls do not decrease as the volume of research increases.) The analyst must adopt a humble and tentative, but useful, stance.

In this spirit, I performed several new analyses of academic prediction in Indonesia, and I pulled together studies done elsewhere in that country. In particular, I analyzed data on a recent entering class of students in the Science Faculty of the prestigious University of Indonesia (U.I.). I also reanalyzed data that Muchkiar compiled from several universities for his doctoral dissertation at the Teacher Training Institute at Bandung. I studied a recent class from the Teacher Training Institute in Jakarta, and I reanalyzed data compiled at U.I.'s Department of Psychology.

Table 14 presents a rough summary of the results. More details are found in the appendix to this chapter.

TABLE 14. Results of Studies of Academic Prediction at Indonesian Universities

University and Faculty	N	Predictors	R
U.I. Faculty of Science, early 1980s	182	PP1 exam	0.41
U.I. Faculty of Psychology, 1975	58	PP1	0.49
U.I. Faculty of Psychology, 1979	78	PP1	0.17[a]
Institute of Technology, Bandung, 1977	33	PP1	0.83
Institute of Technology, Bandung, 1977	33	PP1 + HSGPA + RM	0.85
Institute of Technology, Bandung, 1978	32	PP1	0.85
Institute of Technology, Bandung, 1978	32	PP1 + HSGPA + RM	0.87
U. Gadjah Madah, U.I., and U. Airlangga, 1977	241	PP1	0.59
U. Gadjah Madah, U.I., and U. Airlangga, 1977	241	PP1 + HSGPA + RM	0.70
Teacher Tng. Institute, Jakarta, 1982	242	PP4	0.53

Note: The correlations are not corrected for criterion unreliability or restriction of range. RM = Raven's Matrices, an aptitude test. Author's calculations.

[a]Student disturbances in this year were said to be responsible for this low correlation.

THE EFFICIENCY OF ALTERNATIVE SELECTION POLICIES

What do results like these mean in practical terms? How can we translate what we have learned about prediction into how *useful* better prediction would be? Let me provide several illustrations based on the results from the U.I. Faculty of Science.

1. In my U.I. study, the correlation was 0.18 between the score on the science portion (IPA) of the PP1 examination and the binary variable "*GPA* ≥ 2.0." For illustrative purposes, suppose we found the same predictive relationship between the IPA score and the binary variable "graduates from U.I." How much better do we do by choosing students using the IPA, compared with a random selection from all IPA test-takers? How much better would we do if the correlation were even higher?

The first step is to *correct the observed correlation* for restriction of range.[6] Using the techniques of chapter 3, this correction raises the correlation to 0.32.

The next step is to consider our *selection ratio*. For PP1, it is about 0.08.

Third, we need an estimate about the *likely performance of the applicant pool if admitted*. Imagine we had a randomly selected individual from the PP1 applicant pool. What would be that individual's chance of graduating? It is difficult to say. A plausible guess might be 20 percent.[7] How much better do we do if instead we use the PP1 test to select, with a selection ratio of 0.08 and an adjusted correlation of 0.32 between the test and graduating? From the so-called Taylor-Russell tables,[8] we obtain the answer: the *graduation rate would double*, from 20 percent in the case of random selection to 40 percent with the PP1.

Suppose now that we could raise that adjusted correlation from 0.32 to 0.50. We might obtain this increase by improving the PP1 test or by adding a predictor such as high-school grades or an aptitude test or both. What would happen to our graduation rate? From the Taylor-Russell tables, we learn that the graduation rate would increase from 40 percent to 54 percent, a gain of (54 − 40)/40 = 35 percent.

2. To decide exactly how much we would be willing to pay to obtain that 35 percent increase, we would need a utility measure of "graduate" versus "drop-out/nongraduate." But we can also ask a less difficult question: How much money would the government save in educational costs per successful graduate? This will provide the auspices for my second illustration of utility analysis.

How much does it cost the government to produce a college graduate? To illustrate, let us suppose realistically that the cost to the Indonesian government of educating a university student is U.S.$250 per year, and let us suppose that the average nongraduate stays three years and therefore costs $750. Let us assume that the average graduate takes eight years to obtain a degree, costing therefore $2,000. (Opportunity costs in terms of forgone earnings are omitted from these calculations.)

TABLE 15. Cost Savings from Better Prediction

	% Who Will Graduate	Average Cost per Graduate (Rp. million)
Random selection	20	3.30
Test with $r = 0.32$	40	2.10
Test(s) with $r = 0.50$	54	1.75
Perfect selection	100	1.32

Note: The calculations assume that under random selection 20 percent of those admitted would graduate and that the selection ratio is 0.08.

Under these assumptions, the average costs per graduate, for different percentages of an entering class who graduate, are given in table 15. Moving from a test with an 0.32 correlation to the better test with a correlation of 0.5 leads to *a cost saving of about 20 percent per graduate,* and as noted above, we get about 35 percent *more graduates* per year.[9]

3. A third way to assess the utility of better admissions policies is based on another technique used in chapter 3. About 16,000 university students are being chosen. The selection ratio is 0.08. The correlation between the IPA score and GPA is 0.41; after corrections for restriction of range and unreliability in the GPA measure, the correlation is 0.70.

We also need a measure of the utility of a one standard deviation difference in college grade point average. How might we obtain such an estimate? Following chapter 3, we might ask policy-makers to give a utility value to the difference in performance between a student at the 50th percentile of GPA with the student at the 85th percentile. Let's suppose the answer is $1,000 (the reader may substitute other illustrative values).

How much better do we do by using the IPA to select students than if we selected randomly from the applicant pool? Applying the formula from the appendix to chapter 3, we obtain:

Total utility = 16,000 × 0.7 × $1,000 × 0.1476/0.08 = $20,664,000

That's more than $20 million per year. (If the policy-makers think that the utility of a student achieving one standard deviation higher in GPA is worth more (or less) than $1,000, other numbers could be inserted into this equation.)

Now suppose we could raise that adjusted correlation from 0.70 to 0.80. (Remember that, before statistical corrections, the correlation was 0.41; the corrections raised it to 0.70; so we may think of raising the uncorrected correlation to about 0.50.) With this better predictor, how much "utility" would we gain, compared with random selection? Applying the formula, we obtain $23,616,000. The difference is therefore $23,616,000 minus $20,664,000, or about $3 million per selected class per year. We would compare this with the cost of obtaining and using the better predictor.

This same framework is a way to begin assessing the usefulness of adding other predictors to the PP1 (or PP3 or PP4), for example, an aptitude test, high-school grades, or the high-school certification examination.

Adding an Aptitude Test

As far as adding an aptitude test is concerned, I draw first on data on the 1979 entering class at U.I.'s Faculty of Psychology.[10] The appendix to this chapter gives the results of several regressions. They indicate that it would be quite useful to add the Differential Aptitude Test (DAT) score to the PP1. The multiple correlation R might increase by 0.2. The benefits of this increase can easily be calculated using the formulas we just reviewed. Neither form of another aptitude test, the TIKI, added much to the PP1 and the DAT as a predictor.

Muchkiar's data—with a different aptitude test and a higher base correlation between the PP1 and college grades—led to a weaker result. Adding Raven's Progressive Matrices as a predictor would increase the multiple R by less than 0.1 at three of the universities and by virtually nothing at the Institute of Technology at Bandung.

Adding High-School Grades

In Indonesia, little is known about the predictive power of the HSGPA. Studies at the Agricultural Institute at Bogor (IPB) have correlated grades in each high school course with first-year grades at IPB but have apparently not looked at the *average* high-school grade and its predictive power.[11] Based on IPB data, I suspect that high-school grade point average over all these courses (HSGPA) would have a larger correlation than for any of the individual courses: say $r = 0.35$.

The correlation of high-school grades and PP1 scores is not known, to the best of my knowledge. An as-yet-unpublished evaluation of the twelfth-grade achievement test scores found a correlation of only about 0.2 to 0.3 with teachers' assessments of students in individual courses. If we averaged these assessments, the correlation might be 0.35. We might guess that this was about the correlation between PP1 (another achievement test) and HSGPA (another measure of teachers' assessments). Based on these numbers, the multiple R can be calculated. The answer: with both PP1 and HSGPA as predictors, the multiple R might rise from 0.45 to about 0.50. This is slightly higher than the result obtained through the analysis of Muchkiar's data in the appendix to this chapter, where the multiple R is increased by about 0.02 by adding HSGPA to the regression equation. We now know how to evaluate the gains this increase would entail in terms of graduation rates, cost per successful graduate, and "utility."

Muchkiar's data show correlations of 0.5 to 0.6 between HSGPA and grades at the university, which are lower than the 0.6 to 0.8 correlations for PP1 scores in his sample. This result gives an idea of what would happen if *only* HSGPA were used in admissions instead of *only* PP1 scores: the loss in efficiency can be calculated directly using the techniques above.

Adding the High-School Certification Examination

There is also little evidence on the predictive power of the high-school certification examination (EBTA). The results in the appendix at the end of this chapter and other analyses based on Muchkiar's data seem to indicate that adding the EBTA to the PP1 exam would not significantly enhance the prediction of later grades. Analyses not reported here show that EBTA scores are highly correlated with HSGPA; the correlation of EBTA alone with college grades would be 0.3 to 0.4. Again, our techniques would enable us to calculate the efficiency losses of using EBTA in university selection instead of PP1.[12]

This discussion of the efficiency of selection has been illustrative, not final. Additional research about the connection of test scores, grades, and the rest with performance after school is badly needed. We have had to focus on measures of performance within the university: graduation rates, cost per graduate, and shifts in grades attained (by current standards) among those selected. (In a footnote I address the question "Are the results you have found likely to hold for a broader range of Indonesian universities?")[13] At the end of the chapter, I will summarize the findings, but now let us turn to the second dimension of selection policies: representation. We will look at two examples: students from islands other than Java, and Indonesians of Chinese descent.

THE CASE OF THE OUTER-ISLANDERS

Many Indonesian policy-makers told me that representation was the most important issue in admissions. The current process leads to underrepresentation of the poor and those from outside Java, to name only two groups of interest.

Consider the regional representation. We shall focus on Java and the rest of Indonesia. About 64 percent of Indonesia's population lives in Java, but 80 percent of those taking the IPA track of the PP1 test are from Java. Not only are students from Java overrepresented among test-takers, they also score higher on the IPA than do students from the outer islands (see figure 5). If the highest-scoring 8 percent of those taking the test were admitted, 90 percent of them would be from Java.[14]

Is a cause of these differences predictive bias in the test itself? The data from U.I.'s Faculty of Science were examined in an effort to find out. The PP1 data includes a wealth of information provided by students when they take the test, such as place of birth, location of high school, age, sex, father's level of education, mother's level of education, father's occupation, ethnic group, and type of high school. I added these variables to the equation predicting the first-year GPA.

FIGURE 5. Distributions of Scores on Science Battery of Test-takers from Java and the Outer Islands (Early 1980s)

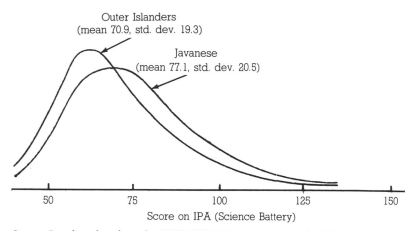

Outer Islanders
(mean 70.9, std. dev. 19.3)

Javanese
(mean 77.1, std. dev. 20.5)

50   75   100   125   150

Score on IPA (Science Battery)

Source: Based on data from the PUSILKOM, Directorate General of Higher Education.

"Location of high-school" was used to create several dummy variables: Java or not, big city or not, Jakarta or not. After controlling for test score, sex, and department, *none of these variables significantly affected GPA.*

For example, see equation (3) in table 21 in the appendix to this chapter. It shows that, on average, students from the outer islands had GPAs 0.10 lower than students from Java, other variables held constant. They were slightly *over-predicted*. But this difference was not statistically significant. Further studies are needed. Based on this small investigation, however, there did not appear to be predictive bias against outer-islanders. If confirmed, the finding of differential performance across regions *and* no regional bias in the predictive sense would modify an assertion by Douglas L. Paauw: "Scrupulous adherence to uniform standards for faculty and student selection from all areas of Indonesia on the sole criterion of scholarly achievement would insure the national character of these university centers."[15]

For a variety of reasons, Indonesian policy-makers would prefer their universities to have a greater representation of outer islanders. Using the techniques of chapter 4, how much would it cost in academic terms to do this? In particular, how much would it cost to increase the proportion of outer-islanders from 10 percent to 20 percent, their proportion in the applicant pool?

Given the distribution of IPA scores for the two groups and a selection ratio of 8 percent, a 20 percent quota for outer-islanders would lead to a cut score of about 98 for non-Java students and a cut score of about 106 for students from Java. Let us suppose that the equation relating GPA to IPA scores is the one we found for U.I.'s Faculty of Science:

$$GPA = 0.38 + 0.018\ IPA$$

FIGURE 6. Marginal Costs of Preferential Treatment for Students from Indonesia's Outer Islands (Excluding Java)

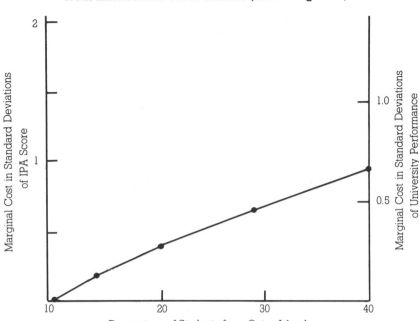

Note: Based on normal approximations assuming that 20 percent of all applicants are from the outer islands, 8 percent of all applicants are accepted, and the equation predicting university performance is that found at the University of Indonesia in 1982. Author's calculations.

Then a 98 corresponds to an expected GPA of 2.15 and a 106 corresponds to an expected GPA of 2.28. The difference of 0.13 GPA points is a measure of the *marginal* cost of a 20 percent quota. If a standard deviation of academic performance equals 0.47 and our utility function for GPA gives a value of Rp. 100,000 to a standard deviation of such performance, then the marginal cost per student for one year is

$$(0.13/0.47) \times \$1,000 = \$277$$

One might also look at the probability of passing as the outcome measure of interest. Figure 6 shows the marginal cost, in terms of the probability of passing, of increasing the proportion of outer-islanders.[16] For a 20 percent non-Java quota, the marginal cost is about a 6 percent difference in the probability of passing.

Policy-makers may prefer to think in terms of total costs. For example, the average IPA score of those admitted is 114.1 without a quota and would be 111.4 with a 20 percent non-Java quota. The expected GPAs corresponding to these scores are 2.434 and 2.385, a difference of about 0.05 of a GPA point. This is $0.05/0.47 = 0.11$ of a standard deviation in GPA. If a one standard deviation were worth $1,000 and there were 16,000 selected students, the total cost of a 20 percent quota would be $1,760,000 per year. Using different assumptions, one may calculate the costs per successful graduate.[17]

Would it be worth these costs to raise the proportion of students from outside Java from about 10 percent to 20 percent? The answer depends on judgments that transcend more statistics. But I hope these numbers would be useful in making the necessary value judgments.

THE CASE OF THE CHINESE QUOTA

In 1982 the Indonesian government had a quota limiting the percentage of Chinese-Indonesians at the major public universities. When students signed up for the PP1 exam, they were asked to indicate their ethnic group. Monitors also examined students' physical features to confirm their self-identification. Chinese test-takers had a red mark put beside their names; this became an asterisk when the IPA scores were computerized.

Much can be said about the desirability, morality, and legality of ethnic quotas in Indonesia and elsewhere, but for our purposes here I wish to focus on a smaller question: What are the academic costs of a quota on Indonesian students of Chinese descent?

Ethnic Chinese make up an estimated 3 percent of Indonesia's population. About 9 percent of IPA test-takers in a recent year were "Chinese"; about 91 percent were "Indonesians." Chinese are not only overrepresented in the applicant pool, they also score much higher on the IPA exam. Figure 7 shows the distributions of scores. The "true" difference in the two cohorts (including non-test-takers) is probably larger still.[18]

In one recent year, the quota on Chinese accepted in PP1 universities was 6 percent, although the quota varied across universities and even across faculties within the same university. For simplicity's sake, I will analyze the selection process as if only one quota were operative. I also assume that the scores for each ethnic group is normally distributed: for the Chinese the mean is 90.7 and the standard deviation is 24.4; for Indonesians the mean is 74.3 and the standard deviation is 19.3. This is a fair assumption when we are working in the area of the distributions near the cutoff for admissions.

Let us assume that IPA scores are related to GPA in the way described above for the Science Faculty of the University of Indonesia:

(1) $GPA = 0.38 + 0.018\ IPA$

(2) $p(GPA \geq 2.0) = -0.095 + 0.0077\ IPA$

Let us also assume, as before, that the average governmental cost per student per year is $250, that a graduate on average takes eight years to graduate, that a nongraduate stays three years in the university on average, that the standard

FIGURE 7. **Distributions of Scores of Indonesian and Chinese Test-takers on Science Battery (Early 1980s)**

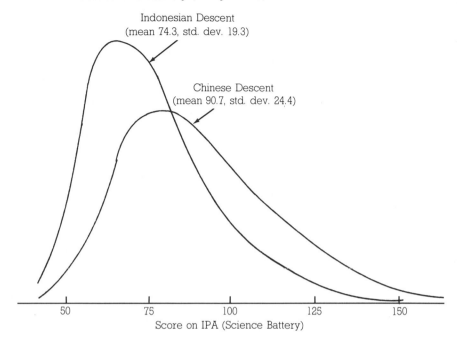

Indonesian Descent
(mean 74.3, std. dev. 19.3)

Chinese Descent
(mean 90.7, std. dev. 24.4)

Score on IPA (Science Battery)

Source: Based on data from the PUSILKOM, Directorate General of Higher Education.

deviation of first-year GPA is 0.47, and that the "utility" for this standard deviation is $1,000.

Table 16 shows the differences in IPA cut scores for Indonesian and Chinese students, under various quotas for Indonesians. Corresponding to these cut scores are expected first-year GPAs and expected probabilities of $GPA \geq 2.0$. These correspond to the *marginal* academic costs of the quota, compared with no quota. Figure 8 shows the marginal cost in IPA scores of various quotas on Chinese students.

Let us examine the marginal costs of a 6 percent Chinese quota or a 94 percent Indonesian quota. Table 16 tells us that the difference in expected GPA at the margin is −0.50, which is 1.064 standard deviations, which is worth $1,064 per student. The difference in p ($GPA \geq 2.0$) is −0.21 (or 0.89 − 0.68). If this same difference held for probability of graduating, then the difference in expected cost per successful graduate at this margin would be $258, or 12.3 percent, and a loss of 0.21/0.89 = 24% in the probability of graduating.

The *total* costs of a 6 percent Chinese quota can be compared with the no quota situation—where approximately 30 percent of those admitted would be Chinese.

**TABLE 16. Differences between Marginal Admissions
(Indonesian minus Chinese) for Various Quotas
of Indonesians Admitted**

Indonesian Quota (%)	Difference in IPA Cut Scores	Difference in Expected GPA	Difference in Expected P (GPA $\geq$ 2.0)
70	0.1	0	0
80	−8.8	−0.16	−0.07
90	−20.7	−0.37	−0.16
94	−27.8	−0.50	−0.21
96	−32.7	−0.59	−0.25

Note: Based on an overall selection ratio of 0.08 and the regression results of the U.I. Faculty of Science. For convenience, normality of each group's distribution of IPA scores is also assumed.

**FIGURE 8. Marginal Costs of Preferential Treatment for Students
of Indonesian Descent**

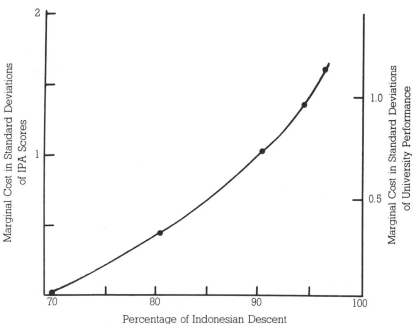

Note: Based on normal approximations assuming 91 percent of applicants are Indonesian, 8 percent of all applicants are accepted, and the equation predicting university performance is that found at the University of Indonesia in 1982. Author's calculations.

With 6 percent Chinese, the expected average GPA of all those admitted would be 2.39. With 30 percent Chinese, it would be 2.44.[19] The difference is 0.05, or 0.11 of a standard deviation. If the utility for one standard deviation per student per year were Rp. 100,000, this difference would be worth $110 per student. Multiply this by 16,000, and the total cost of a 6 percent quota versus a 30 percent nonquota would be *$1,760,000.*

Let us suppose, as we have before, that the findings for p $(GPA \geq 2.0)$ would hold for p (graduates). With 6 percent Chinese, their average IPA score would be 139.6, so their average probability of graduating would be 0.98. For Indonesians, the corresponding figures would be 110.0 and 0.75. Consequently, the weighted average probability of graduating for all admitted with a 6 percent Chinese quota would be 0.766. The average cost per successful graduate would be $2,227.

The same calculation for 30 percent Chinese yields an average cost per successful graduate of $2,197, or about 1.4 percent lower. The percent who graduate would be 0.786, or 2 percentage points higher, a 2.5 percent increase in the graduate rate.

BIAS AGAINST WOMEN

The data set from the University of Indonesia study revealed an extraordinary result: the women outperformed the men. Even after controlling for test scores and the department in which the student was enrolled, the estimated difference between women's and men's GPAs was about 0.35. In predictive terms, this is equivalent to $0.35/0.018 = 19.4$ points on the IPA. A typical woman in the U.I. Science Faculty did about as well as a man with an IPA score 19 points higher! The IPA score seems to be predictively biased against women.

Further analysis of these data confirmed this finding.[20] Of course, additional studies are needed, based on other universities and bigger samples, before this result can be confirmed. *If* further research showed an intercept bias of about 0.35 units of GPA, or the equivalent of 19 points on the IPA exam, drastic steps would need to be taken. The IPA test questions should be investigated for item bias. Alternatively—and surely controversially—one might simply add 19 points to the IPA scores of all women, to compensate for the predictive bias against them of selecting students with the IPA exam.

Several Indonesian policy-makers told me they were not surprised by this finding. "Girls study harder than the boys, who are distracted by all manner of nonacademic diversions," one said. Another said that even if women were underpredicted academically, they should not be admitted in greater numbers, because in Indonesian society female graduates would make a less notable contribution. He was saying, in effect, that academic performance *overpredicts* the later-life contributions of women. Whether this is so in sexist Indonesia, should be so, or should make a difference to admissions policies—these vital questions obviously deserve a much longer discussion. Studies of bias may at least be a way to get such discussions going.

INCENTIVE EFFECTS

Indonesian policy-makers worried particularly about two sorts of incentive effects. First, by ignoring high-school grades, did the current system fail to induce high-school students to work hard in all their courses? Second, would alternative admissions policies be prone to corruption and abuse?

High-school performance was used in admissions by only four universities in Indonesia, and then only at the Faculties of Science. This method of admitting students is called the PP2, and it works as follows. High-school principals are asked to recommend outstanding students and give ratings for academic record, expectation that the student will pass at the university, leadership, getting along with others, and "politeness." Students who are nominated are asked their preferences about areas of study and universities. Then faculties are sent lists of recommended students who want to study with them. Depending on the particular science faculty at these four universities, from one-quarter to over half the entering class is admitted by means of PP2, the rest by the PP1 examination. The Agricultural University of Bogor is said to admit 90 percent in certain faculties by the PP2. Those admitted through the PP2 find out soon enough so that they do not need to go through the PP1 examination. A dean explained:

> A faculty committee evaluates the PP2 applications. We look to see if the grades are above 7 in all subjects and at the class rank. If we do not know about the quality of the high school, we take only the top one to three students. We have two or three meetings. For the biology department, a biology professor decides; for physics, a physics professor; and so forth. As a committee we look at the rest to make sure no one with a high standard has been overlooked.
>
> Frankly, we don't look at leadership or politeness, unless the latter is very low; we only look at academics. No extra weight is given to women. We sometimes in very exceptional cases give weight to father's occupation and try to help those from remote areas. But you can't take the tenth student from the top at a good high school and not the seventh from the top. We have to be open to all. If I do that, I am false, and the principals do not trust me.

The PP2 apparently was begun by the Agricultural University of Bogor, which believed it could recruit able students and lure them away from the University of Indonesia, Gadjah Madah University, and others by offering them admission without the duress of examinations. According to one professor, the university at Bogor believes that "PP2 students do as well as PP1 students in their university marks, and secondly, you may get a more representative student body." Studies on the first point are rare and of dubious quality.[21] On the second point, no comparisons exist.

The four universities using the PP2, which happen to be four of the best academically, invite about 600 high schools from around Indonesia to nominate students (about four-fifths public high schools and one-fifth private schools, most from Java—certainly not all the high schools in the country but the "best" ones). In 1981, some 6,193 candidates were nominated, of whom 1,731 were accepted by the various science faculties at the four universities.

Why don't other faculties use the PP2 system? It is still relatively new. "The Faculty of Arts is now thinking about it," said the dean. "Medicine doesn't need it, because their scores are so high. Before we had to go down to a score of 80 on the PP1 examination in our entering class, but now our threshold is above 100. We want to study how well the PP2 does." The dean also noted a problem with the PP2:

> I am worried about influence. It's the easiest way to get into the university, you see. Only 10 percent or so get in. But here a principal can get someone in. So, if I get bad people from a certain high school, we blackball them. They have to be honest. Till now the PP2 is an honest system, carefully controlled by Bogor [which centrally administers the PP2 process]. But I am worried about the potential for influence.

So far, the PP2 has apparently done a good job avoiding inflated recommendations and corruption.

What about the incentive effects of the PP2 on high-school students? Interviews with officials at Bogor revealed that no studies of this issue had been done. We can speculate that the effects would be small. After all, only a few students each year would be admitted via PP2, and it is unlikely that high-school students in earlier years would change their study habits markedly in hopes of being one of those few.

More central for policy purposes is another incentive question. Suppose PP1 scores were supplemented with high-school grade point averages, or with the results of the high-school certification exam, or both. Would students be motivated to study more of their subjects in high school? (Recall that the PP1 exam called IPS—the nonscience battery—includes only four of the seventeen subjects in the secondary school curriculum.) Would they study in a different way, for example, work harder in laboratory subjects and in writing, neither of which is measured by the PP1 exam?

In the absence of an experiment, it is difficult to know. Here is an area where international comparisons could be helpful. Could Indonesia learn from other countries where both high-school performance and the results of an entrance exam were used in selection? One could also imagine surveys and other studies that could be carried out in Indonesia to shed light on the matter.[22]

As mentioned in chapter 5, the consideration of incentive effects is much more qualitative than the calculations that can be carried out regarding the other two dimensions of selection policies—efficiency and representation. This does not mean that incentive effects should be given less emphasis. These inherently difficult-to-gauge effects should be widely discussed in advance and carefully monitored after new policies are implemented.

TABLE 17. A Schematic Representation of the Possible Costs and Benefits
of Alternative Admissions Policies in Indonesia

Policy	Efficiency	Equity	Costs	Incentives
Current system	0	0	0	0
Combine PP1, 3, 4	0	0	+[a]	0
Add aptitude test	+	0	+	−, 0
Add high-school grades, EBTA	+	+	+ +	+
Representational quotas for:				
Outer-Islanders	−	+ +	0	+
Women	+	+	0	+
Chinese[b]	+ +	− −	0	−?

Note: As the baseline for comparison, the current system is arbitrarily given values of zero
for all variables, + + means great increase, + means increase, 0 means unchanged, − means
decrease and − − means great decrease. "Efficiency" refers to the average academic quality of
those selected. "Equity" refers to the increased enrollment of underrepresented or disadvantaged groups. "Costs" refers to the direct and indirect cost of administering the selection
policy. "Incentives" refers to the effects on students and teachers at previous levels of the
educational system.

[a]Would rise in the short run, but might well decline in the longer term.

[b]The current system has a 6 percent maximum quota on students of Chinese descent. The
policy considered here is removal of that quota.

A SUMMARY OF THE POLICY ANALYSIS

We can now pull together some rough estimates of the benefits and costs of the
main policy alternatives for university selection in Indonesia. Table 17 provides a
summary. Some of the entries are guesses, badly needing further study, but they
are a start.

We have learned how well the PP1 and PP4 examinations predict later
academic performance at the university. The correlations between scores on
these tests and first-year grades are as high or higher than similar correlations in
the United States. They compare favorably with the correlations discovered in
Pakistan and Philippines in previous chapters.

We have also seen that adding an aptitude test—a straightforward IQ test or
Raven's Matrices—to the PP1 would slightly improve the prediction of later
academic performance. The improvement would probably be worth the costs,
although there might be problems with redesigning the exact test questions year
after year. Adding high-school grades to the prediction equation had mixed
results, often leading to only marginally better predictions. But since Indonesia's
top universities are so selective, even tiny improvements in predictive power lead
to sizable gains in efficiency. It therefore seems worthwhile on efficiency grounds
alone to add high-school grades or the EBTA to the PP1 as criteria for admission.
At least, we know enough after these analyses to recommend that the govern-

ment of Indonesia seriously consider adding these other variables to the admissions process. The final answer will probably depend on the costs and likely incentive effects of such additions.

We have also examined possible biases in the current selection system. In 1981, only a quarter of the students at the prestigious University of Indonesia were women. And yet, women obtained significantly better university grades than men, even after controlling for test scores. This indicates biased prediction: it appears that the PP1 system is *biased against* women.

This result, however, is based on only one study. It demands confirmation based on other universities, other years, and other fields of study. *If* further research showed that sexual bias did exist, two remedial steps should be considered. First, the questions on the PP1 exam should be analyzed for sexual bias. Techniques for doing such "item analysis" go beyond the scope of this book, but as mentioned earlier, the idea is to look for questions that women miss much more often than men (compared with the rest of the questions on the test). If biased questions are discovered, they should be deleted from the examination. Second, points could be added to women's scores on the examination—exactly enough points to compensate for the underprediction of their later performance.

For now, we can conclude that our results are so suggestive of sexual bias that the topic should be studied carefully, in depth, and soon.

Our research does *not* reveal predictive bias against students from particular regions of Indonesia or from particular socioeconomic backgrounds. Even if the selection system is unbiased in the predictive sense, there still may be good reasons to give preferential treatment to members of disadvantaged or underrepresented groups. We analyzed two interesting cases: the possibility of implementing a quota for "outer-islanders," who are heavily underrepresented among those admitted to the best universities, and the possibility of removing or easing the existing quota for students of Chinese descent. Both possibilities seemed worthwhile, in terms of academic costs and benefits, but as emphasized in chapter 4, the issue of representation and preferential treatment involves many other considerations as well.

For a country of Indonesia's size, and given the importance of higher education in the nation's future development, the lack of previous research and analysis on these issues is remarkable. This chapter is only a beginning, as much more research needs to be done. For example, the analyses presented here should be carried out for other universities in Indonesia, with longer-term performance measures, and with larger samples. There are now under way "tracer" studies of recent graduates that will provide a good data base for additional research. More work needs to be done on the incentive effects of alternative selection policies.

Even with more research, the issues raised in this chapter will never be "resolved," since policy choices depend so much on value judgments and politics. It is good to close a long and technical chapter like this one with such a reminder. Policy analysis is only part of the answer, and policy analysts have only a modest role in areas as important as selecting the next generation of a nation's leaders. By advancing our tools of analysis and marshaling appropriate data, we can hope that this humble role may nonetheless be a useful one.

APPENDIX: STATISTICAL ANALYSIS OF ACADEMIC PREDICTION IN INDONESIA

The results of the analysis of first-year academic performance of science students at the University of Indonesia are presented here first and in some detail. Then, more briefly, the results of other studies of academic prediction are summarized.

University of Indonesia

Table 18 provides some of the basic information about the data set from the U.I. Science Faculty. These students had taken the IPA examination, which is the science track of the PP1 exam described above. In the analysis below, I assume realistically that the average score on the IPA exam in the entire pool of those taking the test was 76 with a standard deviation of 20.4. The students actually accepted at U.I. scored much higher; their average was 104, with a standard deviation of 10.9.

Their academic performance was measured by first-year grade point averages (GPA), measured on a scale of 0 to 4 with 4 = A, 3 = B, 2 = C, and so forth.

TABLE 18. Basic Data on Recent First-Year Science Class at U.I.
($N = 182$)

Variable	μ	σ	Variable	%
GPA	2.24	0.47	Father's occupation	
IPA test	104	10.9	Government official	38.5
Math	27.5	5.1	Military	5.5
Biology	28.4	4.9	Private sector	14.3
Physics	23.6	4.7	Business	11.5
Chemistry	24.7	4.7	Professional	1.1
			Agriculture/fishing	3.3
			Worker (*buruh*)	3.3
			Pensioner	17.0
			Public school	78.0
			"Big city" background	87.9
			Jakarta	72.5
			Not from Java	9.3
			Male	70.0
			Chinese	6.0
			GPA ≥ 2.0	70.0

TABLE 19. Part of the Correlation Matrix for 182 Science Students at U.I.

	GPA ≥ 2.0	IPA	Math	Biology	Physics	Chemistry	Sex
GPA	.72	.41	.37	.19	.13	.20	−.44
GPA ≥ 2.0		.18	.18	.07	.00	.14	−.35
IPA			.62	.39	.60	.64	−.11
Math				−.13	.27	.20	−.07
Biology					−.07	.07	−.20
Physics						.16	.10
Chemistry							−.08

Faculty members told me that grades below 2.0 (about 30 percent of the class fell below this average) were considered unsatisfactory.

It is useful to begin any analysis of such data by describing the data variable by variable (see table 19). Then one moves to the relationships among variables. Table 19 shows the correlation matrix for many of the variables in table 18. Table 20 shows for two categorical variables—sex and whether or not the student achieved a GPA above 2.0—a contingency table approach to two-at-a-time analysis.

Then we move to regression analysis. For our purposes, the first thing we wish to check is the entrance examination score (IPA). In a linear regression, the ordinary least squares line was:

$$GPA = 0.38 + 0.018 \; IPA \qquad \bar{R}^2 = 0.16$$
$$(0.31) \quad \underline{(0.003)}$$

The figures in parentheses are the standard errors of the regression coefficients; underlining indicates that the regression coefficient is statistically significant at the $\alpha = 0.05$ level.

We might interpret this equation as follows: "If the IPA score is increased by 10 points, the expected GPA rises by 0.18 units." The standard deviation of GPA is 0.47, so this increase corresponds to about 0.38 standard deviations in GPA. And if the IPA score were raised by 20.4 points, which was the standard deviation among all IPA test-takers, we would expect the GPA to increase by about 0.37 grade units, or 0.37/0.47 = 0.79 of a standard deviation.

The correlation coefficient r is the square root of R^2, and in this case $r = 0.41$. For our purposes, we need to correct this correlation for restriction of range and for unreliability in the measurement of GPA. Using the formulas in chapter 3 (and assuming optimistically that GPA has a reliability coefficient of 0.8), the adjusted correlation becomes 0.70.[23]

When working with small samples, a few deviant observations may "distort" the regression equation. To assess such possible distortions and to over-

TABLE 20. Sex and GPA ≥ 2.0 for 181 Science Students at U.I.

	Females	Males	Total
GPA ≤ 2.0	3	51	54
	(16.1)	(37.9)	
GPA ≥ 2.0	51	76	127
	(37.9)	(89.1)	
	54	127	181

Note: Figures in parentheses are the expected values for each cell if females and males had equal academic performance (i.e., assuming independence).

TABLE 21. Selected Multiple Regressions on 182 Science Students at U.I. (Early 1980s)

(1) $GPA = 0.89 + 0.016\ IPA - 0.41\ Male$
      (0.29) (0.003)   (0.06)

(2) $GPA = 0.62 + 0.018\ IPA - 0.35\ Male - 0.010\ math$
      (0.29) (0.003)   (0.07)   (0.10)
      $- 0.16\ phys + 0.09\ biol - 0.06\ pharm + 0.27\ geog$
        (0.09)   (0.12)   (0.11)   (0.11)

(3) $GPA = 0.71 + 0.018\ IPA - 0.33\ Male - 0.013\ math$
      (0.31) (0.003)   (0.075)   (0.11)
      $= 0.18\ phys + 0.08\ biol - 0.08\ pharm + 0.24\ geog$
        (0.09)   (0.12)   (0.11)   (0.11)
      $= 0.005\ f.ed + 0.025\ m.ed - 0.15\ city - 0.10\ non\text{-}Java$
        (0.25)   (0.028)   (0.09)   (0.10)

Note: Figures in parentheses are standard errors. Underlining indicates statistical significance beyond $p < 0.05$. The variables *math*, *phys(ics)*, *biol(ogy)*, *pharm(acy)*, and *geog(raphy)* are dummy variables representing departments within the Faculty of Science; the chemistry department has been left out and so is the point of comparison for the other departments. The variables *f.ed* and *m.ed* are six-category classifications of the father's and mother's level of educational attainment. *City* means that one's secondary school was located in an urban area; *non-Java* means that one's secondary school was not located on Java.

come them, we have several alternatives. We might perform the analyses twice, once with outliers and once without them in the sample. Another alternative is to use methods of statistical analysis that are more "resistant" to outliers and other problems. The details exceed the scope of this book.[24]

A host of multiple regressions were tried. Several results are given in table 21. In the first equation, sex is added as a predictor. Females, on average had college GPAs 0.46 higher than the males. Equation (1) tells us that, after statistically "controlling" for the IPA score, females still do better than males on average: about 0.41 higher in GPA. We shall consider this result in more detail below. For now, note that the efficiency of our prediction of a student's GPA in U.I.'s Faculty of Science could be improved by taking into account sex as well as IPA score.

The second equation in table 21 includes dummy variables for five of the six departments in the Faculty of Science. Chemistry is left out; therefore, the coefficients on the other departments should be interpreted compared with the chemistry department. For example, the coefficient of 0.27 on "geog" means that, after controlling for both IPA score and sex, students in the geography department had average GPAs 0.27 points higher than students in the chemistry department.[25]

The third equation in table 21 includes still other predictors. By adding father's education, mother's education, city, and non-Java as variables, the prediction of GPA was *not* significantly improved. Putting it another way, once we know a student's IPA score, sex, and department, these other variables add no significant new information, as far as predicting GPA is concerned.

This does not mean that IPA scores, or even GPA, was not related to these other variables. In fact, those whose parents have better educations and are from Java did better on the IPA and got better grades. But if we have two students in the same department who are of the same sex and have the same IPA scores, those whose parents have better educations or who are from Java do *not* get better grades at the university.

This is an important result. For this data set, it also holds for other variables: father's occupation; public/private/vocational high school; and Jakarta or not. It appears that the admissions test was not predictively biased across these various categories of student backgrounds.

Teacher Training Institute (IKIP), Jakarta

Based on a sample of 185 who finished their first year of study at the Teacher Training Institute in Jakarta, I calculated this regression equation:

$$GPA = -0.66 + 0.020 \, PP4 \quad R^2 = 0.27 \quad \overline{R} = 0.53$$

In other regressions, the coefficient on "male" was -0.05, not significant. A 10-point increase in the PP4 score corresponded to about an 0.2 increase in GPA, or about one-third of a standard deviation in this truncated sample.

Muchkiar's Data

Indonesian educator Muchkiar Suradinata collected small random samples of data from 1977 in four universities. His predictors went beyond the entrance exams; he also had data on students' performance on the high-school certifying test (EBTA), high-school GPA (HSGPA), and the nonverbal "intelligence test" called Raven's Progressive Matrices (RM).[26]

In order to minimize problems of comparing different grading scales, I

TABLE 22. Selected Regression Results for Muchkiar's Data (1977)

(a) *ITB* ($N = 41$)

1. $GPA = -5.31 + 0.048\ PP1$ $\overline{R}^2 = 0.647$ $R = 0.80$
   (0.62) (0.006)

2. $GPA = -6.63 + 0.043\ PP1 + 0.035\ RM$ $\overline{R}^2 = 0.657$ $R = 0.81$
   (1.10) (0.007) (0.025)

3. $GPA = -7.76 + 0.036\ PP1 + 0.029\ RM$ $\overline{R}^2 = 0.691$ $R = 0.83$
   (1.16) (0.007) (0.025)
   $+0.30\ HSGPA$
   (0.13)

(b) *UI, UGM,* and Airlangga ($N = 241$)

1. $GPA = -2.51 + 0.028\ PP1$ $\overline{R}^2 = 0.346$ $R = 0.59$
   (0.23) (0.002)

2. $GPA = -4.56 + 0.017\ PP1 + 0.061\ RM$ $\overline{R}^2 = 0.468$ $R = 0.68$
   (0.34) (0.003) (0.008)

3. $GPA = -6.17 + 0.013\ PP1 + 0.056\ RM$ $\overline{R}^2 = 0.491$ $R = 0.70$
   (0.58) (0.003) (0.008)
   $+0.33\ HSGPA$
   (0.10)

Note: Figures in parentheses are standard errors. Underlining indicates statistical significance beyond $p < 0.05$. *ITB* = Institute of Technology at Bandung; *UI* = University of Indonesia, *UGM* = University of Gadjah Madah. My calculations, based on data collected by Muchkiar.

TABLE 23. Regression Analyses on 78 Entering U.I. Psychology Students (1979)

	$\overline{R}^2$	R
(1) $GPA = -0.05 + 0.17\ PP1$ (0.10) (0.11)	0.016	0.13
(2) $GPA = -0.03 + 0.13\ PP1 + 0.34\ DAT$ (0.10) (0.11) (0.11)	0.119	0.34
(3) $GPA = -0.03 + 0.13\ PP1 + 0.32\ DAT + 0.03\ LTIKI$ (0.10) (0.11) (0.15) (0.15)	0.108	0.33
(4) $GPA = -0.03 + 0.12\ PP1 + 0.24\ DAT + 0.15\ STIKI$ (0.10) (0.11) (0.14) (0.14)	0.121	0.35

Note: Figures in parentheses are standard errors. Underlining indicates statistical significance beyond $p < 0.05$. The dependent variable is an average of eight normalized course grades (each with mean = 10 and std. dev. = 3) in the first year of study. *LTIKI* = long form of the Indonesian intelligence test; *STIKI* = short form of same.

transformed all grades within a given university into standard normal scores (with a mean of 0 and a standard deviation of 1). Regressions having universities as dummy variables showed that, after controlling for PP1 scores, the Institute of Technology at Bandung (ITB) had much tougher grading. So I stratified the sample, computing separate regressions for ITB and for the other three universities (see table 22). Grades at ITB were more predictable. The correlation at ITB was a thumping 0.80, compared with a lower but still impressive 0.59 for the other three. This high correlation is all the more surprising given ITB's restriction of range: the average PP1 score in the ITB sample was 111.[27]

The Psychology Department at U.I.

Table 23 describes the results of an analysis of a small data set ($N = 78$) of students. It is helpful for its indication that the Differential Aptitude Test (DAT) would be a useful addition to the PP1 examination. The multiple R increases from 0.13 to 0.34 with the addition of the DAT.

7

CONCLUSIONS AND EXTENSIONS

A society faces few questions more important than how it allocates positions on the fast track. Will those chosen for universities or the civil service be the fittest in terms of serving social ends? Will important groups in society, such as classes and regions and races and sexes, be appropriately represented among the chosen few? Will the system used for selecting such future elites create the right kinds of incentives? In short, how can societies make merit systems work?

This book has examined these questions in the context of choosing students for universities in developing nations. This final chapter recapitulates the major findings. It also briefly extends the analysis to encompass a broader domain of policies for allocating scarce positions or resources according to the "merit" of the applicants.

CHOOSING ELITES IN CHINA

The central importance of university admissions as an economic and political issue is clearly portrayed in the turbulent case of China. "The general psychology of the Chinese," Sun Yat-sen said in 1924, "is that a man possessing marked ability should become king."[1] The traditional Chinese way of measuring marked ability was the written examination, through which aspirants displayed their command of the classics of the culture. Already at the time of Charlemagne, China had a nationwide system of competitive examinations for selecting the future elite. The status of one's parents remained important in the determination of one's own status, and opportunities were foreclosed to women, but compared with other cultures, the Chinese gave great emphasis to academic merit as the criterion for honor and political power. "The question usually put to a stranger of unknown rank," noted Max Weber about Imperial China, "was how many examinations he had passed."[2]

Over the centuries, China's system for making merit work was the subject of constant debate. Some said that the tests stressed memorization, not creativity or reasoning. Therefore, in A.D. 1044 new questions were introduced, which involved imaginative solutions and original discussions of the broad meaning of classical texts. Soon, however, problems became apparent with this seemingly attractive change: the examinations were costlier to grade, less reliable and therefore less accurate as predictors of "intellectual merit," and more subject to bias and corruption. The old questions, "which could be graded objectively, if mechanically, on the basis of set rules," were soon reintroduced, despite their evident disadvantages.[3] Other critics pointed out that tests should be supplemented with recommendations, especially when deciding on appointments or promotions to senior ranks. The Chinese found that letters of recommendation were useless because flattery was commonplace, and so they invented the system called sponsorship, where the recommender could be rewarded or punished depending on how well his protégé later did on the job.[4]

Throughout Chinese history, the rich did better than the poor on the examinations, in part because the rich had more access to libraries, tutors, and good schools. Consequently, some criticized the examination system as regressive. To others, however, the tests were not regressive enough: too many brilliant sons of the poor were being selected. After all, these critics argued, the purpose of both selection and the subsequent education was to produce leaders for Chinese society, and the sons of the upper class, by dint of their privileged upbringing, would be best suited to command. As statesman Li Ti-yu put it in the ninth century:

> The outstanding officials of the government ought to be the sons of the highest officials. Why? Because from childhood on they are accustomed to this kind of position; their eyes are familiar with court affairs; even if they have not been trained in the ceremonies of the palace, they automatically achieve perfection. Scholars of poor families, even if they have an extraordinary talent, are certainly unable to accustom themselves to [its routine].[5]

In Imperial China, some groups did better on the examinations than others, leading to charges of what we now call "test bias" and calls for "preferential treatment." For example, in the fourteenth century, southerners tended to be overrepresented among the top scorers on the exams. Northerners complained that the examiners were biased. Eventually, separate lists of selectees—in effect, quotas—were installed for candidates from the South, the North, and the Central regions of China.[6]

Indeed, almost every "modern" criticism of testing and selection can be found, exhaustively discussed if without statistical evidence, in the history of Imperial China. Some of the same, classic tensions and problems were played out in university selection during the first decade and a half of Communist rule. But it was not until 1966 and the Cultural Revolution that the ageless criticisms of testing were carried to their logical extreme. Entrance examinations were condemned as inefficient, unfair to workers and peasants, and the creator of perverse and reactionary incentives throughout the education system and, indeed, Chinese society. Using empirical rather than moral arguments and citing the negative effects of the traditional selection system, the Chinese authorities abolished examinations in 1966. Instead, university admissions would be according to political as well as intellectual criteria, and decisions would be made by the Communist Party, not by the universities or a central examination board.

What ensued was a social experiment in education of unprecedented scope and impact. The radical shift in selection criteria was part of a thorough recasting of the educational system and in many ways symbolized the Cultural Revolution.

By 1977, many Chinese had concluded that the experiment had failed. Examinations were reintroduced; soon they became the dominant criterion for university admissions, along with "weights" for members of racial minority groups. The shift back to examinations had undeniable political implications and overtones. "The entrance examination was suspended. This interference of the Gang of Four in education was one of their greatest crimes," said a top official in the Chinese Higher Education Bureau in 1977. "We must hate and criticize them for it. They have spoiled two generations."[7] Again, however, a remarkable shift in policy was justified primarily with empirical arguments about effects, and not through appeals to moral principle or political justice. As a matter of fact, it was now argued, getting rid of entrance examinations had led to great inefficiencies in terms of the quality of students admitted to universities and therefore of the quality of university graduates. As a matter of fact, abandoning tests had not led to large improvements in the representation of important subsets of the population. And as a matter of fact, the incentives created had turned out to be awful: high-school students no longer were motivated to master their academic lessons, teachers were rendered powerless, and political influence was used to gain the admission of less qualified but well-connected students. This latter process was called "entering through the back door."

China's rich history of making merit work, then, contains several lessons. It is not that examinations are good or bad per se; that depends on the objectives of the selection process and the form and content of the specific examinations. Rather, the point is that debates about choosing future elites, over centuries and regimes, have rotated around fundamental themes. I call them dimensions of the problem of making merit work:

- *The efficiency of selection.* What is the "quality" (in whatever terms happen to be dominant, but including sheer technical capability, intelligence, and motivation) of those chosen? How expensive is the selection system to administer?

- *Representation and bias.* To what extent are important groups and classes proportionally represented among those chosen? Are selection criteria biased against certain groups, in the sense of systematically understating their later performance? What is the ideal extent of preferential treatment, which balances the costs and benefits of rectifying underrepresentation?

- *The incentives created by selection systems.* How do selection criteria affect applicants and potential applicants? With what social repercussions? How do the criteria affect what schools offer, what teachers implement, and what educational policies pursue? In what ways are selection processes open to whim, abuse, influence, and corruption?

The issue is whether it is *right*, in the words of protesting students at the No. 1 Girls' Middle School in Peking in 1966, that "book learning stands above all" or whether "education must serve the politics of the proletariat and be integrated with productive labour."[8] But the issue also concerns the *consequences* of various policies for doing what seems to be right—consequences in terms of efficiency, representation, and incentives. Judging and predicting these effects, and combining these dimensions in a prescriptive framework for policymaking, is a task that goes beyond moral and political arguments, not supplanting those considerations but clarifying their role in deciding how to make merit work.

UNIVERSITY ADMISSIONS AROUND THE GLOBE

The same dimensions can be found in selection policies in other developing countries. Too often one finds anecdotal evidence of inefficient admissions systems that cost a fortune in time and money and end up choosing large numbers of students with neither the inclination nor the ability to complete their university studies. Too often one learns of the underrepresentation, even exclusion, of students from certain regions, races, classes, or sexes (i.e., women). Too often one is told of selection systems that create perverse incentives for students—inducing cramming and memorization rather than problem-solving—and allow influence-peddling and corruption. One result of all this is the crisis in which many universities in the developing countries find themselves. Standards slide with no new standards to replace them, teachers and students pretend to be teaching and learning, and what comes out of the educational process is of little use to the needs of a developing country. According to former Ecuadorian President Osvaldo Hurtado, the failure of entrance policies in his country had led to educational disaster:

> The rapid decline in academic levels has passed critical limits, to the extent that, according to some professors, new professionals being graduated from the university are totally unqualified to work in their areas of specialization. Given this situation, it is unlikely in the near future that the university can satisfactorily assume its proper scientific and academic roles at a time when the cultural and technological dependence of the country is rapidly increasing.[9]

Unfortunately, these topics have received little systematic study from a policy perspective. The literature contains hints and suggestions, but it falters when it comes to empirical analysis (as opposed to description).

There have been tantalizing beginnings. Take, for example, the efficiency of educational selection. Studies in the West suggest that, holding constant years of education, a 1 point increase in a person's intelligence score is associated with a 1 percent increase in the person's later earnings. Thus, a one standard deviation increase in IQ among those completing college is associated with about a 15 percent increase in later earnings. Economists Sebastian Piñera and Marcelo Selowsky ask us to suppose that a similar association holds in the developing

WHEN STANDARDS FALL

A monumental analysis of the "brain drain" contains an incisive description of the paradoxical appearance in many developing countries of "educated unemployment" and a "shortage of high-level talent." Among the causes are declining standards of selection and education in universities:

When nationalism, egalitarianism, and strong personal motives combine to force universities toward mass output of poorly trained people, the pressure is often irresistible.

By and large, it has been easier to expand universities, and to do so without calculated attention to the demand for graduates and their quality. . . . The quality of graduates has often been deficient, so that in some nations shortages of highly qualified people exist simultaneously with a glut of those with mediocre training.

[The] fierce pressure for entry to universities [has resulted] in a general decline in standards of admission, expansion of enrollment at rates precluding the maintenance of standards of instruction, all ending with the production of masses of students who are in theory but not in fact trained for available jobs.

These same "surplus" countries (with more graduates than jobs—India, Korea, Egypt, Colombia, Mexico, and others) have shortages of highly talented people with rigorous and relevant advanced training, and often have foreign experts at work within their boundaries. Simultaneously, they have unemployed or underemployed people with average intelligence, mediocre training, and a low-quality university degree.

Such a widespread and serious imbalance which transcends continents, ideologies and stages of development can only reflect difficulties inherent in the development process or grave misjudgments in educational planning, both domestic and foreign. We think that both explanations share the blame.

Source: Charles V. Kidd et al., *The International Migration of High-Level Manpower: Its Impact on the Development Process* (New York: Praeger, 1970), pp. 686–89.

world. Then, with further heroic assumptions, they tried to calculate the benefits of allocating educational opportunity strictly according to "ability"—which to them, but not necessarily to us, is associated with intelligence. Their answer was interesting: the result would be about a 5 percent increase in the gross national product. This number should not be taken seriously by itself, but it can usefully be compared to other theoretical estimates made by economists on the basis of other heroic assumptions. For example, completely efficient selection in this sense would have about twice the effect on the GNP of a developing economy as the complete correction of welfare losses due to domestic tariffs, and perhaps three times the effect of the complete removal by all the industrialized countries of their protective tariffs on exports of less developed countries.[10] More plausibly, if the correlation between admissions criteria and later performance could be raised from, say, 0.3 to 0.5, Piñera and Selowsky's work might lead us to guess that the result would be a 1 percent gain in GNP.[11]

We also know that in many ways the stakes in terms of efficiency and equity are great in the developing nations, certainly when compared with the industrialized West. For example, only about 5 percent of the relevant age-group is enrolled at the tertiary level in the developing countries, compared with about 25 percent in the developed countries (and 50 percent in North America). The children of the poor and of disadvantaged ethnic groups are usually underrepresented among those enrolled; males and the offspring of government officials are usually heavily overrepresented. A year of higher education costs about ten to twenty times as much as a year of primary education in the developing countries, compared with three to four times as much in the industrialized nations. And in the developing countries, the state typically pays 90 percent and more of the costs of higher education.

In many developing countries, then, being admitted to a university gives a very few young (and often already relatively advantaged) people an expensive government subsidy—and a significant lifetime advantage. This "very privileged minority," in the words of Zimbabwe's Prime Minister Robert G. Mugabe, is "of vital importance to Zimbabwe. Much has been given to the students, and an equal measure will be expected of them in return"[12]—or a more-than-equal measure, for how else can such a limited and regressive process of elite formation be justified? As Tanzanian President Julius Nyerere put it,

> There is, in fact, only one reason why underdeveloped societies like ours establish and maintain universities. We do so as an investment in our future. We are spending large and disproportionate amounts of money on a few individuals so that they should, in the future, make a disproportionate return to the society. We are investing in a man's brain in just the same way as we invest in a tractor; and just as we expect the tractor to do many times as much work for us as a hand-hoe, so we expect the student we have trained to make many times as great a contribution to our well-being as the man who has not had this good fortune.[13]

And so, Nyerere concluded in another writing, "At any university some of the best brains of the day should be living together."[14] In this situation, if better selection policies could reduce the typical failure rates of 30 to 70 percent, the cost savings and social benefits could be sizable. Selection policies could also be used to increase the representation of disadvantaged groups among the future "tractors" of society.

But the usual literature, and the usual policy-making, give little guidance about how to achieve these laudable ends. There is a shortage of available information about the effects of alternative selection policies, in terms of efficiency, representation and bias, and incentives. Moreover, we lack an analytical tradition and a set of tools for dealing with this class of problems in developing nations. The aim of this book has been to begin to rectify this situation.

ANALYZING THE EFFICIENCY OF SELECTION

The case of the School of Pharmacy of the University of Karachi provided the occasion to develop a method for analyzing the efficiency of alternative selection systems—a method later applied to the University of the Philippines and to a number of institutions in Indonesia. "Efficiency" refers in the first instance to the productivity of those chosen for the few available positions. For example, consider trials for an Olympic track team. Which selection system will choose the fastest runners? One could rank alternative methods for choosing the team according to the average times of those chosen, or the proportion who ended up winning medals, or some other grounds. Indeed, as chapter 3 stressed, the choice of measures of performance and "utilities" for those measures is of decisive importance *before* one thinks about which selection system is most efficient. The prior question is always, "Efficient for what?"

Once we have those measures and utilities, we can apply the techniques illustrated in this book to assess how efficient various selection policies are. These techniques, for the most part drawn from psychometrics and rarely if ever applied to problems of developing countries, show that the answer depends on three broad considerations:

- *value judgments* about objectives, performance measures, and utility functions for those measures
- how well alternative selection criteria *predict* later performance
- particular features of the *decision context*, such as how many people apply, how many can be admitted, and the cost of obtaining and using various selection criteria.

In the cases of university admissions in Pakistan, the Philippines, and Indonesia, the objectives and performance measures were academic in nature—such variables as grades in the university, the chance of passing or graduating, and the cost per graduate. These are hardly ideal measures of the efficiency of an educational system, or therefore of a selection system. In the real world of policy-making, one often encounters partial and inexact proxies for the subtle and multiple objectives sought. We can usefully analyze such proxies without endorsing them as ultimate goals; indeed, in doing so we may stimulate a deeper and more fruitful analysis of our broader aims.[15] Decision-making may also be improved. Our analyses enabled us to estimate the difference that one or another selection policy would make in terms of the average grades earned by those admitted, the percentage who would eventually graduate, and the average cost per graduate. Calculating these aspects of educational "efficiency" does not mean that the policy-maker must choose the most efficient policy in these narrow academic domains. I insist only on a weaker proposition: policy-makers should be aware of these predicted effects and should debate them with the best information available, before making decisions.

This book has given considerable emphasis to the second consideration in the analysis of the efficiency of selection: how well we can predict. Prediction usually involves statistical techniques like correlation and regression analysis. When applied to the problem of selection of a few among the many, these techniques are easy to misuse and their results easy to misinterpret.[16] For example, correlations that appear by conventional social scientific standards to be quite "weak"—say, 0.4—can in the context of selection be quite "powerful." In what sense? Using predictors with such "weak" correlations can lead to dramatic improvements in the quality of those selected. This remark has particular force when applied to university admissions in developing countries, which often show that only one in five or one in ten of those who apply are selected. A corollary is that even what look to some like "small" increases in our ability to predict later performance can lead to large gains in efficiency.

We have seen that the efficiency of alternative policies also depends on the particular context in which selection decisions are made. For example, how selective is the institution? And what are the costs of obtaining and using various admissions criteria? Consider two hypothetical universities. Suppose that they have exactly the same objectives, performance measures, and utility functions. Let us further posit that their admissions criteria predict later performance equally well. With all this in common, should both universities use the same admissions criteria? Perhaps not, if the context of decision-making differs. If the first university admits one in ten applicants and the other admits one of every two who apply, the value of better prediction is much greater for the first. So if getting and using information for selection is costly, the less selective university should probably not employ the same criteria as the first. (It is not just a question of different cutoffs on the same criteria.)

In analyzing these three considerations, we have also discovered some interesting facts about the efficiency of selection in universities in three Asian nations. The unadjusted correlations between entrance examinations and grades at the university ranged from 0.4 to 0.8, with a modal figure of around 0.45.[17] (If one "corrects" the 0.45 correlation for unreliability of the criterion and for restriction of range, the correlation will rise to 0.6 to 0.7.) Adding high-school grades to the prediction equation raises the correlation by about 0.05. Using an intelligence test as a predictor along with the entrance examination score raises the correlation by about 0.10. These findings are approximations, unlikely to hold for each and every institution and badly in need of confirmation at other universities and in other countries. It is interesting to note that these figures are not dissimilar to the modal correlations found in colleges and graduate schools in the United States.[18]

What do these numbers mean in practical terms? It depends on one's utilities and the context, as emphasized above. An illustration based on the case of the University of Indonesia suggests that the gains from improvements in the prediction of academic performance could be substantial. If we could increase the adjusted correlation between admissions criteria and the probability of graduation from 0.32 to 0.50, the cost to the government of each successful graduate would go down 20 percent, and 35 percent more students would graduate each year. Moreover, the quality of the graduates would be higher. The 50th percentile student chosen through the improved prediction would be as good as about

TABLE 24. Illustrative Calculations of the Efficiency of Various Selection Criteria, Based on Indonesia

Performance Measure	Random Selection	Admissions Test Only	Admissions Test and HSGPA	Admissions Test + HSGPA + Aptitude	"Perfect Selection"
Predicted % who would graduate	20	40	48	54	100
Average government cost per graduate	$5,000	$3,200	$2,800	$2,650	$2,000
Academic benefit if 1 std. dev. in university grades is worth $1,000	Baseline = 0	$20.7 mil.	$23.3 mil.	$24.7 mil.	$29.3 mil.

Note: HSGPA = high-school grade point average. *Aptitude* = the use of an aptitude test of the kind discussed in chapter 6. "Perfect selection" = what would occur if we could forecast academic success perfectly in this applicant pool. All estimates are approximate. They depend on a number of arbitrary (though plausible) assumptions as explained in chapter 6. The exchange rate used for Indonesian rupiah is the 1982 rate of U.S.$1 = Rp. 660.

TABLE 25. Checklist for Studying Efficiency of Selection

1. Define performance measure(s).
   a. Academic
      i. Short-term measures
      ii. Long-term measures
   b. Later-life contributions to society
      i. Short-term measures
      ii. Long-term measures (A problem: society changes, so long-term studies may not be valid.)
2. Define a utility function for the performance measure(s).
   a. How much are various-sized increases in performance measures worth, in terms of current expenditures?
   b. One technique: Ask policy-makers and knowledgeable observers about the difference in the social value of one person at the 50th percentile of the performance measure and another at the 85th percentile. This estimates the utility of a one standard deviation change in the performance measure.
3. Assess the predictive power of alternative selection policies.
   a. Experimental design: Assess effects directly by comparing many policies. (A problem: such experiments are usually not politically or economically feasible.)
   b. No experimental design: Use correlation and regression analysis.
      i. Assess the assumption of linearity (e.g., via the analysis of residuals); transform variables as needed.
      ii. Correct correlations for unreliability in the performance measure(s) and for restriction of range.
      iii. Given 2, above, and the selection ratio, assess the utility of alternative selection policies.
4. Assess the costs of alternative selection policies.
   a. Costs of design
   b. Costs of administration, including data collection
   c. Costs of using the information in the selection process
5. Compare the benefits and costs of alternative policies.

the 67th percentile student in today's university. We would be able in effect to replace today's average student by one in the top third of the class.[19] Table 24 provides other illustrative results, based on Chapter 6's analyses of university selection in Indonesia.

A shortcoming of the techniques presented for analyzing the efficiency of selection is that they do not lead smoothly and unequivocally to the choice of optimally efficient policies. Our science is limited: we cannot measure all the outcomes we care about, nor can we usually assess the predictive power of various criteria *over time,* as we would like. Moreover, we probably will not obtain agreement about objectives, appropriate measures, and utility functions for those measures.

On the other hand, the techniques have some virtues. They put science in its proper place. They exhibit clearly the limitations and usefulness of analysis. They show where value judgments enter. Thus, using these techniques may help us get beyond a sterile dichotomy, acting *as if* policy choices were all a question of statistics and predictions and social science, or acting *as if* such choices were entirely determined by values and politics. Actually, both matter, and by working systematically through the combined, complex problem of efficient selection, we may improve both our theorizing and our decision-making. Table 25 is a heuristic checklist for doing this sort of analysis of the efficiency of selection policies.

REPRESENTATION

The second dimension of making merit work is achieving the appropriate representation of social groups among the chosen few. In some ideologies and social systems, this is not an issue; indeed, to some people it is offensive to talk about the representation of "groups." But according to other ways of looking at the world, it is crucial that future elites be representative of the society's regions, classes, races, sexes, communal groups, or religions. Especially when the process for creating elites is as limited and potentially regressive as in the case of university selection in most developing countries, one worries about a self-perpetuating, inbred elite, which may, despite its technical excellence or cultural advantages, serve its own interests rather than the nation's as a whole. As Max Weber observed, "Special examinations, on the one hand, mean or appear to mean a 'selection' of those who qualify from all social strata rather than a rule by notables. On the other hand, democracy fears that a merit system and educational certificates will result in a privileged 'caste.' "[20]

The greater inclusion of underrepresented groups may reduce these fears. Preferential treatment for such groups has several possible benefits, as discussed in chapter 4. Some might be called philosophical, including the compensation of certain groups for past injustices: this has been an important justification of preferential treatment for "Untouchables" and Scheduled Tribes in India. Apart from making reparations for the past, one may also look to future social benefits. As part of a national policy to overcome ethnic or regional or sexual inequalities, universities may be able to accelerate the advance of some members of backward groups into leadership positions in government, the professions, and business, and this may in turn lead to a more integrated, stable, and efficient society. This argument too has been used in Indian law—even in a nation that *constitutionally* forbids the use of caste, community, religion, and other characteristics as grounds for rejecting anyone from the university.[21]

On the other hand, preferential treatment usually entails costs as well. Some people argue that group thinking is reinforced at the cost of individualism and nationalism. It has been contended that preferential policies reinforce prejudices by admitting visibly less-qualified students to the university and that, rather than leading to integration, such policies exacerbate intergroup tensions, leading to social conflict.[22]

More narrowly, preferential treatment usually costs something in terms of the performance of those selected. If we want more members of a group with lower predicted performance, we give up something to get them—and the more such people we select, the more we give up. At some point, the benefits from increasing the representation of that group will be offset by the costs in terms of lower predicted performance. Economic reasoning suggests, therefore, that the optimal degree of preferential treatment would exactly balance the marginal benefits and marginal costs of representation.

Unfortunately, in analyzing these benefits and costs of representation, reality intrudes harshly. As in the case of efficiency, we are unable with our current science to measure many of the benefits and costs of greater representation of certain groups. And once again it will be difficult to agree on the value judgments involved. For example, what magnitude of social benefits should be attributed to having 20 percent rather than 10 percent of the students at the top ten universities in Indonesia be from the "outer islands" or to having half rather than one-third of the students at the elite University of the Philippines be from families with annual incomes less than P30,000? And so, as in the case of our analysis of efficiency, we must rely on incomplete proxies for our complicated and controversial objectives. We hope that analysis will advance our understanding—in part by showing where facts are lacking and where value judgments must enter—with no illusion of solving the problem of the optimal degree of preferential treatment.

We looked at a narrow but important question: "What are the academic costs of increasing group representation?" Answering this query involved two distinguishable steps:

1. *Assessing the bias of alternative selection criteria.* To what extent do they systematically misrepresent the capabilities of various groups?

2. *Assessing the costs of various degrees of preferential treatment.* For various degrees of greater representation, how much is lost in terms of predicted performance?

We explored statistical methods for discovering bias in the prediction of later performance by different groups. Usually, one must make inferences from complicated regression analyses. Once in a while, an experiment will be carried out, as in the remarkable XDS program we analyzed at the University of the Philippines. The basic idea is to see whether a given "score" on a selection criterion means the same thing on average for members of different groups, in terms of forecasting later performance.

For example, in the case of Indonesia, students from the outer islands (that is, all but Java) made up 20 percent of the applicant pool but only 10 percent of those admitted. On average, they scored about one-third of a standard deviation lower on the entrance examination for the top ten universities than did students from Java. Did this group difference in scores mean the entrance exam was biased? Not according to our preliminary findings. Among those admitted, students with the same test scores received about the same university grades on average, whether the students were from Java or the outer islands. In this sense, the entrance exam was predictively unbiased.

In the case of students from poor families (less than P30,000 annual incomes) at the University of the Philippines, if anything the bias was the other way. True, these students were underrepresented; they made up about half of the applicant pool but only about one-third of those admitted. This appeared to indicate that students from poor families scored about half a standard deviation lower on the combined admissions index than did students from families with incomes above P30,000. But during the experimental program that admitted lower-scoring, poor students to U.P. and gave them special counseling and financial aid, these students on average earned worse grades than would have been predicted on the basis of their scores on the admissions index. The index overpredicted rather than underpredicted their later performance at the university. (This is a common finding concerning the academic performance of black students at American universities: admissions tests are biased in their favor, in the sense of overestimating their later performance compared with white students.)[23]

On the other hand, we found preliminary evidence of predictive bias against female students at the University of Indonesia. Women, who were underrepresented in the student body, did better at the university than men with the same entrance examination scores. If this finding were confirmed, it would mean that the representation of females could be increased with a *gain* in overall performance.

But as our other examples show—and as, I believe, is evident in the case of the People's Republic of China—this result is not common. Contrary to popular belief, the usual finding is that entrance examinations of the usual sorts are *not* biased against members of various social groups, in the sense of misreporting or underpredicting their academic achievement and promise. This is an unfortunate result, because it means that we usually cannot blame the tests or the grading system for the group inequalities we observe, nor can we usually have both greater representation and greater efficiency.

On the other hand, we still may wish to give lower-scoring groups preferential treatment. It was a mistake, in the case of the admirable experiment at the University of the Philippines, for the committee evaluating the experiment to conclude automatically that because no predictive bias was found the experiment should be terminated. After assessing bias, the next question is this: To what extent do we wish to use the selection system to redress some of the group inequalities? It should not surprise us or shock us that in this policy area, as in so many others, we face a trade-off between efficiency and equity (in this case, to groups). It is a peculiar and lamentable feature of most discussions of educational policy that it is thought that efficiency and equity *must* run together.

The chapters on the Philippines and Indonesia developed new tools for examining these trade-offs. In the case of the outer-islanders applying to the ten top universities in Indonesia, our analysis showed that their numbers could be doubled (from 10 to 20 percent of those admitted) with these likely marginal costs: a 6 percent lower probability of passing and a grade point average 0.13 points lower. This means that with a 20 percent quota the differences between the lowest-scoring outer-islander admitted and the highest-scoring Javanese student rejected would be 6 percent in terms of passing the first year and 0.13 in GPA on a 4.0 scale. To many Indonesian policy-makers, these costs seemed "low," and the case for preferential treatment was strengthened. (Since that case depends on other benefits and costs, as emphasized above, this analysis is not decisive.)

Recall too the interesting findings concerning affirmative action for poor students at the University of the Philippines. Our analysis estimated that increasing the proportion of poor students from 33 percent of the student body to 50 percent (this being their proportion in the applicant pool) would have a marginal cost of about 0.30 in GPA.

These tools can also be used to estimate the costs of existing quotas. For example, Indonesians of Chinese extraction make up about 9 percent of the applicant pool to the top ten universities. In 1982 the government had a quota that restricted their percentage among those admitted to only 6 percent. The Chinese did much better on the entrance examinations than "Indonesian" students: the difference was about five-sixths of a standard deviation. Since only one in twelve applicants is chosen, if admissions had been done strictly on the basis of the examinations, Chinese students would have made up 30 percent of those admitted. The marginal costs of the existing policy of restricting their representation to 6 percent can be calculated in several ways: about 0.5 in GPA, about a 24 percent lower probability of passing, and about a 12.3 percent higher cost per successful graduate.

When does preferential treatment cost us a lot in forgone performance and when only a little? The answer depends on several specific features of our selection problem. The costs in forgone performance will be greater

- the greater the differences in groups' qualifications
- the less the predictive bias in qualifications against the lower-scoring group
- the higher the correlation between the qualifications and the later performance we care about
- the larger the value to us of gains in later performance
- the more selective our institution, in terms of how small a proportion of applicants we are able to accept.

Chapters 4 and 6 provided more precise mathematical ways of making the appropriate calculations of costs in terms of forgone performance. Roughly speaking, in cases such as those we have examined it seems to cost "a lot" at the margin to have preferential treatment if one group is one standard deviation lower on the criterion for selection than another group and only one in ten applicants in the combined pool can be accepted. But it seems to cost only "a little" if the lower-scoring group is only one-third of a standard deviation behind and the institution accepts one of every two applicants. (The final assessment of the magnitude of "costs" is a value judgment that depends on the institution's utility function; and even if preferential treatment costs "a lot" in terms of forgone performance, it may be worthwhile for other reasons, and conversely.)

A corollary emerges about the "right" size of a quota or the "optimal extent" of preferential treatment. We have seen that the costs in terms of efficiency of a quota of a given size or a given degree of preferential treatment depend on a host of specific features of the applicant pool and the institutional context. So as applicant pools vary or institutions differ, affirmative action will have different costs. Thus, in theory, from year to year within a given institution or across different institutions, to have a constant degree of preferential treatment will not lead to the same results. A fixed quota or degree of preference is not, in this sense, an optimal policy over time or across institutions. Put another way, even given identical values regarding the benefits and costs of preferential treatment, there is no one "correct" percentage quota or weight that holds for all contexts, circumstances, and institutions.

This is a theoretical point, but it has a practical side. As legal scholar Marc Galanter observes in his monumental study of preferential treatment in India,

> In the delicate task of balancing the merit principle with other interests, a flat percentage limitation on the extent of reservations is of less use than it might appear. . . . The size of a reservation is not necessarily directly related to the amount of distortion of the merit principle in a given competition. . . . The real impact of a scheme on the chances of others and on the merit principle cannot be known from the percentage of places reserved.[24]

Galanter documents the failure of the Indian courts to come up with even a rough system for empirically assessing the "real impact" of different degrees of preferential treatment, even in the narrow domain of forgone academic or administrative performance. In this context, a framework like that proposed in this book might be helpful. What we have discussed is a start to the problem of balancing efficiency and representation. In the case of the elaborate Indian system of preferences for Untouchables and members of Scheduled Tribes, our framework might help policy-makers, in the words of an Indian Supreme Court decision regarding preferential treatment in government hiring, "to strike a reasonable balance between the claims of backward classes and the claims of other employees as well as the important consideration of the efficiency of administration."[25]

**TABLE 26. Checklist for Calculating the Benefits and Costs
of Representation**

1. Calculate the academic costs of additional representation.
   a. Obtain the distributions of predictors for each group.
   b. Calculate prediction equations for criteria you care about for each group separately. (Notice that this adjusts for over- or underprediction by group.)
   c. Define what percentage of the combined applicant pool you can accept.
   d. For various proportions of each group in your student body, use a, b, and c to calculate differences in the predicted criterion for the marginal admit in each group.
   e. Evaluate the predicted criterion in terms of your utility function.
   f. Graph the marginal costs against the proportion of each group's representation in the student body.
   g. Consider qualitatively any ecological costs—for example, costs arising from disproportionate numbers of the bottom of the class being from one or another group.
2. Consider the benefits of additional representation.
   a. For different proportions of group representation, calculate how much better it is if you replace one non-group member with a group member. The benefits may be to students' educations, their later-life success, the contributions you thereby make to a just or mobile or stable society, or the satisfaction of your constituencies. The result is your marginal benefit function.
   b. Alternatively, looking at the marginal cost curve, ask yourself how much you are willing to give up in terms of that criterion for one additional group member.
3. Calculate optimal representation for you. Notice that the answer depends on what percentage of the applicant pool you select, the group distributions of predictors, and the equation relating predictors to your criterion. It also depends, of course, on your utility function for the criterion and for group representation.

In my limited experience working with policy-makers on problems of preferential treatment and affirmative action, I have seen that it can be a breakthrough to work together through even tentative estimates of the costs and benefits of group representation. The level of discussion improves when people work through frameworks like that given in table 26. At the least, simple mistakes can be avoided—for example, presuming that group differences imply biased measurements or that if predictions are unbiased it means that we should not give preference to lower-scoring groups.

THE INCENTIVE EFFECTS OF SELECTION POLICIES

There is a third dimension to the problem of making merit work. Beyond the static efficiency of selection and apart from questions of the representation of groups are the incentives that selection policies create. In many contexts, this can be the most important aspect of the policy problem.

Take, for example, the case of designing a national policy for university admissions. Suppose 5 percent of the relevant age-group goes to university, but 40 percent go to secondary school and most of that 40 percent wish they could continue their schooling. The choice of admissions policies affects the quality of the 5 percent (the one in eight secondary school students) who are selected for university; this is the dimension of static efficiency. It also affects the proportions of various groups among those selected; this is the dimension of representation. But selection policies create powerful incentives for the secondary school students who are *not* chosen. Their curricula will be shaped by what the universities deem valuable: if lots of science, students will study science courses; if Islamic ideology, then that; or if vocational skills, then the secondary schools will tend to give courses in those areas. The results may be fine for the few who will go on to college, but they will be of decidedly less use for the majority of students who will not.

This problem was faced by universities in the United States at the turn of the century, when about 5 percent of the age cohort went to college. Secondary school curricula were being driven in unhealthy ways by excessively "academic" and "irrelevant" admissions requirements to colleges, such as stiff exams in Greek and Latin and a dozen other subjects. The president of Harvard University lamented the faulty "articulation" between selection criteria and high-school curricula: "The secondary schools of the United States, taken as a whole, do not exist for the purpose of preparing boys and girls for college. Only an insignificant percentage of the graduates of these schools go to college or scientific schools."[26] Consequently, as the president of Columbia University wrote in 1898, "the relation usually existing hitherto between secondary school and college must be reversed; instead of the secondary-school program having to conform to college entrance requirements, college entrance requirements must be brought into harmony with secondary school programs."[27] As a result of this problem, a national entrance examination was born, which gave emphasis to "aptitude" for higher studies and less weight to "achievement" in particular subject areas. The result was that secondary schools could feel free to teach subjects relevant to the vast majority of students who would not go on to universities, without worrying that thereby the prospects of the college-bound students on the entrance examination would be damaged. The confining incentives created by the former university selection systems were removed.

A second sort of incentive created by the choice of selection policies concerns students at previous levels of the educational system. They will tend to undertake the sorts of activities rewarded by college admission. What they study, how they study it, and how hard they work—all these will be shaped not only by the kinds of entrance examinations but also by the weights given in admission to other criteria such as high-school grades, political activities, family background factors, extracurricular achievements, and so forth. The Chinese case provides an excellent illustration of this phenomenon.

A third incentive effect pertains to those doing the selecting. If admissions criteria are vague and the process is politicized, one can anticipate opportunities for influence-peddling, abuse, and corruption. The removal of entrance examinations in China led to such abuses. In the case of the University of the Philippines, we saw a classic case of "discretion," first introduced for entirely reasonable and laudable purposes, that snowballed into an abusive system for getting large numbers of students into the university not on the basis of their merit but on the grounds that they were well connected to important people. Thanks to an unsparing analysis of these abuses by a faculty review committee at the university, the policy of "presidential discretion" was finally removed in 1984.

In general, when an allocation system involves the combination of monopoly power, discretion, and little accountability, it will tend to breed corruption.[28] On the other hand, the effort to avoid corruption will have its own costs. Selection criteria may become more mechanical, bureaucratic, and standardized, even in the face of variation in local conditions. As Brazilian educator Anísio Teixeira pointed out, guarding against corruption can lead to unhealthy centralization, with political implications.

As with other dimensions of selection policies, then, the creation of incentives involves trade-offs. The ideal system will depend on the stage of development and the values of the society. For example, as societies become more developed and good information becomes more widespread, it is more feasible to hold institutions and individuals accountable for their choices; selection systems that involve more discretion can begin to replace those with little discretion. On the other hand, in a society where information is scarce, accountability is difficult, and corruption is widespread, the best choice may be an admittedly narrowly based and mechanical selection system that, however, is relatively immune to the cancerous effects of corruption. Designers of selection systems will be well advised to take these aspects of the policy problem into account.

This and other incentive effects of selection systems were analyzed in chapter 5. The treatment was necessarily less rigorous than for the dimensions of static efficiency and representation. Economists in particular are contributing useful theoretical research about the incentive-creating properties of allocation by contest and other selection systems, but their findings have remained at the qualitative level until now. We know we should watch out for incentives in the design of selection systems; we have seen some cases where these effects were of first-order importance. And yet the topic remains one where the informed judgments of local experts, rather than rigorous policy analysis, will be the main source of insight. Table 27 provides a framework that may be useful in culling and assimilating those informed judgments.

THE OTHER SIDE OF WEBER: THE BUREAUCRATIC COSTS OF RIGID, CENTRALIZED SELECTION

Although he was speaking in a different context, one can infer from the comments of Brazilian educator Anísio Teixeira some of the potential costs of a selection system that is designed to be completely free of discretion.

Why decentralize? Anísio found the deepest reason in a philosophical reflection:
"The longer I live, the more I perceive that human nature is neither good nor evil, but that it makes an enormous difference whether we confide in it or do not confide in it. Latins have preferred not to confide, and with this they have created confusion and corruption. Anglo-Saxons have preferred to confide, and they have established in the world the closest thing to a possible art of human government, the closest thing to a possible human order. From this comes my conviction—*tactically* we ought to have confidence in human nature. Moreover, it is the wisest rule, without in any way supporting Rousseauism. Now, *decentralization* is this tactical attitude of confidence, whose results always surpass our best expectations.

"Bureaucracy in Brazil is not just a fact, it is an ideology. It means above all action that is rigid, centralized, repressed, imposed from top to bottom, with the known results from any imposed order: leadership without imagination and, at the bottom, passivity, apathy, 'sullenness,' 'dullness.' . . . For me, the important thing [about an educational institution] is what I would call the university spirit: a college of people who are free, imaginative, open, studying and doing research about the problem of education in Brazil. But Brazil has no precedents for such a thing, because the university is part of the famous Brazilian 'bureaucracy.' This bureaucracy is really the most important aspect of Brazil. It is a bureaucracy like those of the Crown in the time of absolutism, like that of the Catholic Church in Rome, like that of communism."

Source: Hermes Lima, *Anísio Teixeira: Estadista da Educação* (Rio de Janeiro: Editora Civilização Brasileira, 1978), pp. 175–76, 193–94, emphasis in the original; my translation.

IMPLICATIONS FOR FURTHER RESEARCH ON UNIVERSITY ADMISSIONS

Much more research on all these questions is needed in the developing nations. Theoretical work may help to advance the analysis of static efficiency, representation, and incentives and how these three parts of the selection problem might be combined. There is great room for empirical analysis in this area. We are at a primitive stage in the assessment of the efficiency and equity of existing admissions policies.

The tools, frameworks, and examples presented here may be of use in such work, both as methods for analysis and as illustrations of the possibilities and limitations of social-scientific research about making merit work. In addition, it may be stimulating to append a list of highly tentative hypotheses for further

**TABLE 27. Incentives Created by Selection Systems:
A Checklist for Policy-Makers**

Selection policies may affect all of the following:
1. Students at prior levels of the educational system
   a. What subjects they will study and how hard
   b. How they will study them (e.g., memorization)
   c. What extracurricular activities will be pursued and to what extent
   d. Possibilities for cheating, coaching, etc.
   e. Anxiety, stress, etc.
2. Teachers and principals at prior levels
   a. What courses they will offer (e.g., freedom to evolve locally relevant curricula)
   b. Facilities they will provide (e.g., books, labs)
   c. Power relations with students
3. Those doing the selecting
   a. Who they will be
   b. Opportunities for whim, abuse, nepotism, corruption
   c. Power relations among affected parties (e.g., government officials, university staff, center/periphery)
4. Teachers at the university
   a. Pressures to lower/retain academic standards
   b. Pressures to provide counseling/remedial help
   c. What courses they will offer
5. The job market
   a. The types and economic value of various "signals" sent to future employers

---

investigation. In this spirit of provoking additional research rather than reporting well-established or even probable generalizations, here is a set of ten "stylized facts," or hypotheses about what *might* exist in various as yet unstudied examples of university selection.

Hypothesis 1: Entrance examinations will predict grades in the university with an adjusted correlation of 0.5 or higher. Adding an IQ test will raise that correlation by about 0.1. Adding high-school grades will raise the correlation by about 0.05.

Hypothesis 2: Using correlations that are not adjusted for restriction of range and unreliability of the criterion will lead some critics to underestimate the predictive power of entrance examinations.

Hypothesis 3: Unless the decision context is considered, the analysis of the *usefulness* of alternative selection criteria will be badly handled by all sides of the policy debate over selection policies.

Hypothesis 4: Entrance tests will correlate about 0.3 with family income;

therefore, using a test as the criterion for admission will lead to underrepresentation of the offspring of the poor. Members of various ethnic groups will tend to perform differently on the examinations. As a rough and suggestive figure only, it might be hypothesized that Caucasians and Orientals will tend to perform about half a standard deviation better than Latin Americans, who will in turn perform about a quarter of a standard deviation above Malays and Indonesians, who will tend to be about a quarter of a standard deviation above blacks. Women will tend to do slightly worse than men on mathematical portions, slightly better on verbal portions. There is no supposition in conveying these tentative hypotheses that these differences in performance on typical academic tests are permanent, and research concerning the existence and magnitude of the hypothesized tendencies is needed so that we can understand their causes, consequences, and cures. Given the actual group differences in average performance, the groups' proportions in the population and in the applicant pool, and the selection ratio, the tools developed in this book can be used to predict the degree of under- and overrepresentation.

Hypothesis 5: The careful analysis of entrance tests will not show much predictive bias by income level, social class, or ethnic background. Students from different groups with the same scores will tend on average to do equally well in their later studies. However, there will be evidence of predictive bias for members of different language groups on tests written in one of those languages. Entrance tests may also underpredict the later academic performance of female students.

Hypothesis 6: The representation of low-scoring groups among those admitted can often be significantly increased without incurring large costs in terms of forgone performance. (Guidelines for making more precise predictions on this score are provided above and in chapter 4.)

Hypothesis 7: Preferential treatment for low-scoring groups will lead, among those groups once admitted, to higher flunk-out rates, disproportionate representation in "easier" academic specializations, and lower grades.[29]

Hypothesis 8: The general public, and especially members of groups not receiving preferential treatment, will tend to greatly overestimate how much preference is actually being given. This phenomenon will be fed by the reluctance of authorities to publicize exactly how decisions are made and what the true degree of preference is.

Hypothesis 9: Declining academic standards in selection will lead to the greater admission of heretofore underrepresented groups but also to declining standards in the later academic evaluation of students, including the criteria for the awarding of degrees and professional certificates.

Hypothesis 10: Discussions of alternative selection policies will tend to focus on one or another dimension or aspect; trade-offs will be avoided. Indeed, discussions will tend to involve particular good or bad features of two polar policies, which have these characteristics:

	Policy A: *Measures of merit are narrow,* *short run, easy to measure and* *observe, mechanical.*	*Policy B:* *Measures of merit are broad,* *long run, difficult to measure* *and observe, discretionary.*
Efficiency	Predicts fairly well in short run, less well in long run.	In theory, more in accord with true goals and better predictions; in practice, poor predictions.
Representation	Tends to exclude poor, disadvantaged groups.	May be used to include poor, but may be used to help privileged.
Incentives	Leads to narrow students (but rigorous?); constrained schools (but disciplined?); little corruption; tends to be centralized.	Leads to broader students (but lax?); flexible schools (but wishy-washy?); corruption and abuse; decentralized.

It is evident upon reflection, but not in the heat of the usual debate, that both polar policies have attractive and unattractive aspects. The choice between them—or the choice of an intermediate or hybrid policy—will depend on value judgments. It will also depend on a host of factual questions about the effects of alternative policies on efficiency, representation, and incentives—questions that can be answered authoritatively only with knowledge of the local context and the particular institutions involved.

EXTENSIONS

> O! that estates, degrees, and offices
> Were not deriv'd corruptly, and that clear honour
> Were purchased by the merit of the wearer.
> How many then should cover that stand bare;
> How many be commanded that command;
> How much low peasantry would then be glean'd
> From the true seed of honour; and how much honour
> Pick'd from the chaff and the ruin of the times
> To be new varnish'd!
>
> —William Shakespeare
> *The Merchant of Venice*, act 2, scene 9

This passionate wish for the just allocation of scarce positions speaks of "estates" (in the sense of the three social classes having specific political powers)[30] and "offices" as well as "degrees." What do these have in common? They are all positions carrying honor and power, and they are positions that Shakespeare's character wished were allocated according to merit instead of through the ancient and disreputable means of hereditary privilege, violence, or corruption—or, as one could add in a more modern reference, instead of through the untrammeled market.

The problem of making merit work goes well beyond the domain of university degrees, and so does the applicability of the tools and frameworks developed in this book. As pointed out in chapter 2, the selection problem we have been discussing is a general one. It comes into play when markets are not allowed to allocate scarce positions and resources, as, for example, when universities do not meet their problems of excess demand simply by raising tuition.[31] Markets can be resisted for good and bad reasons. Sometimes a freely operating market will allocate efficiently, but sometimes—particularly in developing countries where information is scarce, indivisibilities frequent, buyers and sellers few, and externalities and complementarities many—markets malfunction. So we *may* prefer to allocate the scarce positions in some other way. (Then again, we may stick to the market, despite its imperfections, because the alternatives are subject to their own, more severe malfunctionings.)

Then there are certain goods that by their very nature should not be auctioned off. The Nobel prize, the soccer championship of Mexico, the title of Miss Venezuela, or awards on the regional examination in Islamic studies are examples. When it comes to the awarding of positions carrying honor and merit and prestige, simply giving them to the highest bidders does violence to the very honor being accorded. In most societies, the same goes for positions of political leadership. It is not nowadays thought proper to select members of the Chamber of Deputies or Parliament according to who offers the most to get the job—at least, not overtly to do so. Instead, the candidates should present their qualifications in the broadest sense to the people, or the party, or the king, and through a political process such as voting the scarce slots will be filled.

Societies use still other mechanisms to allocate scarce positions. Sometimes random assignment is thought the fairest. Examples include lotteries for mandatory military service or, more frivolously, for tickets to overbooked concerts by luminaries of rock music. In other cases, the rule of "first come, first served" holds. Seniority systems are an example. When the person with the longest tenure is chosen for an assignment or a promotion, it is because he or she was "first come." In the famous biannual sales that pack customers into Harrod's Department Store in London, the person at the head of the line gets the most outrageous loss leader. At the other extreme, "first come, first served" is the allocation rule in ration lines.

But there is another mechanism, besides the market and the political process and random assignment and first come, first served. This is the allocation of scarce positions or resources on some basis of the "merit" of the candidates. One example is the selection of university students. But as table 28 shows, other examples abound, and they may in the aggregate be more important than selection for higher education. A common characteristic of all these examples is that

TABLE 28. Other Examples of Making Merit Work

			Dimensions of Alternative Policies	
Example	The Problem	Efficiency	Representation	Incentives
Selecting entry-level civil servants	Set up criteria and a selection process for many young applicants	Predicting who will become the "best" civil servants (e.g., via exams and job records)	"Appropriate" shares for regions, sexes, races, perhaps political orientations	Levels and types of education and work experience; possibilities for corruption
Allocating scarce foreign exchange	Set up criteria and a selection process for many firms, state agencies, etc.	Predicting which uses of foreign exchange will have the largest social benefits (e.g., cost-benefit studies)	"Appropriate" shares for sectors, regions, activities, etc.	How applicants will spend their foreign and domestic resources; possibilities for corruption
Awarding research grants	Set up criteria and a selection process for many universities, research organizations, etc.	Predicting which proposals by which institutions will lead to the "best" findings—scientifically, practically, etc. (e.g., via peer review of "scientific merit")	"Appropriate" shares for various universities, disciplines, regions, perhaps also races and sexes of investigators	Emphasis given to various aspects of research; composition of research team; opportunities for corruption
Awarding large government contracts	Set up qualifications, specifications, and a selection process for domestic and foreign contractors	Predicting which proposals will be cost-effective in advancing the contract's objectives (e.g., via low bid, "quality of contractor," work records)	"Appropriate" shares for domestic firms, regions, type of ownership	Types of firms that enter certain fields; types of bids submitted; opportunities for corruption

we are unwilling or unable to use the market or a political process to allocate a scarce position or resource to a few of the many who have applied. Instead, we choose the few on the basis of "merit," usually vaguely defined. I have argued that we should do this taking into account three distinguishable effects: efficiency, representation, and incentives. With appropriate changes in terminology, the tools we have developed to analyze these three dimensions in the case of university admissions are also applicable to other versions of the selection problem (see table 28).

These other examples of selection policies are amenable to the kinds of analysis we have been carrying out. In each example, the question of *efficient* selection is at the heart of the matter. Many apply for the scarce position or resource. Which among them will do the job best if chosen? To answer this question, we predict future performance on the basis of things we can observe in the candidates now. We look at their past performance in similar endeavors, at the results of special contests or tests, at background variables with independent predictive power, and other information. We carry out forecasting studies and do project appraisals. How well can we predict who will do best? This is a statistical question, one whose often tricky and surprising features we have examined in this book. How useful would it be to improve our predictions of later performance, or to substitute a new selection system altogether? We have seen that the answer to this question depends on how well we can *predict* with various brands of partial and imperfect information, but it depends in addition on *value judgments* about the "utility" of various kinds of later performance and on the *context* of the particular selection problem.

The literature on developing countries contains little analysis of the efficiency of alternative policies for selecting university students, designing civil service recruitment policies, or choosing those who should receive research grants or scarce rations of foreign exchange or large government contracts. There is a vague "ideology of merit" with regard to such problems—that selection should be done by academic merit or scientific merit or lowest bid for an agreed-upon specification. But for real situations, where "quality" and "performance" are imperfectly measured and have multiple dimensions, the ideology of merit provides little operational guidance about the design of selection policies.

Matters get worse. As in the case of university admissions, these other selection problems have dimensions beyond static efficiency. In most of them, the problem of the *representation of groups* emerges at a crucial juncture. As emphasized in this book, policy-makers then face a trade-off between efficiency and representation. The answer depends on value judgments, but it also depends on such factual questions as "How much do we give up in performance to get so many more members of group X among those selected?"

Then too, we must consider the *incentives* created by alternative selection policies. A merit-based system creates various incentives among actual and potential candidates. The "prize" of being chosen leads to competition among aspirants. One question is what this does to the quality of those who actually are selected. Another is what effects it has on the later productivity of those not chosen. The answers lie beyond the domain of static efficiency.

Since the scarce positions are highly valued, applicants will be willing to pay for them, and this raises the constant threat of corruption. Some systems for allocating scarce positions by "merit" are more prone to corruption than others. In areas ranging from the awarding of contracts to promotions on the job to decisions about research grants, problems will tend to emerge that are not unlike those of "getting in through the back door" to universities in China during the Cultural Revolution, or of "presidential discretion" at the University of the Philippines. Here again, what we have learned about university admissions may help us to analyze seemingly unrelated selection problems with a common analytical core.

NOTES

Introduction

1. The word "meritocracy" was coined by British sociologist Michael Young in his classic satire *The Rise of the Meritocracy, 1940–2033* (Hammondsworth, Eng.: Penguin, 1957). Young described a society increasingly dominated by allocation and promotion by merit instead of by privilege or political allegiance or chance. This development would seem to be an advance in terms of efficiency and fairness. After all, what is more just than choosing and promoting those with merit? But even in the future, "merit" cannot be measured perfectly, and in Young's fable meritocracy leads to rigidity, dehumanization, and stratification. The story ends with the overthrow of the meritocracy in a revolution led by kindhearted women.

2. Max Weber, "Bureaucracy," in *From Max Weber: Essays in Sociology,* ed. and trans. Hans H. Gerth and C. Wright Mills (New York: Oxford University Press, 1946), p. 240.

3. Charles Elliott, assisted by Françoise de Morsier, *Patterns of Poverty in the Third World: A Study of Social and Economic Stratification* (New York: Praeger, 1975), chap. 5.

4. Dorotea Furth, "Selection and Equity: An International Viewpoint," *Comparative Education Review* 22 (June 1978): 260.

5. See, e.g., Lee J. Cronbach and G. C. Gleser, *Selection Theory and Personnel Decisions,* 2nd ed. (Urbana: University of Illinois Press, 1965); Frederic M. Lord and Melvin R. Novick, *Statistical Theories of Mental Test Scores* (Reading, Mass.: Addison-Wesley, 1968); and John E. Hunter and Frank L. Schmidt, "Fitting People to Jobs: Implications of Personnel Selection for National Productivity," in *Human Performance and Productivity,* ed. E. A. Fleishman (Hillsdale, N.J.: Erlbaum, 1982).

Chapter 1. The Policy Problems: The Case of the People's Republic of China

1. *Peking Review,* no. 26 (June 24, 1966), pp. 18–19.

2. Hans Bielenstein, *The Bureaucracy of Han Times* (New York: Cambridge University Press, 1980), chap. 6.

3. Max Weber, "The Chinese Literati," in *From Max Weber: Essays in Sociology,* ed. and trans. Hans H. Gerth and C. Wright Mills (New York: Oxford University Press, 1946), pp. 416, 423.

4. E. A. Kracke, Jr., *Civil Service in Early Sung China, 940–1067, with Particular Emphasis on the Development of Controlled Sponsorship to Foster Administrative Responsibility* (Cambridge: Harvard University Press, 1953), chap. 4. Those who failed the exams had a second chance: "The unsuccessful candidates were processed once more through facilitated examinations to yield a further gleaning of potentially useful officials" (ibid., p. 58).

5. "[The candidate in letters] wrote carefully composed papers proposing solutions to five complex problems assigned him, usually based on seeming conflicts in the text he

had studied. In addition, he composed a discussion, a poetic description, and a piece of poetry.

"The examinations in history, law, ritual, and classics, on the other hand, called for none of these original compositions. They depended entirely on the memory test passages and written elucidations, which were multiplied in number. And even the elucidations seem to have been rather routine, stressing memory more than originality" (ibid., p. 62).

6. Ibid., p. 64.

7. Karl A. Wittfogel, "Public Office in the Liao Dynasty and the Chinese Examination System," *Harvard Journal of Asiatic Studies* 10, no. 1 (1947): 28.

8. "The method of competitive examination offered a way of testing abstract reasoning powers and skills that could be formally taught, but it could not foretell how a man would meet the practical challenges that faced an official. Merit ratings attempted to measure energy, zeal, and ability in the actual performance of duties, but were almost inevitably deficient in objectivity. Sponsorship, however, gave greater emphasis to the act of appraising merit, and strengthened the incentives to perform it objectively and responsibly. Thus sponsorship seemed particularly suited to supply the deficiencies of the examination method" (Kracke, *Civil Service*, p. 195).

9. E. A. Kracke, Jr., "Family vs. Merit in Chinese Civil Service Examinations Under the Empire," *Harvard Journal of Asiatic Studies* 10, no. 2 (1947): 121.

10. James B. Parsons, "The Ming Dynasty Bureaucracy: Aspects of Bureaucratic Forces," in *Chinese Government in Ming Times: Seven Studies,* ed. Charles O. Hucker (New York: Columbia University Press, 1969), p. 223.

11. Wittfogel, "Public Office," p. 28.

12. Kracke, *Civil Service,* p. 68.

13. Weber, "The Chinese Literati," pp. 424–25, emphasis and exclamation point in the original.

14. Otto van der Sprenkel, "The Geographical Background of the Ming Civil Service," *Journal of Economic and Social History of the Orient* 4, no. 3 (1961): 302–36.

15. One can raise the possibility without endorsing it that testing in the classics may inadvertently have tested for "general intelligence." At least in England—where incidentally civil servants were often chosen on the basis of academic performance in curricula heavily saturated with Greek and Latin—some older studies suggest it. Spearman computed correlations (adjusted for measurement error) between "general intelligence" and performance in various academic subjects. "The whole thus forms a *perfectly constant Hierarchy* in the following order: Classics, French, English, and Mathematics. . . . However it may be with these or any other special facts, here would seem to lie the long-wanted general rational basis for public examinations. Instead of continuing ineffectively to protest that high marks in Greek syntax are no test as to the capacity of men to command troops or to administer provinces, we shall at last determine the precise accuracy of the various means of measuring General Intelligence" (C. Spearman, " 'General Intelligence': Objectively Determined and Measured" [1904], in *Intelligence and Ability,* 2nd ed., ed. Stephen Wiseman [Middlesex, Eng.: Penguin, 1973], pp. 57, 60; emphasis in the original).

16. Sun Yat-sen, *The Three Principles of the People* (lecture given in 1924), 4th ed., abridged from the translation by Frank W. Price (Taipei: China Publishing Co., 1982), p. 94.

17. Robert Taylor, *China's Intellectual Dilemma: Politics and University Enrolment* (Vancouver: University of British Columbia Press, 1981), p. 107.

18. In a speech, "Correct Handling of Contradictions," cited in ibid., p. 28.

19. Jan-Ingvar Löfstedt, *Chinese Educational Policy: Changes and Contradictions, 1949–79* (Atlantic Highlands, N.J.: Humanities Press, 1980), p. 70.

20. This practice was particularly common in the early years, when large enrollment

plans and limited candidate pools meant that universities or departments fell short of their allotted numbers of students (Taylor, *China's Intellectual Dilemma*, pp. 106, 87).

21. At one point the director of the prestigious Peking Steel Institute was prompted to write a public letter expressing his dismay that the use of outlines had led to a decline in the quality of the students admitted. He said many students lacked any real understanding of the principles of natural science or even Chinese grammar; they merely repeated what had been memorized (ibid., p. 93).

22. Ibid., pp. 106, 58.

23. Löfstedt, *Chinese Educational Policy,* pp. 95–98.

24. Taylor, *China's Intellectual Dilemma*, p. 168. Figures on enrollments of people from worker or peasant families in this period are not available.

25. Löfstedt, *Chinese Educational Policy,* p. 98.

26. Taylor, *China's Intellectual Dilemma*, p. 33.

27. Löfstedt, *Chinese Educational Policy,* p. 109.

28. A speech to the National People's Congress, quoted in ibid., p. 102.

29. Löfstedt, *Chinese Educational Policy,* p. 124.

30. Ibid.

31. Alexander Casella, "Recent Developments in China's University Recruitment System," *China Quarterly,* no. 62 (June 1975), p. 300; Löfstedt, *Chinese Educational Policy,* pp. 123–24.

32. Ibid., pp. 300–301.

33. Löfstedt, *Chinese Educational Policy,* p. 132.

34. Marianne Bastid, "Economic Necessity and Political Ideals in Educational Reform During the Cultural Revolution," *China Quarterly,* no. 41 (January-March 1970), pp. 21, 25.

35. *Peking Review,* no. 51 (1965), p. 5.

36. Bastid, "Economic Necessity," p. 29.

37. Foreign Broadcast Information Service (FBIS), *Daily Report* (China), July 22, 1968, p. 131.

38. Bastid, "Economic Necessity," p. 21.

39. Löfstedt, *Chinese Educational Policy,* p. 126.

40. Jan S. Prybyla, "Notes on Chinese Higher Education: 1974," *China Quarterly,* no. 62 (June 1975), pp. 271–95.

41. Ibid., p. 285.

42. Löfstedt, *Chinese Educational Policy,* p. 136.

43. *Peking Review,* no. 46 (November 11, 1977), p. 17.

44. Quoted in Suzanne Pepper, "An Interview on Changes in Chinese Education after the 'Gang of Four,'" *China Quarterly,* no. 72 (December 1977), p. 281. "Comrade Chang concluded the interview declaring that, 'of all the things the "gang of four" did, what they did in education was the worst. We must hate and criticize them for it. They have spoiled two generations'" (ibid., p. 285).

45. *Peking Review,* no. 2 (January 13, 1978), p. 15.

46. "New College Enrolment System," *Peking Review,* no. 46 (1977), p. 16.

47. For more details on changes in the educational system, see Suzanne Pepper, "Chinese Education After Mao: Two Steps Forward, Two Steps Back and Begin Again?" *China Quarterly,* no. 81 (March 1980).

48. From 1949 to 1979, enrollments in secondary schools increased by a factor of 36, while tertiary enrollments grew four-and-a-half-fold. Consequently, admissions to higher education have become much more competitive.

49. Bejung Xenhua, "New Regulations on College Enrollment," FBIS, *Daily Report,* (China) May 13, 1980. Prescreening at the local level has been tried in several provinces "with relatively good results" (ibid., p. L7).

50. U.S. Department of Education, "1979 National Unified Entrance Examinations for Institutions of Higher Learning," *Chinese Education* 12, no. 3 (1979).

51. Based on interviews with Jay Henderson, National Committee on U.S.-China Relations, and Robert Barendsen, Office of International Education, U.S. Department of Education.

52. FBIS, *Daily Report* (China), May 13, 1980, p. L4.

53. Quoted in Löfstedt, *Chinese Educational Policy,* p. 141.

54. From his speech at the opening ceremony of the first major science conference since the Cultural Revolution, March 18, 1978; quoted in *Encyclopedia of China Today,* ed. Frederic M. Kaplan, Julian M. Sobin, and Stephen Andors (New York: Harper & Row, 1979), p. 226.

55. Ibid.

56. *Chronicle of Higher Education,* June 8, 1981, p. 16.

57. U.S. Department of Education, "1979 National Unified Entrance Examinations."

58. Testing may also enable a more efficient allocation of students to slower and faster—or simply different—courses. At least, Chang Hsue-hsin and other Chinese officials now emphasize this lesson: "As a result [of the suspension of examinations during the Cultural Revolution], the level of education in any given class was not uniform. Some of the students had only been to junior middle school. This presented great difficulties for the teachers. If they taught the more advanced students, then the less advanced complained that they could not keep up. But if the teachers taught at their level, then the senior middle school students were dissatisfied" (quoted in Pepper, "An Interview," p. 281).

59. FBIS, *Daily Report* (China), May 13, 1980, p. L6. Some of these arguments are reminiscent of Confucius: "With a good student, the teacher doesn't have much to do and results are double, besides getting the student's respect. With a bad student, the teacher has to work hard and the results are only half of what is to be expected, besides getting hated by the student" (*The Wisdom of Confucius,* ed. Lin Yutang [New York: Random House, 1958], p. 249).

60. FBIS, *Daily Report* (China), May 13, 1980, p. L3. The Cultural Revolution's admissions system also entailed considerable financial costs, but comparative cost figures are not available.

61. William L. Parish, "Egalitarianism in Chinese Society," *Problems of Communism* 30, no. 1 (1981), table 7.

62. Casella, "Recent Developments," p. 301.

63. Pepper, "Chinese Education," p. 15.

64. Minority groups are admitted with lower test scores—perhaps 10 to 30 points, depending on the field and university. In 1979, proportionally fewer minorities than Hans enrolled at each additional level. See table N1.1, below.

TABLE N1.1

Level	Percentage of National Population Who Are Enrolled	Percentage of Minorities Who Are Enrolled
Primary	15.00	14.000
Secondary	6.30	4.600
Tertiary	0.15	0.065
Total	21.40	18.600

Source: Peking Review, nos. 1 and 10 (1980).

Note: These figures do not adjust for the age distributions of the two groups.

65. Students at the Beijing Foreign Language Institute—a key institution—told Dr. Jayjia Hsia that "female candidates must score higher than males to be accepted—because the institution wants a predominantly male student body, and girls receive higher mean scores than boys in foreign languages" (Personal communication from Dr. Hsia, June 16, 1982).

66. Robin Munro, "Settling Accounts with the Cultural Revolution at Beijing University, 1977–78," *China Quarterly*, no. 82 (June 1980), p. 310.

67. "Towards the end of the Manchu Dynasty, when corruption ran rampant in many branches of government, the Imperial examination system remained independent and free alike of external interference and internal corruption. This was one reason why the degrees conferred were so much honored in China" (Chiang Monlin, *Tides from the West* [Taipei: World Book Co., 1963], p. 55). Note also that by removing the power to admit from local production units and the Communist Party, the new admissions system hurt these groups and helped educators—not least the secondary school teachers, whose wares now were in demand.

68. Foreign language test scores have recently been given equal weight with the other five examinations. As a consequence, "course offerings and parental demand for excellence in foreign languages—especially English—have risen sharply" (Dr. Jayjia Hsia, Personal communication, June 16, 1982).

69. FBIS, *Daily Report* (China), May 13, 1980, p. L6.

70. See *Chronicle of Higher Education*, November 17, 1980, p. 17, and November 4, 1981, p. 21, for examples.

71. FBIS, *Daily Report* (China), May 13, 1980, p. L4. In 1979, Minister of Education Jiang Nanxieng noted a related issue: "We must not overemphasize the proportion of students who are graduating to higher levels. . . . We must not only be responsible to the advanced classes but also to the slower ones. What merits our attention at present is the situation in the slow classes. Students there often give themselves up as hopeless and drift along" (Löfstedt, *Chinese Educational Policy*, p. 154).

72. FBIS, *Daily Report* (China), May 6, 1981.

73. Richard P. Suttmeier, "Politics, Modernization and Science in China," *Problems of Communism* 30 (January-February 1981): 22–36.

74. Pepper, "Chinese Education," p. 17.

Chapter 2. Selection Policies in Developing Countries

1. Max Weber, "The Chinese Literati," in *From Max Weber: Essays in Sociology*, ed. and trans. Hans H. Gerth and C. Wright Mills (New York: Oxford University Press, 1946), pp. 416–17.

2. See, e.g., Harold Lasswell, Daniel Lerner, and C. Easton Rothwell, *The Comparative Study of Elites: An Introduction and Bibliography* (Stanford: Stanford University Press, 1952); Joel D. Aberbach, Robert D. Putnam, and Bert A. Rockman, *Bureaucrats and Politicians in Western Democracies* (Cambridge: Harvard University Press, 1981); and I. William Zartman et al., *Political Elites in Arab North Africa: Morocco, Algeria, Tunisia, Libya, and Egypt* (New York: Longman, 1982).

3. Victor Azarya, *Aristocrats Facing Change: The Fulbe in Guinea, Nigeria, and Cameroon* (Chicago: University of Chicago Press, 1978), p. 1. See also this conclusion: "With the opening of the new center to indigenous participation and control in the period of decolonization and after independence, the maintenance of a dominant position within the group's own area became closely dependent on the given group's ability to dominate, or at least be influential in, the central positions whose control passed to indigenous elements" (ibid., p. 227).

4. Many members of Pakistan's economic elite, e.g., have had little formal education.

See Gustav Papanek, *Pakistan's Development Experience II* (Cambridge: Harvard University Press), 1970.

5. Pierre L. Van den Berghe, *Power and Privilege at an African University* (London: Routledge & Kegan Paul, 1973), p. 72, cited in Irving Markovitz, *Power and Class in Africa: An Introduction to Change and Conflict in African Politics* (Englewood Cliffs, N.J.: Prentice-Hall, 1977), p. 222.

6. Rudolf P. Atcon, "The Latin American University," *Die Deutsche Universitätzeitung* 17 (February 1962): 16, cited in *Elites in Latin America*, ed. Seymour Martin Lipset and Aldo Solari (New York: Oxford University Press, 1976), p. 46.

7. Edgar O. Edwards and Michael P. Todaro, "Education and Employment in Developing Nations," in *Employment in Developing Nations*, ed. Edgar O. Edwards (New York: Columbia University Press, 1974), pp. 313–29.

8. Robert Klitgaard, "Education on the Auction Bloc: An Admissions Fable," *Change* 15, no. 2 (1983): 44–47.

9. George Psacharopoulos, *Higher Education in Developing Countries: A Cost-Benefit Analysis* (Washington, D.C.: World Bank, November 1980).

10. Ibid.

11. Ibid.

12. Ingvar Svennilson in association with Friedrich Edding and Lionel Elvin, *Targets for Education in Europe in 1970*, vol. 2 of *Policy Conference on Economic Growth and Investment in Education* (Paris: OECD, 1962). See also Frederick Harbison and Charles A. Myers, *Education, Manpower, and Economic Growth: Strategies of Human Resource Development* (New York: McGraw-Hill, 1964), chap. 3, where the correlation between GNP per capita and a measure of enrollment in higher education was 0.735.

13. Psacharopoulos, *Higher Education*.

14. Ibid.

15. Michael Nacht, "Internal Change and Regime Stability," in *Third World Conflict and International Security* (London: International Institute for Strategic Studies, Summer 1981), pp. 52–58.

16. Julius K. Nyerere, "The Intellectual Needs Society," in *Freedom and Development: A Selection from Writings and Speeches 1968–1973* (London: Oxford University Press, 1964), p. 23.

17. Julius K. Nyerere, "The Rule of Universities," in *Freedom and Socialism: A Selection from Writings and Speeches 1957–1967* (Dar es Salaam: Oxford University Press, 1968), p. 181.

18. Alan H. Goldman derives the idea of the right of the most qualified job-seeker (or applicant) to the job (*Justice and Reverse Discrimination* [Princeton: Princeton University Press, 1979]).

19. See the discussion in Robert A. Dahl, *After the Revolution? Authority in a Good Society* (New Haven: Yale University Press, 1970), pp. 40–58.

20. Robert M. Spaulding, Jr., *Imperial Japan's Higher Civil Service Examinations* (Princeton: Princeton University Press, 1967), p. 323.

21. Sebastian Piñera and Marcelo Selowsky, "The Optimal Ability-Education Mix and the Misallocation of Resources within Education Magnitude for Developing Countries," *Journal of Development Economics* 8 (1981): 111–31; Marcelo Selowsky, "Women's Access to Schooling and the Value Added of the Educational System: An Application to Higher Education," in *Women and Poverty in the Third World*, ed. Mayra Buvinić, Margaret A. Lycette, and William Paul McGreevey (Baltimore: Johns Hopkins University Press, 1983), esp. pp. 177–79.

22. Dorotea Furth, "Selection and Equity: An International Viewpoint," *Comparative Education Review* 22 (June 1978): 260.

23. Spaulding, *Imperial Japan's Higher Civil Service Examination*, p. 324.

24. Ibid., pp. 300–305.

25. Charles Elliott, assisted by Françoise de Morsier, *Patterns of Poverty in the Third World* (New York: Praeger, 1975), p. 261.

26. The corresponding figures were 36 females for every 100 males in higher education in Africa, 41 in the Middle East, 34 in South Asia, 57 in the Far East, and 77 in Latin America (Ruth Leger Sivard, *Women: A World Survey* [New York: Rockefeller and Ford Foundations and the Carnegie Corporation, 1985]).

27. Selowsky, "Women's Access to Schooling," provides a step in the right direction.

28. Elliott, *Patterns*, esp. table 9-10; see also Seth Spaulding and Arka Kargorian, "Democratization of Higher Education through New Admissions Strategies: A Comparative Study of Theory and Practice," UNESCO ED-81/WS/4, February 1981.

29. Elliott, *Patterns*, p. 253.

30. Color categories were white (54 percent of the population), brown or "parda" (39 percent), black or "preta" (6 percent), and yellow (1 percent).

31. Robert Klitgaard, "Institutionalized Racism: An Analytical Approach," *Journal of Peace Research* 9, no. 1 (1972): 41–49.

32. FBIS, *Daily Report* (China), May 15, 1980, p. L6.

33. *Report on Secondary Education* (Lahore, Pakistan: Board of Secondary Education, 1956), p. 19.

34. David Riesman, "Educational Reform at Harvard College: Meritocracy and Its Adversaries," in Seymour Martin Lipset and David Riesman, *Education and Politics at Harvard* (New York: McGraw-Hill, 1975), p. 392.

35. E.g., Robert Klitgaard, "On the Economics of Indonesian Economics" (Jakarta: Ford Foundation, 1978).

36. Derek Bok, David Bell, Harvey Brooks, Edward Keenan, Robert Klitgaard, Dwight Perkins, and Francis X. Sutton (consultant), *Possible Courses for Development of the Aga Khan University* (Cambridge: Harvard University, October 1983), esp. part 3.

37. Psacharopoulos, *Higher Education*, pp. 58–59.

38. Douglas M. Windham, *The Benefits and Financing of American Higher Education: Theory, Research, and Policy*, No. 80-A19 (Stanford: Institute for Research on Educational Finance and Governance, Stanford University, November 1980), pp. 5–6.

Chapter 3. The Efficiency of Selection

1. Robert Klitgaard, *Choosing Elites* (New York: Basic Books, 1985), chaps. 6, 7.

2. W. D. Furneaux, *The Chosen Few: An Examination of Some Aspects of University Selection in Britain* (London: Oxford University Press, 1961), pp. 94–95.

3. H. C. Taylor and J. T. Russell, "The Relationship of Validity Coefficients to the Practical Effectiveness of Tests in Selection: Discussion and Tables," *Journal of Applied Psychology* 23 (1939): 565–78; C. W. Brown and E. E. Ghiselli, "Per Cent Increase in Proficiency Resulting from the Use of Selective Devices," *Journal of Applied Psychology* 37 (1953): 341–44.

Chapter 4. Representation and Bias: The Case of the Philippines

1. Quoted in Program Development Staff, *Democratization of Admissions* (Office of the President, University of the Philippines, March 1977), p. 4.

2. World Bank, *World Development Report 1983* (New York: Oxford University Press, 1983), table 25. Other sources give slightly different numbers:

	CIA	U.S. State Dept.	UNESCO
Philippines	83	88	83
Indonesia	60	64	57
Pakistan	24	24	21
People's Republic of China	75	"over 75"	NA

Sources in the above table are as follows: CIA = Central Intelligence Agency, *The World Fact Book Nineteen Hundred and Eighty-three* (Washington, D.C.: Central Intelligence Agency, 1983); U.S. State Dept. = U.S. Department of State, Bureau of Public Affairs, *Background Notes* (Washington, D.C.: Department of State, 1983 [Philippines, Indonesia, China] and 1981 [Pakistan]); UNESCO = *Statistical Yearbook,* 1983 (Paris: UNESCO, 1983). The UNESCO estimates are based on older data: the Philippines, 1970; Indonesia, 1971; Pakistan, 1972. No estimates were given by UNESCO for the People's Republic of China.

3. Richard Lynn, "Ethnic and Racial Differences in Intelligence: International Comparisons," in *Human Variation: The Biopsychology of Age, Race, and Sex,* ed. R. Travis Osborne, Clyde E. Noble, and Nathaniel Weyl (New York: Academic Press, 1978); Arthur R. Jensen and Cecil R. Reynolds, "Race, Social Class, and Ability Patterns on the WISC-R," *Personality and Individual Differences* 3 (1982): 423–38.

4. Robert E. Klitgaard and George R. Hall, "Are There Unusually Effective Schools?" *Journal of Human Resources* 10, no. 1 (Winter 1975): 90–106.

5. Robert Klitgaard, Sadequa Dadabhoy, and Simin Litkouhi, "Regression Without a Model," *Policy Sciences* 13, no. 1 (1981): 99–115; see also John Simmons and Leigh Alexander, "Factors Which Promote School Achievement in Developing Countries: A Review of the Research," in Simmons et al., *The Education Dilemma: Policy Issues for Developing Countries in the 1980's* (London: Pergamon Press, 1979).

6. Stephen P. Heyneman, with William A. Loxley, "The Effect of Primary School Quality on Academic Achievement Across 29 High and Low Income Countries," *American Journal of Sociology* 88, no. 6 (May 1983): 1162–94.

7. See, e.g., Christopher Jencks et al., *Inequality: A Reassessment of the Effect of Family and Schooling in America* (New York: Basic Books, 1972), Appendix A; Bernard D. Davis and Patricia Flaherty, eds., *Human Diversity: Its Causes and Social Significance* (Cambridge, Mass.: Ballinger, 1976), pp. 97–241; and L. J. Eaves, "Inferring the Causes of Human Variation," *Journal of the Royal Statistical Society,* Series A, vol. 140, pt. 3 (1977): 324–55.

8. Bruce C. Eckland, "Social Class Structure and the Genetic Basis of Intelligence," in *Intelligence: Genetic and Environmental Influences,* ed. Robert Cancro (New York: Grune & Stratton, 1971).

9. "Report of the PDS Study Team on University Admission" (University of the Philippines, May 19, 1982, Mimeographed), p. 3.

10. It is not clear from the study, but this may be the ratio of completers to completers plus those who dropped out for academic reasons. In other words, it is not clear whether these percentages exclude those who drop out even in academic good standing.

11. Based on unpublished statistical background papers by the Research Subcommittee on Freshman Admission, University of the Philippines (1983). The definition of the regions changed over time. Metropolitan Manila now includes several municipalities that used to belong to the Southern Tagalog region.

12. Program Development Staff, *Democratization of Admissions,* p. 12. In 1976 about three-quarters of the applicants were from families with annual incomes less than P20,000, but this group made up only 58 percent of those actually admitted. Based on these data, I calculate that the difference in average test scores between students whose

families had less than P20,000 annual incomes and those whose families had greater than P20,000 annual incomes was about two-thirds of a standard deviation in 1976.

13. Presumably, students who did take these tests, or did apply to the University of the Philippines, were better prepared academically than those who did not take it. In other words, there is self-selection that is positively correlated with the expected test score. Students from Manila are disproportionately likely to apply to the University of the Philippines, compared with those not from Manila. One can infer that if we had a census of all the students of the relevant age-groups, the differences between those from Manila and those not from Manila would be larger than those we have observed.

14. P. Richards and M. Leonor, *Education and Income Distribution in Asia* (London: Croom Helm, 1981), pp. 93, 95.

15. Cecil R. Reynolds suggests a slightly different method: "In this procedure, a multiple regression equation for the prediction of performance on the criterion variable is determined using all independent variables with a single collapsed group of subjects. Using this equation based on the total sample, the investigator predicts criterion scores and calculates a residual score ($\hat{Y}_i - Y_i$) for each individual. Standardized residual scores are then examined by ANOVA with group membership as a main effect to determine if there are any mean differences in errors of prediction as a function of group membership. . . . The direct examination of residuals is also more readily interpretable to nonstatistical audiences" ("Methods for Detecting Constructed and Predictive Bias," in *Handbook of Methods for Detecting Test Bias*, ed. Ronald A. Berk [Baltimore: Johns Hopkins University Press, 1982], p. 222).

16. Recall that CGPA at U.P. is scaled in such a way that lower CGPAs represent better performance (most universities proceed in the opposite fashion).

17. To see this point, return again to the example of weighing children from poor and rich families. Suppose one used the weights themselves as a dependent variable in a regression equation and the right-hand side had variables like income, region, and so forth. Suppose there were in fact systematic differences across income groups and regions in the weight of children; in this case, we would expect the regression coefficients on those variables to show up as significant. But this would not imply that the measuring scale of weight was biased. It would mean that if we used weight in selecting children, this criterion would lead to adverse impact by those groups. But it does not show that the measurement of weight itself is biased in the sense we wish to determine.

18. One of the statistical background papers for the subcommittee noted that the income data for the 1982 UPCAT sample were unbelievably low, and it concluded: "In all probability, as a consequence of the publicity on the Democratization of Admissions, which may have given U.P.C.A.T. applicants the impression that only lower-income students will be admitted into the University, U.P.C.A.T. applicants have become accustomed to lying about their annual family income."

19. Arthur Jensen, *Bias in Mental Testing* (New York: Free Press, 1980); and the various articles in *Handbook of Methods*, ed. Berk.

20. If the old predicted grade (call it UPG) predicted the four-year CGPA without bias, the coefficient would equal 1.0: a one-unit increase in UPG would lead to a one-unit increase in four-year CGPA. In fact, however, the regression coefficient on UPG is 0.91, with a constant term of 0.22. For students admitted with predicted grades below the 2.5 approximate cutoff, the equation tends to overestimate their true performance: the students did slightly worse in grade point average than they were expected to based on the 1973 equation.

21. Eleanor C. Folke-Olsen, "An Academic Profile of the Experimental Democratization Students 1977–1982" (University of the Philippines, n.d. [1983?], Mimeographed), p. 9.

22. For other statistical reasons, too, it is difficult to say whether the slopes of the two

equations are really different. With so restricted a range on UPG, that predictor is very unreliable, and disattenuation could radically increase the slope. It is perilous to extrapolate the two lines beyond the bounds of their respective data sets, which must be done to make the comparisons I have been attempting. For our purposes, what matters is that there is no evidence that the XDS students did *better* than their test scores and high-school grades would have predicted.

23. Robert Linn, "Ability Testing: Individual Differences, Prediction and Differential Prediction," in *Ability Testing: Uses, Consequences, and Controversies,* Report of the Committee on Ability Testing, National Research Council, vol. 2, ed. Alexandra K. Wigdor and Wendell R. Garner (Washington, D.C.: National Academy Press, 1982).

24. Robert Klitgaard, *Choosing Elites* (New York: Basic Books, 1985), chap. 8.

25. See the papers in *Handbook of Methods,* ed. Berk.

26. There are, of course, legal and moral arguments relevant to the question of the preferential treatment of groups. My point is not to shortchange these other dimensions, but rather to present a technique for analyzing the efficiency costs of greater group representation.

27. In 1983, some 47.6 percent of U.P. applicants were from families with incomes less than P30,000, and 52.4 percent were from families with incomes above P30,000. The university accepted 19 percent of all applicants, and among those selected, 32.6 percent were from families with incomes less than P30,000. (Source: Computer printouts in the U.P. Registrar's Office.)

28. If one does not know the standard deviation of the combined sample, it can be calculated from the standard deviations of the two (or more) groups. The basic idea is that the variance of the combined sample σ_T^2 is equal to the sum of the variance within groups and the variance between groups:

$$\sigma_T^2 = \underbrace{p(\mu_A - \mu_T)^2 + (1 - p)(\mu_B - \mu_T)^2}_{\text{variance between groups}} + \underbrace{p\sigma_A^2 + (1 - p)\sigma_B^2}_{\text{variance within groups}}$$

where p is the proportion in the sample from group A, μ_A is the mean of group A, and so forth. If the two groups have equal standard deviations ($\sigma_A^2 = \sigma_B^2$) and the two group means differ by k standard deviations ($\mu_A - \mu_B = k\sigma$), this formula simplifies to:

$$\sigma_T^2 = [1 + k^2 p(1 - p)]\sigma^2$$

In our hypothetical but realistic example, $k = 0.5$, $p = 0.5$, and $1-p = 0.5$, so $\sigma_T^2 = 1.0625 \, \sigma^2$. The standard deviation σ_T is $1.031 \, \sigma$. If the two groups' means differed by one standard deviation, σ_T would be $1.118 \, \sigma$.

29. The calculations behind this figure appear in table N4.1:

TABLE N4.1

Proportion of Student Body Who Are PF	Students from Poorer Families (PF) (50% of Applicants)			Students from Richer Families (RF) (50% of Applicants)			
	Cut Score in:		Proportion of PF Admitted	Cut Score in:		Proportion of RF Admitted	Marginal Cost in σ_T
	σ_T	σ_{PF}		σ_T	σ_{RF}		
0.33	0.840	1.11	0.13	0.840	0.62	0.27	0
0.35	0.805	1.08	0.14	0.863	0.64	0.26	0.058
0.40	0.728	1.00	0.16	0.931	0.71	0.24	0.203
0.45	0.640	0.91	0.18	0.990	0.77	0.22	0.350
0.50	0.572	0.84	0.20	1.057	0.84	0.20	0.485
0.55	0.504	0.77	0.22	1.125	0.91	0.18	0.621

30. Assuming the reliability of these GPAs is 0.7, then $0.6/\sqrt{0.7} = 0.72$ and $0.5/\sqrt{0.7} = 0.69$. I do not adjust for restriction of range for reasons of simplicity: the calculation would turn out slightly differently for each proportion of poorer students admitted (the new σ of the selected group would change). By not correcting for restriction of range, I have slightly underestimated the marginal costs of representation.

31. With a common cut score for both groups, the *marginal* cost will be zero, but there still will be a difference in the *average* scores of those above the cutoff in each group.

32. One must remember to keep calculations in terms of the mean and standard deviation of the combined applicant pool. A 40 percent quota means that the probability of a poor student's being admitted is 0.16, compared with 0.24 for a rich student (see table N2). The formula $\mu_A + \sigma_A (\phi_A/\pi_A)$, translated into units of the combined applicant pool μ_T *and* σ_T, becomes

$$\frac{\mu_A - \mu_T}{1.031} + \frac{\sigma_A}{1.031}(\phi_A/\pi_A).$$

The calculations for a 40 percent quota are:

$$\mu_{\underline{PF}}: \frac{-0.25}{1.031} + \frac{\sigma_{PF}}{1.031}(0.242/0.16) = 1.225$$

$$\mu_{\underline{RF}}: \frac{0.25}{1.031} + \frac{\sigma_{RF}}{1.031}(0.311/0.24) = 1.499$$

And for a 50 percent quota, $\mu_{PF} = 1.115$ and $\mu_{RF} = 1.6$.

Chapter 5. The Incentives Created by Selection Policies

1. Humaira Akhtar, Azizeh Currimbhoy, Robert E. Klitgaard, and Sayeed A. Shaikh, "Can We Afford a Half-time University?" Discussion Paper No. 15 (Applied Economics Research Centre, University of Karachi, December 1976).

2. Wilson Farrand of Neward Academy, writing in 1895, quoted in Harold S. Wechsler, *The Qualified Student: A History of Selective College Admission in America* (New York: John Wiley & Sons, 1977), p. 88.

3. Nicholas Murray Butler, quoted in ibid., p. 87.

4. Charles W. Eliot, writing in 1892, quoted in ibid., p. 84.

5. Ibid., p. 104. Wechsler goes on to note that "many reputable colleges accepted considerable amounts of vocational work toward college admission . . . that efforts to facilitate the selective function were being abused . . ." (p. 105).

6. From the letter written by graduating members of the Peking No. 1 Girls' Middle School in 1966, *Peking Review*, no. 26 (June 24, 1966), p. 19.

7. Jan S. Prybyla, "Notes on Chinese Education 1974," *China Quarterly*, no. 62 (June 1975), p. 389.

8. Speaking in about 500 B.C., Confucius shows a remarkably jaundiced (and modern?) view of the shortcomings of teachers: "The teachers of today just go on repeating things in a rigamarole fashion, annoy the students with constant questions, and repeat the same things over and over again. They do not try to find out what the students' natural inclinations are, so that the students are forced to pretend to like their studies, nor do they try to bring out the best in their talents. What they give to the students is wrong in the first place and what they expect of the students is just as wrong. As a result, the students hide their favorite readings and hate their teachers, are exasperated at the difficulty of their studies and do not know what good it does them. Although they go through the regular course of instruction, they are quick to leave it when they are through. This is the reason for the failure of education today" (*The Wisdom of Confucius*, ed. and trans. Lin Yutang [New York: Modern Library, 1938], p. 246).

9. Robin Munro, "Settling Accounts with the Cultural Revolution at Beijing University 1977–78," *China Quarterly*, no. 82 (June 1980), p. 310.

10. E. A. Kracke, Jr., *Civil Service in Early Sung China, 960–1067, with Particular Emphasis on the Development of Controlled Sponsorship to Foster Administrative Responsibility* (Cambridge: Harvard University Press, 1953), chaps. 10, 12.

11. "Report of the PDS Study Team on University Admission" (University of the Philippines, May 19, 1982, Mimeographed), p. 10.

12. Ibid., p. 11.

13. Ibid., p. 16.

14. Ibid., pp. 18–19. The report contains no analysis of under- or overprediction.

15. Ibid., p. 20.

16. A. Michael Spence, *Market Signaling: Informational Transfer in Hiring and Related Screening Processes* (Cambridge: Harvard University Press, 1974), p. 80.

17. Randall Collins, *The Credential Society: A Historical Sociology of Education and Stratification* (New York: Academic Press, 1979).

18. Joseph E. Stiglitz, "The Theory of 'Screening,' Education and the Distribution of Income," *American Economic Review* 65, no. 3 (1975): 298. See also Kenneth Wolpin, "Education and Screening," *American Economic Review* 67, no. 5 (1977): esp. 952–53.

19. M. Boissiere, J. B. Knight, and R. H. Sabot, "Earnings, Schooling, Ability and Cognitive Skills" (World Bank, April 1984), p. 31.

20. John G. Riley, "Testing the Educational Screening Hypothesis," *Journal of Political Economy* 87, no. 5, part 2 (1979): S227–S252.

21. Mary O'Keeffe, W. Kip Viscusi, and Richard J. Zeckhauser, "Economic Contests: Comparative Reward Schemes," *Journal of Labor Economics* 2, no. 1 (Winter 1984): 48.

22. The achievement/aptitude distinction is a cloudy one. Though a rigid line cannot be drawn between "performance to date" and "potential for the future," selection systems must struggle with both ideas, worrying especially about incentive effects. F. F. Ridley comments on the parallel struggle in selection systems for civil service: "What *balance is drawn between assessment of competence in present work and predictions about ability to perform well at a higher level?* The British civil service was long organized on the basis of classes recruited at different educational levels, on the assumption that there were such qualitative differences in the work involved that they required different intellectual capacities. The dangers inherent in promotion on the basis of present competence are encapsulated in the 'Peter Principle', which states that this will eventually lead to the promotion of all staff to a level above their capacity. A possible solution is the *German rule* that aptitude for higher level work must be proved by a probationary period during which the official works in a higher level post but remains in the present grade" (F. F. Ridley, "Career Service: A Comparative Perspective on Civil Service Promotion," *Public Administration* 61, [Summer 1983]: 189, emphasis in the original).

23. Robert Klitgaard, *Choosing Elites* (New York: Basic Books, 1985), chap. 7.

24. A. M. Rosenthal, "Memoirs of a New China Hand," *New York Times Magazine*, July 26, 1981, p. 23.

25. Robert Klitgaard and Ruth Katz, "Overcoming Ethnic Inequalities: Lessons from Malaysia," *Journal of Policy Analysis and Management* 2, no. 3 (1983): 333–49.

26. Sunil Bastian, "University Admission and the National Question," in *Ethnicity and Social Change in Sri Lanka,* Papers presented at a seminar organized by the Social Scientists Association, December 1979 (Colombo: Karunaratne & Sons, 1984), pp. 166–78; A. Sivanandan, "Sri Lanka: Racism and the Politics of Underdevelopment," *Race & Class* 26, no. 1 (1984): pp. 21ff.; Marc Galanter, *Competing Equalities: Law and the Backward Classes in India* (Berkeley: University of California Press, 1984), esp. chaps. 4, 16.

Chapter 6. Integrating the Analysis: The Case of Indonesia

1. World Bank, *Indonesia: Development Prospects and Policy Options* (April 1981), p. vii.

2. Agency for International Development, *Indonesia: Country Development and Strategy Statement, FY 82* (January 1980), p. 18.

3. The average recurrent cost per student was about Rp. 320,000 per year; at the University of Indonesia, the figure was closer to Rp. 650,000.

4. Note that as enrollments expand and pressures mount to produce more graduates, there will also be strong incentives to lower academic standards. If this "lowering" is simply a way of making the curriculum more relevant to the needs of the nation, it is to be welcomed. But the experience of many other developing countries—from Morocco to Mexico, from Ecuador to China—shows that lowered standards may induce a dynamic of educational mediocrity, producing graduates who are not qualified to assume a leadership role in the society. Admissions policies may be able to forestall lower standards, if qualified students can be more accurately pinpointed in advance.

5. Notice that some equity arguments can be based on efficiency considerations. Take regional representativeness. If it were true that only those *from* a region would go back *to* it to work, then to meet social needs it might be desirable to admit certain proportions of students from the different regions.

6. We might want to correct some performance measures (like GPA) for their unreliability of measurement. As noted earlier, we would then divide the correlation by the square root of the reliability coefficient. In the case of graduation as a criterion, however, this adjustment does not seem helpful.

7. Two studies at the University of Andalas and Gadjah Madah University showed that only 20 percent of those who entered the universities in 1969 had graduated after ten years. Admission in 1969 was not based on the PP1 test, but it was not random either. Thus, we might tend to conclude that the probability of a random PP1 test-taker's graduating would be less than 0.2. On the other hand, graduation rates have been improving. So let us take the figure of 0.2 as an example. Let us suppose that if a person were selected at random from the PP1 test-takers (for IPA, mean = 76, standard deviation = 20.4), the person would have a 20 percent chance of graduating.

8. H. C. Taylor and J. T. Russell, "The Relationship of Validity Coefficients to the Practical Effectiveness of Tests in Selection," *Journal of Applied Psychology* 23 (1939): 565–78.

9. I *assumed* that the probability of graduating for a randomly selected student would be 0.2, but we can try other assumptions too. We might ask experts and policymakers to give their estimates, and do the calculations for these different numbers. For example, suppose the probability were as high as 0.50. Then under random selection, the cost per successful graduate is Rp. 1.83 million. With selection by a test with $r = 0.32$, the percentage graduating rises from 50 percent to 73 percent and the cost declines to Rp. 1.5 million. With selection by a test with $r = 0.50$, the graduation rate rises to 85 percent and the cost goes down to Rp. 1.4 million.

10. The original data were generously provided by E. Bonang and R. W. Matindas of that faculty. The data set came to my attention thanks to their article "Penelitian Variabel-Variabel Peramal Untuk Keberhasilan Studi di Fakultas Psikologi Universitas Indonesia" (March 3, 1982), in *Kerabat Psikologi, Universitas Indonesia 1982* (Jakarta: U.I.F. Psikologi, 1982), pp. 245–61. Their analyses do not address the question posed here, and most of the results I will report are not in their informative article.

For each student, the following information was available: scores on various tests of the Differential Aptitude Test (DAT), translated and adapted from the Psychological Corporation's (U.S.) tests; scores on the eleven tests of the Test Intelligensi Kolektip Indonesia

(TIKI), developed by a team of Indonesian and Dutch psychologists in the early 1970s (P. J. D. Drenth, B. Dengah et al., *Test Intelligensi Kolektip Indonesia: Buku Pegangan* [in English] [Vrije Universiteit Amsterdam and Universitas Padjadjaran Bandung, 1976]); sex; and grades in eight first-year psychology courses, where each course's grades had been converted to standardized scores with a mean of 10 and a standard deviation of 3. PP1 scores were also available (the IPS track, including Bahasa Indonesia, English, mathematics, and social sciences). The data therefore enable us to ask, for this small sample, whether aptitude tests would improve the prediction of first-year grades which is made on the basis of the PP1 test alone.

I will report only a few of the results here. I calculated total scores for the DAT, TIKI, first-year GPA, and PP1. I also calculated the score of the "short form" of the TIKI, namely, the first four tests. Drenth et al. showed that this short version, which can be administered in only an hour, had considerable predictive power for college performance.

11. Table N6.1, below, shows the same results from IPB.

TABLE N6.1. Correlations for 1,887 IPB Students Entering in 1976–78

High School Grade in	Correlation with First-Year GPA in IPB, All Subjects
IPA (1st year)	0.27
Math (1st)	0.29
Biology (2nd year)	0.16
Physics (2nd)	0.26
Chemistry (2nd)	0.23
Math (2nd)	0.28
Biology (3rd year)	0.18
Physics (3rd)	0.20
Chemistry (3rd)	0.24
Math (3rd)	0.24

Source: Amril Aman, Endang Sjamsudin, Bambang Sumantri, and Andi Hakim Nasoetion, "Suatu Profil Keberhasilan SMA dan Daerah Tingkat I Diukur Atas Dasar Prestasi Akademik Siswa-Siswanya di Institut Pertanian Bogor," *Buletin Penelitian Institut Pertanian Bogor* 1, no. 1 (1980): 10.

12. But notice that using only the EBTA would save all the costs of designing and administering the PP1 exam.

13. Are these results likely to hold for other faculties and other schools? Only more research can tell us for sure. But research is expensive, and it would be helpful if we could estimate how different the results are likely to be. My hunch is that *predictive relationships will not vary much across universities.* Various statistical artifacts probably explain most of the differences in the correlations we have reviewed. Since the sizes of samples vary, the correlations actually calculated will vary for purely statistical reasons. And samples will also vary in the amount of restriction of range and in the unreliability of GPA and other measures. But once we take these sources of variation into account—they mask the true, underlying relationships between predictors and outcome—there are reasons to believe that the "corrected" results will be similar across institutions and subject areas. As I say, only research can tell us this for sure, but let me give the reasons for my hypothesis:

> *Research in the United States.* In a persuasive set of recent papers, John Hunter and Frank Schmidt have shown that, once adjustments are made for the statistical artifacts just listed, aptitude tests have almost the same correlations with performance in similar jobs, regardless of geography, the particular company, and so forth (e.g.,

John E. Hunter, Frank L. Schmidt, and J. Rauschenberger, in *Perspectives on Bias in Mental Testing*, ed. C. R. Reynolds and R. T. Brown [New York: Plenum, 1984]; Frank L. Schmidt and John F. Hunter, "Development of a General Solution to the Problem of Validity Generalization," *Journal of Applied Psychology* 62 [1977]: 529–40; and Frank L. Schmidt et al., "Further Tests of the Schmidt-Hunter Validity Generalization Model," *Personnel Psychology* 32 [1979]: 257–81). In the case of academic prediction in the United States, there are variations in prediction across fields and universities, but some of that is explained by varying sample sizes, different restrictions of range, and so forth. Colleges generally find correlations of 0.3 to 0.5 between test scores and college grades. The correlations are higher in law schools and somewhat lower in business schools (Robert Klitgaard, *Choosing Elites* [New York: Basic Books, 1985], chap. 5 and app. 1).

Research in Indonesia.   The pioneering work of Drenth, Dengah, et al. in measuring intelligence in Indonesia included a validation study for nineteen faculties at eleven universities and seven IKIPs. The results appear in table N6.2, below.

TABLE N6.2. **Correlations between Intelligence Test Scores and First-Year "Propedeuse" Exam Scores for 19 Indonesian Faculties (Mid-1970s)**

	Number of Students	Correlation with Total TIKI Score
Arts (alpha) faculties		
1	29	0.22
2	38	0.36
3	29	0.66
4	39	0.41
Science (beta) faculties		
5	43	0.31
6	36	0.23
7	34	0.17
8	34	0.40
9	35	0.37
10	24	0.56
11	44	0.34
12	26	0.39
13	33	0.52
14	36	0.51
15	32	0.30
IKIP faculties		
16	34	0.50
17	35	0.39
18	35	0.42
19	30	0.47
		Median = 0.39

Source: P. J. D. Drenth, B. Dengah, et al., *Test Intelligensi Kolektip Indonesia: Buku Pegangan* (in English) (Vrije Universiteit Amsterdam and Universitas Padjadjaran Bandung, 1976).

Note: The actual date of the testing is not given, although it is mentioned that "the criterion data were collected . . . about one year after the testing had taken place" (Drenth, Dengah, et al., *Test Intelligensi,* p. 45). Eleven universities and seven IKIPs were included in the study (ibid., p. 31, has details); some were eliminated because of too few testees or "almost no variance" in the criterion (ibid., p. 46).

I calculate the median correlation as 0.39. I am impressed by the overall *stability of this coefficient across faculties;* much of the variation we observe in table N6.2 is due to the small numbers of students, around thirty per sample.

Work by Toemin A. Masoem ("Korelasi Antara Hasil Test Prestasi dan Test Kemanpuan Umum Calon Mahasiswa UI Tahun Akademi 1974" [Fakultas Ilmu Pasti dan Ilmu Alam, Jurusan Mathematik, Universitas Indonesia, 1974]) shows that another set of correlations, between entrance examination scores in 1974 and an intelligence test, are remarkably stable across U.I. faculties, with a median correlation of around 0.60. Unpublished research by Susanto Iman Rahayu of ITB suggest relatively stable correlations with medians around 0.5 to 0.6, between PP1 tests and college grades. A recent doctoral dissertation by Agustiar studies twenty-six faculties at six institutions. He finds the standardized regression coefficients (or beta weights) of scores on "high school examination" to be "an important predictor for B.A. graduates grade point average in obtaining the degree" (p. 161), with a median beta weight of about 0.30. This means a one standard deviation change in this examination score (measured among B.A. graduates) corresponds to a 0.30 standard deviation change in GPA among those graduates, after controlling for variables like sex, age, and so forth ("An Evaluation of the Efficiency and Effectiveness of Some Higher Education Institutions in Indonesia" [Ph.D. diss., School of Education, Macquarie University, Sydney, 1982], chap. 5 [quotation from p. 161]. It is never made clear in the dissertation just which "high school examination" this is, nor are correlations with other variables provided for this test). This is remarkably similar to our finding in the Science Faculty at U.I.

I conclude that further research in Indonesia, while warranted, would not greatly alter the findings presented here.

14. The estimated difference in means of 6 points probably *underestimates* the "true" difference between students from Java and outside Java. Presumably, students who take the IPA are, on average, better prepared academically than those who do not take it. In other words, there is self-selection that is positively correlated with the expected test score. Students from Java are disproportionately likely to take the test, compared with those not from Java. The difference in scores actually observed between test-takers from Java and those from outside Java will therefore underestimate the true difference. I suspect that the "true" difference in mean scores would be more like 10 points, or about half a standard deviation.

15. In the short run, at least, he would be mistaken. "Indonesian Universities: The First Generation," *Prisma*, no. 10 (September 1978), p. 62.

16. The calculation is based on an overall selection rate of 0.08 and the equation derived from U.I.'s Science Faculty, $GPA \geq 2.0 = -0.095 + 0.077\ IPA$.

17. Without the quota, suppose the average probability of graduating among those selected is 0.784; with the quota, it is 0.763. The difference is about 0.02. (This is the difference in $P(GPA \geq 2.0)$ using the results of the U.I. science data; I am presuming, unrealistically but for the sake of illustrating the methodology, that the same finding would hold for P(graduates).) As before, let us assume that the government's cost per student per year is Rp. 165,000, that a graduate takes eight years on average, and that a nongraduate takes three years. The cost per successful graduate with P(graduates) = 0.784 is Rp. 1.46 million. The cost for P(graduates) = 0.763 is Rp. 1.47 million. For 16,000 admits, we would have 12,544 graduates in the first case, versus 12,208 in the second. The cost per graduate would be 0.7 percent lower.

18. Data to test whether the admissions test was predictively biased for or against Indonesians of Chinese descent were not available.

19. The calculations are done as follows. The cut score for Chinese would be 129,

which is 1.57 standard deviations above the Chinese mean. Only 5.8 percent of Chinese applicants would be admitted. The average IPA of those admitted is $\mu + \sigma(\phi/p) = 90.7 + 24.4 (0.1163/0.058) = 139.6$. The GPA corresponding to this score is $0.38 + 0.018 (139.6) = 2.89$. The same calculation for Indonesians yields a GPA for them of 2.36. The overall average is $0.06 (2.89) + 0.94 (2.36) = 2.39$.

20. I divided the data set into a male sample and a female sample and analyzed them separately (one female observation was deleted before doing these analyses, as a suspected outlier). The resulting sample of women was small ($N = 54$), so we expect considerable sampling error. Were the regressions of GPA on IPA the same for males and females? Table N6.3, below, gives some relevant facts.

TABLE N6.3. Regressions for Males and Females at U.I.'s Faculty of Science

	R^2	R
Males ($N = 127$)		
(1) $GPA = \quad 0.57 + 0.015\ IPA$ $\qquad\quad(0.35)\quad(0.003)$	0.127	0.36
(2) $GPA = \quad 0.49 + 0.016\ IPA - 0.11\ Math - 0.11\ Phys - 0.09\ Biol$ $\qquad\quad(0.34)\quad(\underline{0.003})\qquad(0.12)\qquad\quad(0.09)\qquad\quad(0.20)$ $\qquad\qquad\qquad + 0.10\ Pharm + 0.27\ Geog$ $\qquad\qquad\qquad\ \ (0.15)\qquad\quad\ (\underline{0.12})$	0.196	0.44
(3) *Resistant Line GPA* $= 1.34 + 0.0072\ IPA$	—	—
Females ($N = 54$)		
(1) $GPA = \quad 0.05 + 0.024\ IPA$ $\qquad\quad(0.50)\quad(0.005)$	0.314	0.56
(2) $GPA = -0.38 + 0.028\ IPA - 0.01\ Math - 0.43\ Phys - 0.15\ Biol$ $\qquad\quad(0.49)\quad(\underline{0.004})\qquad(0.20)\qquad\quad(0.20)\qquad\quad(0.17)$ $\qquad\qquad\qquad - 0.16\ Pharm + 0.32\ Geog$ $\qquad\qquad\qquad\ \ (0.16)\qquad\quad\ (\underline{0.21})$	0.449	0.67
(3) *Resistant Line GPA* $= 1.92 + 0.006\ IPA$	—	—

Note: Figures in parentheses are standard errors of the coefficients. Underlining indicates statistical significance at $p < 0.005$. "Resistant line" is a fitting technique that is not affected as much as OLS by outlying observations; for details, see John W. Tukey, *Exploratory Data Analysis* (Reading, Mass.: Addison-Wesley, 1970).

Notice that equations (1) and (2) in table N6.3 look quite different, and not just in the intercept terms. The coefficients for IPA are 0.015 and 0.024 in the two equations (1); they are 0.016 and 0.028 in the two equations (2). It looks as though a certain-sized increase in IPA scores leads to a greater increase in GPA for females than for males.

But examine the two equations (3). Here the intercepts are different, but the slopes are about the same. These equations were obtained not by ordinary least squares (OLS) but through a "resistant" fitting technique that is not much affected by outliers. Scatterplots show that the two very high-scoring females were greatly affecting the OLS line. When we compare resistant lines, however, we might conclude *that the only bias was "intercept bias,"* not slope bias. This might occur if all females, regardless of the level of their particular IPA scores, did X units better than males with the same scores. (The best guess from these resistant fits is roughly the difference in the two intercept terms.)

21. Table N6.4, below, gives the data I compiled at U.I.

TABLE N6.4. First-Year Academic Performance of PP1 and PP2 Admits at the University of Indonesia (1980–81)

Department		N	% with First-Year Grade Point Average					Academic Dropout
			> 3.5	3.0–3.49	2.5–2.99	2.0–2.49	< 2.0	
Mathematics	PP1	31	3	6	42	29	19	0
	PP2	15	0	27	33	13	27	0
Physics	PP1	33	0	3	0	45	32	19
	PP2	37	0	8	27	24	39	11
Chemistry	PP1	17	12	0	18	29	24	18
	PP2	26	4	12	35	27	19	4
Biology	PP1	13	0	8	50	25	17	0
	PP2	25	4	9	34	43	9	0
Total for four depts.	PP1	94	3	4	23	33	23	10
	PP2	103	2	12	32	28	22	5

Source: Unpublished U.I. documents.

Note: This group is the first class that the University of Indonesia has ever admitted via the PP2. Two other science departments—geography and pharmacy—do not use the PP2 system of admission.

22. I recommended several studies to the Indonesian Directorate General of Higher Education. Two were the following:

(1) A sample of various high schools would be chosen, perhaps stratified along PP2/not PP2, public/private, various geographical areas, percentage of the high school's graduates who go on to higher education, and so forth. Within each school, a small sample of students and a couple of teachers would be chosen. Students would be sent questionnaires asking about their knowledge of the material covered on the entrance exams, their special efforts to prepare for the exams, the time allocated to their various high-school subjects, their self-assessed prospects of admission, and various personal and academic data. Teachers from subjects included and not included on the entrance exams would be asked about their students' efforts in class; the coachability of the entrance tests; how the form of the entrance tests affects students' willingness to learn to write well, to do lab work, and to do field work; and their estimate of the effects of using high-school grades as an additional admissions criterion.

(2) A much smaller sample, perhaps twenty students and twenty teachers, would be chosen for in-depth interviews along the same lines. In the report their answers and explanations would be woven into the questionnaire results.

23. Is the best description of the relationship between GPA and IPA really *linear*? Linearity is often assumed for convenience. As the work of Hunter and Schmidt (see note 13) makes clear, in studies of the linearity assumption in the developed countries, the assumption of linearity usually cannot be rejected. But I believe that in most cases the relationship *would be* nonlinear *if* we greatly expanded the range of observations. Consider the case at hand. Our linear regression of GPA on IPA implies that a student with an IPA score of 40 would be expected to obtain a GPA of $0.38 + 0.018(40) = 1.1$. And yet 40 is the score on the IPA that would be obtained by random guessing! (The IPA exam had 180 questions this year, but in the previous year the test taken by our sample had 200 questions. For each question, the student had a choice of five possible answers, one of which was correct. Random guessing would therefore get 1 in 5 questions right, or 40 in 200 questions. The standard deviation of the total score by guessing would be $\sqrt{npq} = 5.7$, so it would not be impossible for a student to get a 50 simply by guessing.) Do we really

believe that a person with a 40 would on average achieve a 1.1 GPA in the Faculty of Science at U.I.? To put it another way, do knowledgeable Indonesian experts believe that a typical student who obtains a 75 on the IPA would expect to earn a GPA of 1.73 in the first year in the U.I. Science Faculty? Most people would make a lower prediction.

True, all this is guesswork, since no such people have been admitted. The nonlinear relationships I hypothesize are difficult to validate in an already selected sample. The R^2 is typically low, so it is difficult to distinguish a straight line from a curved one. So it remains a question about which *statistically speaking* we must be agnostic. As *educators*, however, we may wish to opine that if we extrapolate too far outside the selected sample the relationship between grades and test scores would be much steeper than a linear regression would predict.

I recommend trying several nonlinear regressions as noted above. The one I found most attractive would predict a GPA of 0 for an IPA score of 58, and a GPA of 1.33 for an IPA of 75. Do these seem more plausible?

For practical policy-making, we will not be considering the admission of students with scores like 58 or 75 to U.I., but we might be interested in scores of 85, especially if we ask what might happen if we admitted more disadvantaged or rural or geographically remote students. Our predictions with the linear and my preferred nonlinear equation do not differ too much over this range, but by the time IPA gets down to 80, the difference starts to look more important. See table N6.5, below.

TABLE N6.5

IPA	Predicted GPA for:	
	$GPA = 0.38 + 0.018\ IPA$	$GPA = 3.29 + 11037\ (-1/IPA^2)$
95	2.09	2.07
90	2.00	1.93
85	1.91	1.76
80	1.82	1.57

My big point should not be lost in all these numbers. Try nonlinear regressions. Use the experienced judgment of educators to help you decide which regression equations make the most sense.

24. Both devices were used in the analysis of these data, although for economy's sake they will not be reported here in detail. The deletion of an apparent outlier made little difference. The "resistant line" computed by the MINITAB program was

$$GPA = 0.70 + 0.015\ IPA,$$

so the regression coefficient was not much different from the ordinary least squares line. (The predicted GPA for an IPA of 95 was 2.13; for 80 it was 1.90.) On these techniques, the reader may wish to consult Frederick Mosteller and Robert Rourke, *Sturdy Statistics* (Reading, Mass.: Addison-Wesley, 1977); Robert Klitgaard, "Identifying Exceptional Performers," *Policy Analysis* 4, no. 4 (1978): 529–47; and John W. Tukey, *Exploratory Data Analysis* (Reading, Mass.: Addison-Wesley, 1970).

25. This equation takes some account of the varying difficulties of departments, but it assumes that the relationship between changes in IPA and changes in GAP is the same across departments. The sample size was so small that checking this assumption does not seem helpful, but in general one would subdivide the data set by department and compute regression equations for each department. In this fashion, one could see whether the relationship between IPA and GPA differed across departments.

26. Muchkiar's work was unfinished in 1982; his dissertation for IKIP Bandung was to have the title "Suatu Studi Tentang Efektifitas Sistem Seleksi Calon Mahasiswa dengan Mempergunakan Prediktor Kiberhasilan Belajar di Perguruan Tinggi: Taraf Inteligensi, Prestasi Belajar di SMA dan Hasil Ujian Masuk Perguruan Tinggi."

27. For ITB, all students took the IPA version of the PP1. In the other three universities, both IPA and IPS scores are included under the variable PP1. This may explain part of the difference in the predictive power of PP1 scores in the two samples. Sampling error may also be at work.

Chapter 7. Conclusions and Extensions

1. Sun Yat-sen, *The Three Principles of the People* (lecture given 1924), 4th ed., abridged from the translation by Frank W. Price (Taipei: China Publishing Co., 1982), p. 94.

2. Max Weber, "The Chinese Literati," in *From Max Weber: Essays in Sociology,* ed. and trans. Hans Gerth and C. Wright Mills (New York: Oxford University Press, 1946), p. 423.

3. E. A. Kracke, Jr., *Civil Service in Early Sung China, 940–1067, with Particular Emphasis on the Development of Controlled Sponsorship to Foster Administrative Responsibility* (Cambridge: Harvard University Press, 1953), p. 64.

4. Ibid.

5. Karl A. Wittfogel, "Public Office in the Liao Dynasty and the Chinese Examination System," *Harvard Journal of Asiatic Studies* 10, no. 1 (1947): 28.

6. Otto van der Sprenkel, "The Geographical Background of the Ming Civil Service," *Journal of Economic and Social History of the Orient* 4, no. 3 (1961): 302–36.

7. Chang Hsue-hsin, quoted in Suzanne Pepper, "An Interview on Changes in Chinese Education after the 'Gang of Four,' " *China Quarterly,* no. 72 (December 1977), pp. 281, 285.

8. Letter to *Peking Review,* no. 26 (June 24, 1966), pp. 18–19.

9. Osvaldo Hurtado, *Political Power in Ecuador,* trans. Nick D. Mills, Jr. (Albuquerque: University of New Mexico Press, 1980), p. 252.

10. Sebastian Piñera and Marcelo Selowsky, "The Optimal Ability-Education Mix and the Misallocation of Resources within Education Magnitude for Developing Countries," *Journal of Development Economics* 8 (1981): 111–131; the estimate concerning the removal of developed-countries' tariffs for less developed countries' exports is based on Naheed Kirmani, Pierluigi Molajoni, and Thomas Mayer, "Effects of Increased Market Access on Exports of Developing Countries," *IMF Staff Papers* 31, no. 4 (1984): 661–84.

11. To make this calculation, I assume that their figure of a 5 percent gain in GNP compares "perfect selection" with "random selection," or a 1.0 correlation between predictor and outcome and a 0 correlation. From psychometric theory, we know that a correlation of 0.3 can be understood as getting 30 percent of the utility of perfect selection, compared with random selection, and a correlation of 0.5 can be understood as getting 50 percent. Thus a gain in the correlation from 0.3 to 0.5 is worth roughly 20 percent of the value of perfect selection compared with random selection. In the Piñera-Selowsky calculation, this would be 20 percent of 5 percent, or 1 percent in GNP. I hasten to add that this calculation is for illustrative purposes only, since I have misgivings about the basic model underlying their analysis (such as the association of "IQ" with the only sort of "ability" that matters, and "inherent" ability at that).

12. Quoted in Avery Russell, "Education in Zimbabwe: The Struggle between Opportunity and Resources," *Carnegie Quarterly* 39, no. 3 (1984): 7.

13. Julius K. Nyerere, "The Intellectual Needs Society," in *Freedom and Development: A Selection from Writings and Speeches 1968–1973* (London: Oxford University Press, 1968), p. 23.

14. Julius K. Nyerere, "The Role of Universities," in *Freedom and Socialism: A Selection from Writings and Speeches 1957–1967* (Dar es Salaam: Oxford University Press, 1968), p. 181.

15. This is a general point concerning the use of imperfect information in policy analysis. I have benefited from the work and example of Howard Raiffa, e.g., *Decision Analysis* (Reading, Mass.: Addison-Wesley, 1968).

16. Robert Klitgaard, *Choosing Elites* (New York: Basic Books, 1985), chap. 4.

17. The measures of university performance varied. Sometimes first-year grades were the criterion, sometimes grade averages across four years, and sometimes the marks obtained on a professional examination at the end of four years of study. For results not presented here, on the various faculties of the University of Karachi and the Dow Medical School, see Robert Klitgaard, *Data Analysis for Development* (London and Karachi: Oxford University Press, 1985), chap. 6.

18. Klitgaard, *Choosing Elites*, chap. 5 and Appendix 1. Comparisons are precarious because both tests and grades may be differently determined in different places. For example, in one university both entrance tests and university grades may depend on memorizing facts. In another, both may instead measure problem-solving skills. If the correlations between tests and later grades at both universities turned out to be the same, we should be reluctant to conclude that the systems were equally efficient.

19. Again, this is a rough calculation, based on an improvement of 0.2 in the correlation of the admissions criterion with college grades and a selection ratio of one in ten.

20. Max Weber, "Bureaucracy," in *From Max Weber*, p. 240.

21. Marc Galanter, *Competing Equalities: Law and the Backward Classes in India* (Berkeley: University of California Press, 1984).

22. The remarkable efforts of Malaysia since 1970 to advance the welfare of the Malay ethnic group through preferential treatment seems to have calmed an explosive political situation; at least, ethnic hostility is down, and democracy is still intact (Robert Klitgaard and Ruth Katz, "Overcoming Ethnic Inequalities: Lessons from Malaysia," *Journal of Policy Analysis and Management* 2, no. 3 [1983]: 333–49). On the other hand, some recent communal violence in India has been directed at the removal of reserved seats and posts for members of backward castes and tribes, and some observers of the tragic ethnic conflict in Sri Lanka attribute part of the hostility to pro-Sinhalese hiring and university admissions policies adopted in the 1970s. Sri Lankan Sunil Bastian writes that the issue of "standardizing" entrance examination scores among ethnic groups has been of immense political importance. "The question of standardisation figured prominently in the formation of the Tamil United Liberation Front. The Vadukkodai resolutions adopted at the formation of the T.U.L.F. gives an important place to the question of standardisation and university admission. It had become a key issue of communal agitation for Sinhala chauvinists and also a topic of much prominence in the mass media." (Sunil Bastian, "University Admission and the National Question," in *Ethnicity and Social Change in Sri Lanka,* Papers presented at a seminar organized by the Social Scientists Association, December 1979 [Colombo: Karunaratne & Sons, 1984], p. 167. See also Galanter, *Competing Equalities,* esp. chaps. 4 and 16; and A. Sivanandan, "Sri Lanka: Racism and the Politics of Underdevelopment," *Race & Class* 26, no. 1 [1984]: 21ff.)

23. Klitgaard, *Choosing Elites*, chap. 8.

24. Galanter, *Competing Equalities*, p. 417.

25. Ibid., p. 412. The Indian courts have made similar statements with regard to the balancing of efficiency and representation in university admissions. "Lowering the quality of graduates, says the Court, is the 'inevitable consequence of reservation.' But the need for technical, scientific, and academic personnel 'is so great that it would cause grave prejudice to national interest if considerations of merit are completely excluded by wholesale reservation of seats in all technical, medical, or engineering colleges or institu-

tions of that kind.' Thus special provisions for the backward must be within 'reasonable limits': 'the interests of the weaker sections of society which are a first charge on the States and the Centre have to be adjusted with the interests of the community as a whole" (ibid., p. 401).

26. Charles W. Eliot, writing in 1892, cited in Harold S. Wechsler, *The Qualified Student: A History of Selective College Admissions in America* (New York: John Wiley & Sons, 1977), p. 84.

27. Nicholas Murray Butler, cited in ibid., p. 87.

28. Robert Klitgaard, *Controlling Corruption* (in press), esp. chap. 3.

29. Galanter (*Competing Equalities*, p. 63) provides these conclusions from the case of the Scheduled Castes (SC) and Scheduled Tribes (ST) in India: "As one might expect, SC and ST students are concentrated in the less prestigious, less demanding, and less potentially remunerative subjects. . . . These students tend on the whole to be less well prepared than their fellows. . . . It seems that the wastage [dropout] rate among SC and ST college students is staggeringly high. For example, a survey conducted in Maharashtra found that 25% to 40% failed in their first-year exams, about 70% failed in intermediate, 10% in their junior year, and between 40% to 60% in their final exams. Only 8% received their college degrees within the prescribed four years, and about 85% left college without a degree. Those who do get through tend to get low grades."

30. Formerly, the first estate was the clergy, the second estate was the nobility, and the third estate was the commons, or bourgeoisie. "Estate" also has the meaning of social status or rank.

31. Many writers on higher education policies in developing nations have called for higher tuition fees (see, e.g., Edgar O. Edwards and Michael Todaro, "Education and Employment in Developing Nations," in *Employment in Developing Nations*, ed. Edgar O. Edwards [New York: Oxford University Press, 1974], pp. 313–29). As noted above in chapter 2, typically the state subsidizes 90 percent or more of the cost of tertiary education. Moreover, a disproportionate number of the beneficiaries of this subsidy come from the middle and upper classes, so that the effect of the subsidy is regressive. The same finding holds, in a less exaggerated form, in the United States. And yet for political reasons it has proved difficult to reduce the subsidies, even in rich countries like the United States (witness the extraordinary opposition to the Reagan administration's plan to reduce subsidies in college loan programs to students from middle- and upper-class families, even though such aid had more than quadrupled since 1976). Similar political factors, involving the middle class (and upper class) protecting its own interest, have been cited to explain the continuation in most developing countries of inefficient and inequitable subsidies for all university students.

But an ideological, symbolic point is also important in this regard. Prior to independence or before modernization, higher education was the preserve of the elite and a springboard into the colonialists' or the modernizers' world. This access is therefore emblematic of the opportunity to obtain power, to be "first class" by international standards, and the idea that the state should do anything but virtually give this opportunity away smacks of restriction, neocolonialism, or worse. Many European countries have a similar aversion to the use of the market mechanism in higher education: if you are good enough to be "qualified" for the university, you have the "right" to attend, at the state's expense.

One final aside: the same ideological, symbolic aspect of university admission may explain why preferential treatment and quotas in this domain often cause a political furor. An analyst may point out that the state carries out many "preferential" policies in its development programs, where efforts are targeted at uplifting backward groups, who may (this is not always true) receive a disproportionate share of public spending. The public may support such redistributive policies. But the public may oppose preferential treatment in university admissions and in hiring. The analyst may wonder what is different between preferentially allocating limited slots at the university and preferentially allocating a limited public budget. The answer has to do with the ideological, symbolic content of access and opportunity that these selection policies convey.

INDEX

affirmative action, 5, 25, 95, 148, 150
Africa, 34, 36, 43–44, 47
Agency for International Development, 110
Algeria, 49
allocation systems, 1, 2, 6, 105, 135, 156–57, 182n.31; and corruption, 8, 152, 160; nonmarket, 35–36. *See also* economics; efficiency
analysis, policy, 58–69, 127–29, 138, 140–45, 153; checklists for, 6, 144; integrating of, 6, 110–34; limitations of, 6, 8, 114, 129, 145, 153; techniques of, 5, 51, 95, 110, 144–45; tools of, 5, 6, 7, 51, 75, 95, 129, 153, 159; value judgments in, 48–52, 65, 67, 93, 95, 141, 145, 146, 149, 156, 159. *See also* efficiency; incentives; representation
aptitude, scholastic, 72–75, 80, 98, 107, 117, 127, 174n.13. *See also* tests

Bandung: Institute of Technology at (ITB), 117, 134; Teacher Training Institute at, 114. *See also* Indonesia
bias, 70, 135, 146; and prediction, 80–88, 93, 147, 155; and representation, 10, 137; sexual, 87, 124–25, 128, 147, 165n.65, 177n.20; techniques for assessing, 5, 80–86; in tests, 74, 113, 118, 136; vs. underrepresentation, 5, 42
Bogor: Agricultural Institute at (IPB), 117; 125, 126
Bok, Derek, 47
Burkina Faso (Upper Volta), 43, 44
Brazil, 7, 44–45, 152, 153
Brown, C. W., 62

case studies, 7, 51; Indonesia, 110–34; Pakistan, 53–69; People's Republic of China, 9–32; Philippines, 70–95
CAT. *See* College Admission Test
CCP. *See* Chinese Communist Party
CGPA. *See* college grade-point average

Chad, 39
Chang Chun-chiao, 23
Chang Hsue-hsin, 22, 33, 164n.58
Charlemagne, 3, 135
Chile, 39
China: Communist Revolution in, 13–15; elitism in, 3, 135–38; examination system in, 3, 5, 7, 9–13, 48, 100, 135–38, 161nn.4,5, 162n.8; incentives in, 6, 152; selection systems in, 7, 9, 33, 39, 100–101, 135–38; sponsorship in, 136, 162n.8. *See also* Cultural Revolution; People's Republic of China
China People's University, 19
Chinese Communist Party (CCP): Communist Youth League of, 21; and education, 17, 19, 136–37; and examinations, 9, 17, 19, 20; university admissions under, 9, 14, 136, 165n.67. *See also* Cultural Revolution; People's Republic of China
Chinese People's Liberation Army (PLA), 20–21
chin-shih degree, 10, 11, 12
Chou En-lai, 16, 21
chu-jen degree, 10
civil service: in China, 10–12; in England, 162n.15, 172n.22; in Japan, 41; selection for, 1, 2, 33, 35, 36, 97, 135, 159
College Admission Test (CAT), 71, 76, 79, 81, 82, 83, 87. *See also* University of the Philippines
College Entrance Examination Board, 98
college grade-point average (CGPA), 81, 82–83, 84, 87, 91, 92
Columbia University, 98, 151
Confucius, 99, 164n.59, 171n.8
corruption: in China, 100, 101, 135, 152, 165n.67; and examinations, 31, 41, 46, 103; and incentives, 6; in Indonesia, 125, 126; in the Philippines, 102–4, 152; and selection policies, 3, 97, 138, 152, 153, 160; Shakespeare on, 156–57

BOOKS IN THE SERIES

Asian Village Economy at the Crossroads:
An Economic Approach to Institutional Change
by Yujiro Hayami and Masao Kikuchi

The Agrarian Question and Reformism in Latin America
by Alain de Janvry

Redesigning Rural Development: A Strategic Perspective
by Bruce F. Johnston and William C. Clark

Energy Planning for Developing Countries: A Study of Bangladesh
by Russel J. deLucia, Henry D. Jacoby, et alia

Women and Poverty in the Third World
edited by Mayra Buvinic, Margaret A. Lycette, and William Paul McGreevey

The Land Is Shrinking: Population Planning in Asia
by Gayl D. Ness and Hirofumi Ando

Agricultural Development in the Third World
edited by Carl K. Eicher and John M. Staatz

Agriculture and Economic Development
by Subrata Ghatak and Ken Ingersent

The Geography of Underdevelopment: A Critical Survey
by D. K. Forbes

Basic Needs in Developing Countries
by Frances Stewart

Western Economists and Eastern Societies:
Agents of Change in South Asia, 1950–1970
by George Rosen

Factories and Food Stamps: The Puerto Rico Model of Development
by Richard Weisskoff

Agricultural Development:
An International Perspective, revised and expanded edition
by Yujiro Hayami and Vernon W. Ruttan

State and Countryside:
Development Policy and Agrarian Politics in Latin America
by Merilee S. Grindle

Neoconservative Economics in the Southern Cone of Latin America, 1973–1983
by Joseph Ramos

Elitism and Meritocracy in Developing Countries:
Selection Policies for Higher Education
by Robert Klitgaard

Robert Klitgaard is associate professor of public policy in the John F. Kennedy School of Government at Harvard University. His previous books include *Choosing Elites* and *Data Analysis for Development*.

The Johns Hopkins University Press

Elitism and Meritocracy in Developing Countries

This book was set in Sabon text and Serifa display type by
The Composing Room of Michigan, from a design by Ann
Walston. It was printed on 50-lb. Warren's Olde Style paper
and bound in Holliston Roxite A by Thomson-Shore, Inc.